Gallica
Volume 31

MARCO POLO'S
LE DEVISEMENT DU MONDE

Gallica

ISSN 1749–091X

General Editor: Sarah Kay

Gallica aims to provide a forum for the best current work in medieval and Renaissance French studies. Literary studies are particularly welcome and preference is given to works written in English, although publication in French is not excluded.

Proposals or queries should be sent in the first instance to the editor, or to the publisher, at the addresses given below; all submissions receive prompt and informed consideration.

Professor Sarah Kay, Department of French, New York University, 13–19 University Place, 6th floor, New York, NY 10003, USA

The Editorial Director, Gallica, Boydell & Brewer Ltd., PO Box 9, Woodbridge, Suffolk IP12 3DF, UK

Previously published volumes in this series are listed at the end of this volume.

MARCO POLO'S
LE DEVISEMENT DU MONDE
NARRATIVE VOICE, LANGUAGE
AND DIVERSITY

SIMON GAUNT

D. S. BREWER

© Simon Gaunt 2013

All Rights Reserved. Except as permitted under current legislation
no part of this work may be photocopied, stored in a retrieval system,
published, performed in public, adapted, broadcast,
transmitted, recorded or reproduced in any form or by any means,
without the prior permission of the copyright owner

The right of Simon Gaunt to be identified as
the author of this work has been asserted in accordance with
sections 77 and 78 of the Copyright, Designs and Patents Act 1988

First published 2013
D. S. Brewer, Cambridge
Paperback edition 2018

ISBN 978 1 84384 352 8 hardback
ISBN 978 1 84384 496 9 paperback

D. S. Brewer is an imprint of Boydell & Brewer Ltd
PO Box 9, Woodbridge, Suffolk IP12 3DF, UK
and of Boydell & Brewer Inc.
668 Mt Hope Avenue, Rochester, NY 14620–2731, USA
website: www.boydellandbrewer.com

A catalogue record for this title is available
from the British Library

The publisher has no responsibility for the continued existence or accuracy of
URLs for external or third-party internet websites referred to in this book,
and does not guarantee that any content on such websites is,
or will remain, accurate or appropriate

CONTENTS

Illustrations	vi
Acknowledgements	vii
Abbreviations and a note on citations and editions	ix
Introduction: *Le Devisement du Monde:* textual tradition and genre	1
1 Narrative voice and style: 'ego Marcus Paulo'	41
2 Language and translation: 'in lingua Galica dicitur'	78
3 Knowledge, marvels and other religions: 'oculis propriis videt'	113
4 Diversity and alterity: 'diversarum regionum mundanas diversitates'	145
Conclusion: 'et ipse non notavit nisi pauca aliqua, que adhuc in mente retinebat'	173
Bibliography	183
Index	195

ILLUSTRATIONS

1 Monstrous Races illustrating *Le Devisement du Monde*. 120
  MS Bodley 264, fol 218 r. Reproduced by permission of the
  Bodleian Libraries, The University of Oxford.
2 The Execution of Nayan. © British Library Board. 132
  All rights reserved. British Library, Royal 19 D 1, fo 85.

ACKNOWLEDGEMENTS

I have incurred many academic debts during the course of researching and writing this book. Stimulating discussions following invited papers/lectures at the following institutions shaped the evolution of this project decisively: Columbia University (2006), University of Glasgow (2006), University College London (2006), University of Oxford (2006), University of Nottingham (2007), University of Cambridge (2007), New York University (2008), Princeton University (2008), University of Illinois at Urbana/Champaign (2009), Washington University in St Louis (2009), University of Michigan at Ann Arbor (2009), University of Texas at Austin (2009) and the University of Geneva (2009). Similarly, feedback from participants at the following conferences was invaluable: Association Portugaise d'Etudes Françaises (Porto, 2006), 'The Persistence of Philology' (Toronto, 2007), Medieval Academy (Toronto, 2007), American Comparative Literature Association (Long Beach, 2008), 'The Spaces and Locations of Medieval Culture' (London, 2009), The Canadian Society of Medievalists (Montreal, 2010) and 'The Ethics of Translation' (London, 2010). Rather than name all the individuals who kindly invited me to speak on these occasions and the many who listened attentively, asked such useful questions and, on occasion, shared their own work with me, I trust they will all recognize themselves in this list and accept my most cordial and grateful thanks.

My colleagues in the French Department in King's College London make it an unparalleled environment in which to teach and think. I have also benefited hugely from working with our outstanding recent and present graduate students and would in particular like to mention Camilla Barker, Gillian Ni Cheallaigh, Tom Hinton, Richard Mason, Hannah Morcos, David Murray, Jessica Stacey, Jessica Stoll and Luke Sunderland, all of whom have contributed to my thinking in this book. Jessica Stoll did heroic work on the index for which I am eternally grateful. In King's special thanks are also due to Jan Palmowski, who engineered study leave when I needed it and whose unwavering support has been invaluable.

In the broader academic community I am particularly grateful to the following for the interest they have shown in this project and in many cases also for the help or advice they have offered: Suzanne Akbari, Stefano Asperti, Bill Burgwinkle, Ardis Butterfield, Emma Campbell, Chris Cannon, Fabrizio Cigni, Philippe Frieden, Jane Gilbert, Miranda Griffin, Elizabeth Guild, Noah

Guynn, Ruth Harvey, Sarah Kay, Sharon Kinoshita, Karla Mallette, Peggy McCracken, Bob Mills, Linda Paterson, Regina Psaki, Zrinka Stahuljak, Eleanora Stoppino, Marion Uhlig-Vuagnoux and Nicolette Zeeman. Sarah Kay offered enormously useful and characteristically incisive feedback as series editor, as did Boydell and Brewer's reader, whose comments led (I hope) to tangible improvements. Patrick ffrench and Mark Treharne both did some last-minute reading that was encouraging and helpful.

Finally, I should like to record some debts of a more personal nature. Bill Burgwinkle, Chris Cannon, Lisa Drew, Elizabeth Edwards, Lizzie Eger, Patrick ffrench, Vanessa Gaunt, Joel Gouget, Belinda Graham, Liz Guild, Nick Harrison, Ruth Harvey, Eddie Hughes, Sarah Kay, Hector Kollias, Phil Levy, Jo Malt, Bob Mills, Daniel Monk, Florence Talks, Mark Treharne, Sarah Westlake and Nicolette Zeeman helped me – practically and otherwise – through some very difficult times while I was working on this book. I thank them all from the bottom of my heart. I dedicate this book to the memory of my late aunt, the incomparable Monette Gaunt, who knew a thing or two about diversity, and to four remarkable people without whom this book would never have seen the light of day: Mr Khalid Gufhoor, Dr James Hardy, Marianne Miller and Dr Amen Sibtain.

SG
London, September 2012

ABBREVIATIONS

DMF   *Dictionnaire du Moyen Français*, consulted on-line at http://www.atilf.fr/dmf/
FEW   Wartburg, Walther von, *Französisches Etymologishes Wörterbuch*, 25 vols (Tübingen: Niemeyer, 1922–2005)
Godefroy Godefroy, Frédéric, *Dictionnaire de l'ancienne langue française et de tous ses dialectes*, 10 vols (Paris: F. Vieweg, 1880–1902)
Niemeyer Niemeyer, Jan Frederik, *Mediae Latinitatis Lexicon Minus* (Leiden: Brill, 1954–77)
TL   Tobler, Alfred, and Lommatzsch, Erhard, *Altfranzösisches Wörterbuch*, 11 vols (Berlin: Weidmannsche, 1925–2002)

Editions of *Le Devisement du Monde*

I refer to a range of editions of different versions of Marco Polo's *Le Devisement du Monde*, each of which uses a different system for referencing the text, and some of which use unusual diacritics. Unless otherwise stipulated, citations are from the so-called Franco-Italian redaction. The following list indicates the editions used throughout, the form of references and any unusual diacritics.

Franco-Italian redaction: Marco Polo, *Milione. Le Divisament dou monde. Il milione nelle redazioni toscana e franco-italiana*, ed. Gabriella Ronchi, intro. by Cesare Segre (Milan: Mondadori, 1982). Reproduces Benedetto's edition, but with some emendations. Uses roman numerals for chapters, arabic for sentences. Single angled brackets (e.g. <>) indicate where text has been supplied; square brackets indicate corrections.

French redaction: Marco Polo, *Le Devisement du monde*, ed. Philippe Ménard et al., 6 vols (Geneva: Droz, 2001–9): I, ed. Philippe Ménard (2001); II, ed. Jeanne-Marie Boivin, Laurence Harf-Lancner and Laurence Mathey-Maille (2003); III, ed. Jean-Claude Faucon, Danielle Quéruel and Monique Santucci (2004); IV, ed. Joël Blanchard and Michel Quereuil (2005); V, ed. Jean-Claude Delclos and Claude Roussel (2006); VI, ed. Dominique Boutet, Thierry Delcourt and Danièle James-Raoul (2009). Uses arabic numerals for chapter and line numbers. Square brackets indicate text supplied from manuscripts other than the base.

Pipino: *Milion: Dle jediného rukopisu spoly s příslušným základem latinským. Vydal*, ed. Justin V. Prášek (Prague: Česká, Akademie Císaře Františka Josefa, 1902). The text is divided into three books. References give page numbers.

Ramusio: *I viaggi di Marco Polo, gentiluomo veneziano*, in Giovanni Battista Ramusio, *Navigazioni e viaggi*, ed. Marica Milanesi, 6 vols (Turin: Einaudi, 1978–88), III (1980), pp. 7–297. The text is divided into three books. References give page numbers.

Tuscan redaction: Marco Polo, *Milione: versione toscana del Trecento*, ed. Valeria Bertolucci Pizzorusso, with an 'indice ragionato' by Giorgio R. Cardona (Milan: Adelphi, 1975). Uses arabic numerals for chapters and sentences. Also reproduced in Ronchi's edition of the Franco-Italian redaction.

Venetian redaction: Marco Polo, *Il «Milione» veneto: ms. CM 211 della Biblioteca Civica di Padova*, ed. Alvaro Barbieri and Alvise Andreose (Venice: Marsilio, 1999). Uses roman numerals for chapters, arabic for sentences.

Z: Marco Polo, *Milione. Redazione Latina del manoscritto Z*, ed. Alvaro Barbieri (Parma: Fondazione Pietro Bembo/Ugo Guanda, 1998). Uses arabic numerals for chapters and sentences.

Other frequently cited editions
Franco-Italian redaction: Marco *Polo, Il milione*, ed. Luigi Foscolo Benedetto (Florence: Olschki, 1928)

French redaction: *La Description du monde*, ed. Pierre-Yves Badel (Paris: Livre de Poche, 1998)

Rustichello da Pisa: *Il romanzo arturiano di Rustichello da Pisa*, ed. Fabrizio Cigni (Ospedaletto: Pacini, 1994)

Editions of other texts cited and all other references are given in footnotes.

A note on place-names and names
With the exception of place-names that are commonly used and that will be instantly recognizable to modern readers (e.g. Japan, Asia, Africa etc.), I adopt, when referring to the *Devisement*, the orthography of the Franco-Italian redaction. Where this might make a place difficult to identify, a modern form is then given in brackets, or in the translation. The modern forms of Chinese and Indo-Chinese place-names are taken from Stephen Haw's catalogue in *Marco Polo's China: A Venetian in the Realm of Khubilai Khan* (London and New York: Routledge, 2006). Modern forms of other place-names are taken from Wikipedia. I realize that the spelling of some names is controversial: here I have opted for recognizability and consistency.

Translations
All translations are my own.

Introduction
Le Devisement du Monde: textual tradition and genre

Marco Polo

'Marco Polo is one of those comparatively few people from the thirteenth and fourteenth centuries of whom everyone today has heard.'[1] Thus begins one of the most authoritative historical studies of this Venetian merchant, who was probably born in 1254 and who died on 9 January 1324. Airports and cars are named after him; he has been the subject of numerous children's books from the nineteenth century onwards; he makes guest appearances in *Dr Who*; and popular histories of his life appear with regularity every few years, which suggests he continues to fascinate.[2] The name Marco Polo remains a byword for intrepid travel, particularly to Asia and the Indian Ocean, and for the observation by Europeans of exotic lands. Marco's fame, however, is not merely a modern phenomenon: his travels in Asia meant he was a celebrity for the last twenty-five years of his life, not only in Venice but throughout Europe, and the memory of his travels remained alive throughout the Middle Ages, inspiring Christopher Columbus, no less, to sail west in the hope of reaching the lands Marco had visited by travelling east.[3] Marco Polo is an iconic figure for European culture and for its relations with the rest of the world.

Although Marco Polo is sometimes presented as an explorer or pioneer, he was in fact neither. Other Europeans had been to Asia before him – merchants,

---

[1] John Larner, *Marco Polo and the Discovery of the World* (New Haven, CT, and London: Yale University Press, 1999), p. 1.

[2] See most recently Laurence Bergreen, *Marco Polo: From Venice to Xanadu* (London: Quercus, 2008).

[3] Christopher Columbus's annotated printed copy of Marco Polo, in the Pipino Latin translation, survives. Though the annotations almost certainly post-date Columbus's first voyage and not all are his, the journal of his first voyage nonetheless suggests familiarity with Marco Polo. For the annotations, see *El libro de Marco Polo anotado por Cristóbal Colon. El libro de Marco Polo, versión de Rodrigo de Santaella*, ed. Juan Gil (Madrid: Alianza, 1987), pp. 11–168 (which is a translation of the Pipino text of Columbus's copy together with a translation of the annotations); for discussion of the likely date of the annotations see pp. vii–ix and Larner, *Marco Polo*, pp. 151–60.

missionaries and diplomats – particularly in the fifty years or so that immediately preceded his own twenty-four-year stay outside Europe (1271–95), some by more or less the same routes along which Marco travelled.[4] Indeed, when Marco set out for China in 1271, he was accompanying his father, Niccolò, and his uncle, Maffeo, who were returning to Asia after a journey they had previously made between 1260 and 1269. Marco's fame thus rested, and indeed continues to rest, not so much on his travels in and of themselves as on a remarkable text originally composed in Italianate French that he probably had a hand in composing (though he was also probably not its sole author), *Le Devisement du Monde* ('the "description", or possibly "division", of the world'),[5] which is less about his travels as such than it is about the world he observed. Even here Marco was not unique, for other thirteenth-century Europeans had composed written texts about their travels to Asia and described what they saw.[6] But Marco's text clearly struck a chord in the European imagination – even though it is poorly structured and apparently sometimes frankly sloppy in its execution – for it was very quickly translated from the hybrid French in which it was composed into a range of European languages (initially at least into a form of French that conformed more to contemporary literary norms in France, then into Tuscan Italian, Venetian and Latin) and copied in its various versions in more than 140 manuscripts throughout the fourteenth and fifteenth centuries.[7] This already makes the *Devisement* one of the most widely disseminated and translated of medieval vernacular texts, but, perhaps even more impressively, the text went quickly into print and has remained so to the present day. The *Devisement* is thus one of the few medieval vernacular texts for which there has been a continuous tradition of readership since it was written, and it has stimulated voluminous scholarship from the early modern period onwards.

Seven centuries (and counting) of popular and academic fascination with Marco Polo himself and with his book (as the *Devisement* refers to itself) have led to an astonishing amount of speculation about the man, his life, his

---

[4] For an overview of merchants in Asia, see J.R.S. Phillips, *The Medieval Expansion of Europe*, 2nd edn (Oxford: Clarendon Press, 1998), and for missionary travel in Asia see Christopher Dawson, *Mission to Asia* (Toronto: Toronto University Press, 1980).

[5] I do not retain Ronchi's spelling of the title (*Divisament*), since this derives from a correction made by Benedetto to the only manuscript of the Franco-Italian redaction.

[6] Dawson, *Mission*, pp. 3–72 and 89–220, offers translations into English of John of Plano Carpini's widely disseminated *Ystoria Mongalorum*, which narrates his journey made in 1245–7, and William of Rubruck's less well-known but remarkable *Itinerarium fratris Willielmi de Rubruquis*, which relates his journey made in 1253–5. John was a papal envoy and sixty-five at the time of his departure; William was the envoy of Louis IX of France.

[7] For an exhaustive study of the manuscripts, see Consuelo W. Dutschke, 'Francesco Pipino and the Manuscripts of Marco Polo's *Travels*', unpublished Ph.D. dissertation, University of California at Los Angeles, 1993.

travels and the text attributed to him. Furthermore the textual tradition of the *Devisement* is complex, and since most readers of the text today encounter it in translations that draw on more than one version, in a range of languages, the original (or, more accurately, the earliest version of the text), its style, content and language, are obscured by centuries of tradition and scholarship. Even among medievalists, adaptations and translations are better known than the earliest version of the text, which is extremely hard to find in a modern printed edition, particularly in the anglophone world.[8] So what can be securely known about Marco and about the *Devisement*? One problem posed by this question is that our main and sometimes only source of information about Marco and his book is the *Devisement* itself, but to facilitate my account I will stick to what is generally accepted by historians about Marco's life.

The Polos were a family of Venetian merchants who traded with Asia through the Black Sea, for which purpose they owned houses in Constantinople and Soldaia (Sudak) in the Crimea.[9] It was from Soldaia that the brothers Niccolò and Maffeo Polo set out in 1260 to trade in jewels with the Mongols of the Golden Horde in central Asia. They had not, it would seem, originally intended to travel to the Far East, but if the *Devisement* itself is to be believed, a series of wars barred their route back to the Mediterranean and, while at Bukhara, in present-day Uzbekistan, they accepted an invitation to accompany an embassy from the Persian Ilkhan, Hülegü, to the Great Khan, Kublai.[10]

The rapid and inexorable rise of the Mongol empire in the thirteenth century is one of the more momentous events in human history, though its scope and significance have often been obscured by the subsequent history of European colonialism and world domination.[11] The first few decades of the thirteenth century had seen the Mongols, previously a relatively insignificant tribe of Nomad herders and warriors from the Asian steppes, establish a pan-Asian empire under the leadership of the redoubtable Genghis Khan. His death in 1227 slowed but did not stop the expansion of the Mongol empire, which in 1237–8 and 1241–2 had attacked eastern Europe with brutal force, leaving Europeans in no doubt as to the incomparable might and violent ruthlessness of the great power that lay to the east, and dashing any hope that the Mongols might be potential allies against the Muslim world. By the time the

---

[8] Benedetto's edition of the Franco-Italian redaction was published in a limited edition of 600 copies; it is now almost impossible to find outside major copyright and older university libraries. This is in sharp contrast to the wide availability of numerous translations into English (all of which draw on several versions) and of the French and Tuscan redactions.

[9] Larner, *Marco Polo*, pp. 32–3.

[10] *Devisement*, III–VI.

[11] See Peter Jackson, *The Mongols and the West, 1221–1410* (Harlow: Longman, 2005), and, for a shorter overview, Larner, *Marco Polo*, pp. 8–30.

Polo brothers were in central Asia in the early 1260s, Genghis's empire had been divided among his heirs, but all still paid tribute to, and were nominally under the authority of, the Great Khan, Kublai, who had acceded to power in 1260 and who was to remain in control of the vast Mongol empire until his death in 1294. Kublai expanded Mongol power into China, threatening Korea, Indo-China, India and Japan. By the standards of the time this was a global empire, stretching from Russia and the Black Sea to the South China Sea. It was also one of astonishing wealth, with well-organized communication networks that allowed travel the length and breadth of Asia, albeit sometimes for a price, in relative freedom and safety, the so-called *pax mongolica*, which proved such an extraordinary stimulus to trade throughout Asia, and indeed in Europe, since it enabled an influx of Oriental goods.[12]

The Polo brothers apparently met Kublai himself, and when they returned to Europe in 1269, they did so as his ambassadors to the Pope.[13] The problem was that Clement IV had died the previous year, and thus far there was no Pope to whom they could deliver their messages and greetings. So they made their way to Venice rather than to the Papal court. Frustrated with the lengthy Papal interregnum, they eventually decided to return to Asia without having fulfilled their mission, taking with them this time Niccolò's seventeen-year-old son Marco. But before they got too far (Ayas, now in Turkey), news reached them that an old acquaintance, Archdeacon Tedaldo Visconti, had been elected Pope Gregory X and, knowing him to be in Acre, they made their way there. When they set out for Asia again (probably in November 1271), they did so with messages from the new Pope and two Dominican friars, who quickly, however, found the journey too arduous and so turned back.[14]

The Polos were not to return to Venice until 1295. The *Devisement* claims they spent seventeen years in the Far East and China (from 1275 to 1292), occupying various offices in Kublai Khan's administration, with Marco apparently enjoying the Great Khan's particular favour because of his gift for languages and for narrating accounts of the places in Kublai's empire that he visited on official business.[15] There is some evidence that members

---

[12] On the implications of the Mongol empire for trade, see Janet L. Abu-Lughod, *Before European Hegemony: The World System AD 1250–1350* (New York and Oxford: Oxford University Press, 1989), pp. 153–247, and for the seminal influence of this trade on European culture and history more generally, see John M. Hobson, *The Eastern Origins of Western Civilisation* (Cambridge: Cambridge University Press, 2004), pp. 44–50.

[13] *Devisement*, VIII–IX.

[14] *Devisement*, X–XIII.

[15] *Devisement*, XIV–XVII; cf. also CV, 1–2. See further pp. 75–7 on Marco's relationship with Kublai. It has recently been argued that, on the one hand, Marco was an official with particular responsibility for the production and transportation of salt and, on the other, that he was a *keshigten* (*quesitan*, see LXXXVI, 1, in the *Devisement*), which is to say a member of Kublai Khan's extensive bodyguard. For the former, see Pierre

of the Polo family in Venice knew their absent relatives to be alive in 1280,[16] so it cannot be excluded that lines of communication were kept open during Marco's extended stay in Asia. In any event, in 1292, we are told, the Polos joined what turned out to be a disastrous marriage party taking a Mongol princess to marry the new Persian Ilkhan, Arghun (possibly precisely as a means of returning to Europe): not only were most of the escort lost en route, but the bridegroom turned out to be dead when they arrived. Nonetheless, this trip apparently afforded the Polos a sea journey round the Indian subcontinent, during which they visited many islands and Indian provinces.[17] A few years after their return to Europe – in 1298 – Marco found himself held for ransom in a Genoese prison (though our only source for this information is the first chapter of the *Devisement*), possibly after capture at the naval battle of Curzola between Venice and Genoa.[18] There, the text tells us, he collaborated (I, 7: 'fist retraire toutes cestes chouses a') with one Rust[c]iaus de Pise to produce the *Devisement du Monde*, in French, as already noted. This Rust[c]iaus is usually identified as Rustichello da Pisa, otherwise known as the author/compiler of an Old French prose romance compilation (which, like the *Devisement,* is frequently marked by Italianisms), whom the Polos could conceivably have met in 1271, either in Italy or in Acre.[19] Released from captivity, most probably in 1299, Marco returned to Venice, where he was to remain not just as a prosperous merchant but also as the celebrated author of the *Devisement*, which within fifteen years had been translated into a range of different languages, including Latin, and was being widely disseminated throughout Europe.

The rest, as they say, is history, except that in this case history seems to be full of holes, uncertainties and controversies. Conventional historical sources for the Polos, though not negligible, tend to tell us little about what scholars have really wanted to know – which is to say, his life and travels in Asia – the composition of the *Devisement* and its early textual history. Thus there are sources concerning the Polos' businesses in Europe, both before and after their travels, and then their wills, but these documents have little concrete to tell us about Marco Polo's travels and nothing substantive about the *Devisement*.[20] While Asian sources make it clear that Europeans

---

Racine, *Marco Polo et ses voyages* (Paris: Perrin, 2012), 'Marco Polo au service du grand khan'; for the latter see Stephen G. Haw, *Marco Polo's China: A Venetian in the Realm of Khubilai Khan* (London and New York: Routledge, 2006), Chapter 11.

[16] Larner, *Marco Polo*, p. 41.

[17] *Devisement*, XVIII–XIX.

[18] This is certainly what Marco Polo's sixteenth-century translator and editor Ramusio alleged in his 'Prefazione' (p. 31), but his information is not necessarily reliable. He says, for example, that Marco's collaborator was 'un gentiluomo genovese molto suo amico'.

[19] On Rustichello and Marco, see Benedetto (ed.), *Milione*, pp. XIII–XXVII.

[20] On surviving documentation relating to the Polos, see Giovanni Orlandini, 'Marco Polo e la sua famiglia', *Archivio Veneto-Tridentino*, 9 (1926), 1–68, and David

were not unheard of at Kublai Khan's court, none of those mentioned can be securely identified with the Polos, and some modern historians have alleged that Marco never in fact went as far as China but rather spent his years away in Persia, where he picked up information about China and the Far East from Arabic travellers.[21] Otherwise widely circulated stories, for example about the Polos' return to Venice dressed as Mongols and initially unrecognized,[22] or about how Marco's account of Asia was questioned by his contemporaries so that even on his deathbed he was asked to recant the lies he had peddled in the *Devisement*,[23] come from later (sometimes much later) sources and are almost certainly apocryphal. But such stories nonetheless point to a number of important features of the medieval and post-medieval reception of the *Devisement*, whether popular or scholarly: first, the apparent need to supplement the information the text supplies; secondly, the drive to romanticize Marco's life (a drive that has also led to novels and films); thirdly, the impulse to question or, alternatively, defend the veracity of the text.[24] One of the arguments of this book will be that these features of the reception of the text are invited and instantiated by the text itself.

Within the vast body of post-medieval writing and scholarship on Marco Polo a number of major and minor strands can be identified, even if they by no means account for all work in the field:

Jacoby, 'Marco Polo, His Close Relatives, and His Travel Account: Some New Insights', *Mediterranean Historical Review*, 21 (2006), 193–218; also on Marco's will, see Larner, *Marco Polo*, pp. 44–5.

[21] See, for example, Frances Wood, *Did Marco Polo Go to China?* (London: Martin Secker and Warburg, 1995), whose argument has elicited several ripostes. For example: Haw, *Marco Polo's China*; Larner, *Marco Polo*, pp. 60–3; and Igor de Rachewiltz, 'Marco Polo Went to China', *Zentralasiatische Studien*, 27 (1997), 34–92.

[22] Ramusio, pp. 28–9.

[23] The account of Marco Polo's deathbed is given in Jacopo d'Aqui's *Chronica* (c. 1334); Marco is said to have replied that he had told only half of what he had seen. This account also echoes a story told ostensibly of Maffeo Polo in Pipino's prologue. See Benedetto (ed.), *Milione*, p. CXCIV, Dutschke, 'Francesco Pipino', p. 1196, and for the text Pipino, p. 2.

[24] Apart from the story of Marco's deathbed, Ramusio reports, while defending the veracity of the book, that it had been for many years 'riputato favola' (p. 22: 'reputed to be a fable'). Dutschke has argued, however, that the evidence of manuscript annotations (principally of Pipino) indicates Marco Polo was widely believed ('Francesco Pipino', pp. 43–99), while Martin Gosman has made the important argument that after c. 1350, following the Black Death and the disintegration of the Mongol empire, Westerners no longer had direct access to the Far East, which made Marco's account no longer verifiable, as well as outnumbered by other accounts that were not grounded in personal experience and often based on fanciful textual traditions (such as Mandeville's). See: 'Marco Polo's Voyages: The Conflict between Confirmation and Observation', in Zweder von Martels (ed.), *Travel Fact and Travel Fiction: Studies in Fiction, Literary Tradition, Scholarly Discovery and Observation in Travel Writing* (Leiden: Brill, 1994), pp. 72–84. Gosman's thesis is consonant with Ramusio's observation that recent explorations have made Marco's account verifiable (pp. 22–3).

- Translations and adaptations of the *Devisement* (which are in fact far more common than editions) with a view to making the contents of the text (and primarily the account of medieval Asia) widely available.[25]
- Attempts to reconstruct exactly the Polos' trajectory by identifying all the places mentioned in the *Devisement*.[26]
- Attempts to deny that Marco did in fact go to China or, alternatively, attempts to prove that he did so.[27]
- Pseudo-biographical accounts of Marco Polo's life and of his travels. This is by far the most common form of popular writing on Marco Polo.[28]
- Scholarly monographs on Marco Polo: these often lean towards biography, and so focus on his travels and/or subsequent reputation. Though some do include consideration of the *Devisement*'s textual tradition and of its literary qualities, this is usually only as an accessory to the main focus on the text's content and on biography.[29]
- Scholarship interested in the medieval European representation of Asia and/ or East–West cultural interchange, travel, contact and conflict, or in post-colonial approaches.[30]

---

[25] There are numerous translations and reprints of translations in almost every language. Widely available English versions include *The Travels of Marco Polo*, trans. with an introduction by Ronald Latham (Harmondsworth: Penguin, 1958), and *The Travels of Marco Polo*, with an introduction by Paul Smethurst (New York: Barnes and Noble, 2005). The former is a translation of Benedetto's edition, but incorporating many passages from the Z redaction; the latter reproduces William Marsden's nineteenth-century translation of Ramusio's text, but with the extensive (early twentieth-century) notes of Ernest Rhys.

[26] Pioneering work here includes: Leonardo Olschki, *L'Asia di Marco Polo: introduzione alla lettura e allo studio del 'Milione'* (Venice: Fondazione Cini, 1957); Paul Pelliot, *Notes on Marco Polo*, 3 vols (Paris: Imprimerie Nationale, 1959–73); Henry Yule, *The Book of Ser Marco Polo the Venetian concerning the Kingdoms and Marvels of the East,* revised by Henri Cordier, 2 vols (London: John Murray, 1903), now also available as a Project Gutenberg e-book. Also indispensable are Giorgio Cardona's 'Indice ragionata' to Bertolucci Pizzorusso (ed.), *Milione*, since this takes previous scholarship into account comprehensively, and Haw's *Marco Polo's China*, which exploits Chinese sources extensively.

[27] See n. 21 above.

[28] For example: Bergreen, *Marco Polo*; Vito Bianchi, *Marco Polo: storia del mercante che capì la Cina* (Bari: Laterza, 2007); or the more solemn Alvise Zorzi, *Vita di Marco Polo veneziano*, 2nd edn (Milan: Bompiano, 2000).

[29] Notable contributions here include: John Critchley, *Marco Polo's Book* (Aldershot: Variorum, 1992); Jacques Heers, *Marco Polo* (Paris: Fayard, 1983); Larner, *Marco Polo*; Marina Münkler, *Marco Polo: vita e leggende*, trans. Giuliana Cavallo-Guzzo (Milan: Vita e Pensiero, 2001); and Racine, *Marco Polo*. Critchley's and Münkler's books, in particular, are worth consulting for their comments on the *Devisement*'s literary qualities.

[30] Olschki, *L'Asia di Marco Polo*, and Yule, *The Book*, contain much useful information on this score. Notable recent contributions (though very different in nature) include: Alvaro Barbieri, *Dal viaggio al libro. Studi sul 'Milione'* (Verona: Fiorini, 2004), pp. 175–251

- Philological studies (i.e. linguistic studies and critical editions of different versions).[31]
- Stemmatic studies (i.e. textual criticism aiming to reconstruct the relation of different versions of the text to each other).[32]

(= five previously published articles: 'Marco Polo e l'altro', 'Marco Polo e la montagna', 'Il popolo degli arcieri: i Mongoli nel *Milione*', 'Usanze e culti nell' Oriente poliano (schede etnografiche dal *Milione*') and 'Marco Polo etnografo: le cortigiane templari nella provincia di Maabar'); Eugenio Burgio, 'Marco Polo e gli idolatri', *L'immagine riflessa*, 8 (2005), 31–62; Michael Calabrese, 'Between Despair and Ecstasy: Marco Polo's Life of the Bhudda', *Exemplaria*, 9 (1997), 189–229; Mary B. Campbell, *The Witness and the Other World: Exotic European Travel Writing, 400–1600* (Ithaca: Cornell University Press, 1988), pp. 87–121; Antonio García Espada, *Marco Polo y la cruzada: historia de la literatura de viajes a las Indias en el siglo XIV* (Madrid: Marcial Pons Historia, 2009); Syed Manzarul Islam, *The Ethics of Travel from Marco Polo to Kafka* (Manchester and New York: Manchester University Press, 1996); Sharon Kinoshita, 'Marco Polo's *Le Devisement dou Monde* and the Tributary East', in Suzanne Conklin Akbari and Amilcare A. Iannucci (eds), *Marco Polo and the Encounter of East and West* (Toronto: University of Toronto Press, 2008), pp. 60–86.

[31] Major linguistic studies of different versions of the *Devisement* (other than those included in the introductions to critical editions) include: Valeria Bertolucci Pizzorusso, 'Lingue e stili nel *Milione*', in Renzo Zorzi (ed.), *L'epopea delle scoperte* (Venice: Leo S. Olschki, 1994), pp. 61–73; Eugenio Burgio and Giuseppe Mascherpa, '«Milione» latino. Note linguistiche e appunti di storia della tradizione sulle redazioni Z e L', in Renato Oniga and Sergio Vatteroni (eds), *Plurilinguismo letterario* (Soveria Mannelli: Rubbettino, 2007), pp. 119–58; Maria Grazia Capusso, *La lingua del "Devisament dou Monde" di Marco Polo: 1 morfologia verbale* (Pisa: Pacini, 1980), and 'La mescidanza linguistica del *Milione* franco-italiano', in Silvia Conte (ed.), *I viaggi del 'Milione': itinerari testuali, vettori di trasmissione e metamorfosi del Devisement du monde di Marco Polo e Rustichello da Pisa nella pluralità delle attestazioni. Convegno internazionale Venezia, 6–8 ottobre 2005* (Rome: Tiellemedia, 2008), pp. 263–83; Gustav Ineichen, 'La mescolanza delle forme linguistiche nel "Milione" di Marco Polo', in Günter Holtus, Henning Krauss and Peter Wunderli (eds), *Testi, cotesti e contesti del franco-italiano: in memoriam Alberto Limentani* (Tübingen: Niemeyer, 1989), pp. 65–74; Philippe Ménard, 'Le mélange des langues dans les diverses versions du *Devisement du Monde* de Marco Polo', in Claire Kappler and Suzanne Thiolier-Méjean (eds), *Le Plurilinguisme au moyen âge: Orient-Occident: de Babel à la langue une* (Paris: L'Harmattan, 2009), pp. 233–49; Barbara Wehr, 'Venetismi e toscanismi nel MS. B.N. FR. 1116 del testo di Marco Polo', in Oniga and Vatteroni (eds), *Plurilinguismo letterario*, pp. 205–23.

[32] The *locus classicus* here is Benedetto's 200-page introduction to his edition, but see also (in addition to the introductions of other editions): Alvaro Barbieri, *Dal viaggio al libro*, pp. 47–91 ('Quale *Milione?* La questione testuale e le principali edizioni moderne del libro di Marco Polo'); Eugenio Burgio and Mario Eusebi, 'Per una nuova edizione del *Milione*', in Conte (ed.), *I viaggi del* Milione, pp. 17–48; Jacques Monfrin, *Etudes de philologie romane* (Droz: Geneva, 2001), pp. 513–33 ('La tradition du texte de Marco Polo'); Mario Roques, 'Les manuscrits de Marco Polo', *Romania*, 76 (1955), 399–408; B. Terracini, 'Richerche e appunti sulla più antica redazione del *Milione*', *Rendiconti della Reale Accademia Nazionale dei Lincei*, ser. VI, 9 (1933), 369–428.

- Studies of the iconography of illustrated manuscripts of the *Devisement*.[33]
- Literary studies, particularly in relation to narrative voice and authorship, the use of formulae, the treatment of marvels and genre, but more recently also adopting post-colonial approaches.[34]

---

[33] Important contributions here include: Laurence Harf-Lancner, 'From Alexander to Marco Polo, from Text to Image: The Marvels of India', in Donald Maddox and Sara Sturm-Maddox (eds), *The Medieval French Alexander* (Albany: State University of New York Press, 2002), pp. 235–57, and 'Divergences du texte et de l'image: l'illustration du *Divisement du monde* de Marco Polo', *Ateliers*, 30 (2003), 39–52; Jean-François Kosta-Théfaine, 'Du récit de voyage et de sa mise en image: l'exemple du manuscrit de New York (Pierpont Morgan Library M 723) du *Devisement du Monde* de Marco Polo', in Jean-Loup Korzilius (ed.), *Art et Littérature: le voyage entre texte et image* (Amsterdam: Rodopi, 2006), pp. 31–60; Philippe Ménard, 'L'illustration du *Devisement du Monde* de Marco Polo: étude d'iconographie comparée', in François Moureau (ed.), *Métamorphose du récit de voyage* (Paris: Champion/Slatkine, 1986), pp. 17–31, and 'Marco Polo en images. Les représentations du voyageur au moyen âge', in Pietro G. Beltrami, Maria Grazia Capusso, Fabrizio Cigni and Sergio Vatteroni (eds), *Studi di filologia romanza offerti a Valeria Bertolucci Pizzorusso*, 2 vols (Pisa: Pacini, 2006), II, pp. 993–1021; Debra Higgs Strickland, 'Artists, Audience, and Ambivalence in Marco Polo's *Divisament dou Monde*', *Viator*, 36 (2005), 493–529, and 'Text, Image, and Contradiction in the *Devisement dou monde*', in Akbari and. Iannucci (eds), *Marco Polo and the Encounter of East and West*, pp. 23–59; and Rudolf Wittkower, *Allegory and the Migration of Symbols* (London: Thames and Hudson, 1977), pp. 76–92 ('Marco Polo and the Pictorial Tradition of the Marvels of the East'). Some important illustrated manuscripts that include the French redaction of the *Devisement* have been the subject of extensive study. See in particular: François Avril, Marie-Thérèse Gousset, Jacques Monfrin, Jean Richard and Marie-Hélène Tesnière, *Marco Polo Das Buch der Wunder. Handschrift Français 2810 der Bibliothèque Nationale de Paris/Le Livre des merveilles. MS fr. 2810 de la Bibliothèque Nationale de France* (Lucerne: Faksimile Verlag, 1996); Philippe Ménard, 'Réflexions sur l'illustration du texte de Marco Polo dans le manuscrit fr. 2810 de la bibliothèque nationale de Paris', in *Mélanges in memoriam Takeshi Shimmura* (Tokyo: France Tosho, 1998), pp. 81–92; Maria Luisa Meneghetti, 'Quando l'immagine dice di più. Riflessioni sull'apparato decororativo del *Livre des Merveilles du monde*', in Beltrami, Capusso, Cigni and Vatteroni (eds), *Studi di filologia*, II, pp. 1023–49; David J.A. Ross, 'Methods of Book Production in a XIVth Century French Miscellany (London, B.M. Royal 19.D.1)', *Scriptorium*, 6 (1952), 63–75.

[34] Apart from Critchley, *Marco Polo*, pp. 1–29, and Münkler, *Marco Polo*, pp. 31–70, notable contributions include: Pierre-Yves Badel, 'Lire la merveille selon Marco Polo', *Revue des Sciences Humaines*, 183 (1981), 7–16; Barbieri, *Dal viaggio al libro*, pp. 129–54 ('Marco, Rustichello, il "patto", il libro'); Valeria Bertolucci Pizzorusso, 'Enunciazione e produzione del testo nel *Milione*', *Studi Mediolatini e Volgari*, 25 (1977), 5–43; Dietmar Rieger, 'Marco Polo und Rustichello da Pisa: der Reisende und sein Erzähler', in Xenia von Ertzdorff (ed.), *Reisen und Reiseliteratur im Mittelalter und in der Frühen Neuzeit* (Amsterdam: Rodopi, 1992), pp. 289–312; Cesare Segre, 'Marco Polo: filologia e industria culturale', in Gabriella Ronchi, Marica Milanesi and Cesare Segre (eds), *Avventure del "Milione"* (Parma: Zara, 1983), pp. 9–20, and 'Chi ha scritto il *Milione* di Marco Polo?', in Conte (ed.), *I viaggi del* Milione, pp. 5–16; Paul Smethurst, 'The Journey from Modern to Postmodern in the *Travels of Sir John Mandeville* and Marco Polo's *Divisament dou Monde*', in Richard Utz and Jesse G. Swan (eds), *Studies in Medievalism XIII: Postmodern*

One striking feature of a good deal of post-medieval writing about the *Devisement* is the tendency to privilege content over form, to see it therefore primarily as a source of information about Marco Polo, his travels and Asia. The form, language and style of the text are rarely mentioned in some writing; sometimes they are explicitly regarded as inconvenient textual barriers that get in the way of what really matters, which is to say, the information that the text contains.[35] Ironically, the form and style of the illustrations in the relatively few illuminated manuscripts have elicited at least as much sustained interpretation as the form and style of the text itself, reflecting the fact that literary studies are by some considerable margin thinner on the ground than other modes of scholarship. And even in many more stylistic or literary studies the aim often seems largely to enable answers to positivist questions such as: who wrote this text, and under what circumstances? Which is to say, did Rustichello, Marco, or Rustichello and Marco together work from notes Marco brought back from Asia?[36] And if Marco Polo did indeed collaborate with Rustichello da Pisa in the composition of the *Devisement*, who is responsible for which aspects of the text? These questions are often answered with the assertion that, while Marco Polo was responsible for the substance of the *Devisement*, Rustichello was responsible for some aspects of its form or style.[37] These questions and assertions in turn dovetail with the concerns of philologists and textual scholars: which is the most authentic or authoritative version of the text, who wrote it, in which language and what was the state of that language?[38] If some historians, and indeed some post-colonial literary scholars, seem in turn rather innocent of textual and

Medievalisms (Cambridge: D.S. Brewer, 2005), pp. 159–79; Marion Steinicke, 'Marco Polo's *Devisement dou monde* as a Narcissistic trauma', in Akbari and. Iannucci (eds), *Marco Polo and the Encounter of East and West*, pp. 87–109.

[35] For example, Heers (*Marco Polo*, pp. 10–11) laments the *Devisement*'s monotonous and heavy style, while Phillips (*Medieval Expansion of Europe*, pp. 109–10) finds the style rambling and the poor French often unintelligible.

[36] The suggestion that while in Genoa Marco sent to Venice for notes he made in Asia seems to derive from Ramusio (p. 31), but it was strongly endorsed by Benedetto (*Milione*, pp. XXXVI–VII), and numerous subsequent scholars have argued or assumed the authors of the text worked from Marco's notes. See, for example: Barbieri, *Dal viaggio al libro*, pp. 138–9; F. Borlandini, 'Alle origini del libro di Marco Polo', in *Studi in onore di Amintore Fanfani*, 6 vols (Milan: Giuffrè, 1962), I, pp. 107–47; Larner, *Marco Polo*, p. 52; Segre, 'Chi ha scritto?', p. 8. It is frequently suggested that, if the notes were in Venetian, this might help explain some of the linguistic features of the text.

[37] To give but one influential formulation of this: 'Compito espresso di Rustichello dev' essere stato quello di stendere in una lingua letteraria accettabile quelle note di che Marco, vissuto così a lungo in oriente, non si sentiva di formulare con esatezza in nessuna parlata occidentale' (Benedetto ed., *Milione*, p. XXVII).

[38] Whereas for some scholars (e.g. Heers, *Marco Polo*, p. 305–7) only Rustichello da Pisa would have had any competence in French, others have argued persuasively that Marco Polo too is very likely to have known French (see, in particular, Bertolucci Pizzorusso, 'Lingue e stili', pp. 62–3).

philological questions and why they might matter, with just a few notable exceptions there is a remarkable proclivity to read the *Devisement* primarily as a vehicle for its outlandish subject-matter, and to fail therefore to explore fully the implications and effects of the way it draws on a range of different textual traditions and antecedents, of its exploitation of a variety of narrative and descriptive techniques to create its own textual dynamic. There seems, in other words, a general reluctance to subject the *Devisement* systematically to the tools of literary criticism.

This book offers a reading of *Le Devisement du Monde* that seeks to do just that, while also taking into account its complex early manuscript tradition and the languages of the earliest versions. If my motivation for writing yet another book on Marco Polo stems in part at least from dissatisfaction with previous scholarship, this is not to say that there is not some excellent work that has informed my own. I would like, in particular, to signal a debt throughout what follows to Valeria Bertolucci Pizzorusso's many erudite and acute essays on the *Devisement*. The books of Alvaro Barbieri, John Critchley, Jacques Heers, John Larner, Marina Münkler and Pierre Racine have likewise been crucial. In the remainder of this introduction I will first go into more detail about the text, its history and languages of transmission, and the scholarly debates that have surrounded the relation of its different versions; I will then discuss the genre of the *Devisement* and scholarly opinion on this, and endeavour to explain why this matters; finally, I will outline my own approach and the structure of this book. My intention here is to set out information that will underpin and inform discussion throughout subsequent chapters.

Le Devisement du Monde: the text and its history of transmission

The following table, which deals only with the main early witnesses of the text, offers a schematic summary of received opinion on the textual tradition of the *Devisement*. I will usually refer to the different vernacular versions under discussion as 'redactions' rather than 'translations' (without entirely abandoning the latter term), in order not to beg the question of whether the different versions are in fact translations or, indeed, rather *remaniements* (re-workings) of texts into different linguistic forms that may or may not have been perceived as distinct languages.

1298	Franco-Italian redaction, represented by just one MS (Bibliothèque Nationale de France fonds français 1116), dated 1310[39]

---

[39] One fragmentary and barely legible manuscript (British Library Cotton Othon D V) was previously thought to be a second witness to the Franco-Italian redaction, but is

1309	Tuscan redaction, deriving from a source similar to BNF f.fr. 1116, six MSS[40]
c. 1310–11	French redaction, deriving from a source similar to BNF f.fr. 1116, eighteen MSS, which divide into three distinct families[41]
c. 1310–14	Venetian redaction: deriving from a source similar to BNF f.fr. 1116, five MSS[42]
c. 1314–24	Pipino's Latin translation and adaptation of the first Venetian redaction (about seventy MSS)[43]
Early 14th century	Z redaction, one MS copied c. 1470 of a Latin translation of a lost Franco-Italian source, similar to BNF f.fr. 1116, but with supplementary material of seeming authenticity[44]
Early 14th century	L redaction, Latin translation of a source similar to BNF f.fr. 1116, but also related to Z's source, six MSS[45]

Most later medieval redactions (in Catalan, Czech, French, Gaelic, German, Tuscan and Venetian) derive either from Pipino or from the first Venetian redaction, but one further important post-medieval witness is the Italian translation of a Latin manuscript, close but not identical to Z, published by Giovanni Battista Ramusio in 1559, which also draws on Pipino.[46]

Much of what we know about this textual tradition rests on the seminal work of Luigi Foscolo Benedetto, whose monumental 1928 critical edition

---

now generally thought to be an Anglo-Norman transcription of the French redaction. See Philippe Ménard, 'Marco Polo en Angleterre', *Medioevo Romanzo*, 24 (2000), 189–208. I abbreviate 'fonds français' hereafter to 'f.fr'.

[40] On the date of this version, see Valeria Bertolucci Pizzorusso, 'Le versioni storiche del *Milione* in Italia. La versione toscana', in Federico Masini, Franco Salvatori and Sandro Schipani (eds), *Marco Polo 750 anni. Il viaggio. Il libro. Il diritto. Congresso internazionale (*Rome: Tiellemedia, 2006), pp. 199–208 (p. 203).

[41] For the dating of this redaction, see Philippe Ménard, 'Intérêt et importance de la version française du *Devisement du Monde* de Marco Polo', in Masini, Salvatori and Schipani (eds), *Marco Polo 750 anni. Il viaggio. Il libro. Il diritto. Congresso internazionale*, p. 187.

[42] The Venetian redaction is not easily datable, but it must pre-date Pipino's translation.

[43] Incredibly the only modern edition of Pipino is published as a support to its medieval Czech translation. For the dating of Pipino's translation see Dutschke, 'Francesco Pipino', pp. 206–19.

[44] A precise dating of Z is difficult, but it must date from before 1341; see Burgio and Mascherpa, '«Milione» latino', p. 123, n. 15.

[45] This version of the text remains unedited. For recent analysis see Burgio and Mascherpa, '«Milione» latino'. A precise dating is difficult: it must have been completed before 1373, but it is likely to be earlier (Burgio and Mascerpa, '«Milione» latino', p. 132, n. 43).

[46] See Ramusio p. 32, n. 1, for his remarks about the manuscript of 'maravigliosa antichità' that he used, a remark dropped from the second edition. Ramusio clearly believed that the text was originally in Latin (p. 32) and that Pipino was translating from an early translation into the vernacular (p. 34).

of the Franco-Italian text includes an extensive analysis of the manuscript tradition (pp. XI–CCXXI). Most, if not quite all, scholars affirm the precedence, 'il posto d'onore' as Benedetto puts it (p. CCXX), that he accorded the text preserved in BNF f.fr. 1116, and which he edits, albeit with frequent critical interventions. BNF f.fr. 1116 is the longest surviving redaction of the text and is dated 1310, so just twelve years after the supposed date of composition, which for a medieval text of this period is relatively unusual.[47] Of Italian provenance, BNF f.fr. 1116 is written in French but riddled with hybrid Italianate forms (hence its language is referred to as 'Franco-Italian'); it also has a fair number of errors and apparent lacunae, and it seems to finish without a conclusion. Benedetto's claim about this manuscript was not that it is the original; indeed, his conclusion was that 'il fr. 1116 della Nazionale di Parigi è già un esemplare abbastanza lontano, nella forma e nel contenuto, dall' archetipo genovese' (p. CCXX: 'fr. 1116 in the National library in Paris is already a quite distant copy, in both its form and content, of the Genoese archetype'). However, the combination of the reproduction of some errors and lacunae in other versions of the text with the preservation of some passages not in BNF f.fr. 1116 (particularly in Z), led Benedetto to argue persuasively that other versions derive not from f.fr. 1116 itself or even from its direct source, but rather from sources close to it. Furthermore, and crucially, the presence in early vernacular versions such as the French and Tuscan redactions of Italianisms and Gallicisms respectively, or of Gallicisms alongside Italianisms in Z, or of hybrid linguistic forms (of which more in Chapter 2) in all parts of the early tradition, suggests again a lost common source for all versions in a hybrid form of French similar to the language of BNF f.fr. 1116. In other words, all early redactors of the text, with the exception of Pipino, seem to have worked from a range of different Franco-Italian exemplars similar, but not identical, to BNF f.fr. 1116, and even Pipino's direct source (the Venetian redaction) clearly has a shorter Franco-Italian model. Thus, on the one hand, because BNF f.fr. 1116 is the only surviving manuscript that preserves the language of the original (or some approximation of this), as well as being the most complete manuscript, it deserves pride of place; on the other, because BNF f.fr. 1116 is believed to be a faulty copy, arguments are made for the value of other versions, either in order to supplement the readings of BNF f.fr. 1116 or, more radically, to supplant it as the best witness to the earliest, most authentic version of the text. However, as we will see, none of the arguments in favour of other manuscripts being more reliable than BNF f.fr. 1116 is unproblematic, which means that the language and length of the *Devisement* in BNF f.fr. 1116 remain, in my view, decisive arguments in favour not only of continuing to give it the 'posto d'onore' in

---

[47] Though it is worth bearing in mind that one MS of the Tuscan redaction (Florence, Biblioteca Nazionale II.IV.88) is dated 1309.

any analysis of the manuscript tradition but also (and more importantly for my purposes) of setting its text at the heart of any comparative analysis of different versions, as a version approximating the source from which other redactions derive.

How can we be so certain that a Franco-Italian source similar to BNF f.fr. 1116 lies behind other early redactions? During the course of this study (but particularly in Chapters 1 and 2) I will offer comparative readings of episodes from different versions of the *Devisement*, together with analyses of how narrative technique varies from version to version that will, I hope, provide cumulative evidence in favour of the Franco-Italian redaction (albeit not necessarily exactly in the form in which it survives in BNF f.fr. 1116) being the earliest version of the text from which other redactions derive. For now I will content myself with just one lexical example that points in this direction (though among many possible instances).

The rare noun and adjective *tramontane* and *tramontain* ('north'), cognates of the medieval Latin *transmontanus*, are Italianisms in Old and Middle French, meaning primarily 'Pole Star' and 'north wind', and then, but only very occasionally, simply 'north': indeed, the very formation of the word implies a world view anchored in an Italian perspective, since the mountains in question, over which the wind will blow and the Pole Star may be seen, are the Alps, to the north. The Italian reflex of *transmontanus*, *tramontana*, primarily means simply 'north' in early Italian texts. It is surely not, then, coincidental that the earliest attestations of *tramontane* in French are in Brunetto Latini and Marco Polo, two Italian writers of French, and that both use *tramontane* to indicate simply the direction 'north', rather than the Pole Star or a wind. In other words, they use the word *tramontane* exactly as *tramontana* is used in Italian. Moreover, the fact that Brunetto Latini feels the need to gloss the term may indicate that he anticipated that some of his initial francophone readers might find the term opaque: 'vers tramontane, c'est en septentrion' (I, 121, 3: 'towards *tramontane*, which is to say the north').[48] Subsequently the word is attested, though infrequently, in Middle French almost exclusively to designate a north wind or the Pole Star, as it still is in French today in regional or archaic contexts; outside Brunetto Latini and Marco Polo, the dictionaries attest only one certain example of *tramontane* in French being used simply to mean 'north' (from the much later Antoine de la Sale).[49] Given that in the French redaction of the *Devisement* the word is only used where the corresponding passage in the Franco-Italian redaction

---

[48] Cited from Brunetto Latini, *Tresor*, ed. Pietro Beltrami, Paolo Squillacioti, Plinio Torri and Sergio Vatteroni (Turin: Einaudi, 2007).

[49] See *FEW*, 13, 211–14; see 212, in particular, for *tramontane* as an Italianism in French. For *tramontane* as an Italianism in the French redaction of the *Devisement*, see ed. Ménard, I, p. 87, and V, p. 53. For other examples, see the *DMF*, sv. the etymon *transmontanus*: http://atilf.atilf.fr/scripts/dmfX.exe?LEX_ENTREE_INITIALES;BALISE=ETYM;BAC

has *tramontane* or *traimontaine* (see, for example, the Franco-Italian redaction V, 2 ('por tramontane et por grec'), XXIII, 19, and CXLVI, 5; French redaction 4, 4, 22, 53, and 145, 14), and given the precise meaning it is accorded, *tramontane* meaning 'north' is almost certainly a peculiarly Franco-Italian word with limited use in French outside this context.[50] *Tramontana* in versions of the text in Italian dialects (for example Tuscan redaction 22, 16, and 142, 6; Venetian redaction XIV, 5, and CXII, 3) is unsurprising, but usage in the Latin text *Z* is more interesting: 'Sed exercitus permanere non poterat, nisi solummodo a facie una, videlicet versus tramontanam' (79, 8: 'but the army could not remain there, except on one side, which is to say to the north', equivalent to CXLVI, 5, in the Franco-Italian redaction and 145, 14, in the French). Here again *tramontanam* clearly indicates a direction (as in contemporary Italian usage), while one might expect in Latin the spelling *transmontanam*. This apparently trivial example offers fascinating insight into the literal (which is to say, to the letter) translation and transcription techniques often deployed in the Middle Ages; it is also suggestive for how a word from one Romance language may become incorporated into another (or indeed into Latin from a Romance vernacular), even if in this instance the word did not really catch on widely in French.[51] But more locally *tramontane* in the French redaction and *tramontanam* in *Z* indicate these texts derive from a source coloured by Franco-Italian usage.

I should pause here to say something briefly about terminology. 'Franco-Italian' is in some respects a misleading designation for the language of BNF f.fr. 1116 (though the text is in a form of French mixed with Italian, and the manuscript itself is from Italy), since it implies a degree of homogeneity with so-called Franco-Italian literature more generally. Yet within this catch-all category we probably need to distinguish at least four rather different types of texts: French texts circulating in Italy more or less unadapted;[52] French texts adapted for circulation in Italy;[53] translations into Italian vernaculars or

---

K;;ISIS=isis_dmf2010L.txt;OUVRIR_MENU=3;s=s105127fc;LANGUE=FR (consulted 07/05/12). Cf. also *ultramontanus*, Niemeyer, 1050.

[50] In the French redaction at 4, 4, several manuscripts have 'par montaignes et par gauz' for 'par tramontane et par grec', which may suggest a failure to understand *tramontane* on the part of some French scribes.

[51] On translation between Romance languages, or between Romance languages and Latin, see most recently the two stimulating contributions of Frédéric Duval and Sarah Kay: Kay, 'La seconde main et les secondes langues dans la France médiévale', and Duval, 'Les néologismes', in Claudio Galderisi (ed.), *Translations médiévales: cinq siècles de traduction en français au Moyen Âge (XIe–XVe siècles). Etude et répertoire*, 3 vols (Turnhout: Brepols, 2011), I, pp. 461–85 and 499–534.

[52] This is most notably the case with the *Tristan en prose* and the *Lancelot en prose*, on which see particularly Daniela Delcorno Branca, *Tristano e Lancillotto in Italia: studi di letteratura arturiana* (Ravenna: Longo, 1998).

[53] This is the case with many texts in the substantial tradition of Franco-Italian *chansons de geste*, which also, however, includes some original compositions. On this

into Latin by Italians of French texts, but retaining many French forms;[54] and finally texts, such as the *Devisement*, composed in French by Italians.[55] We also need to be aware that there was a wide spectrum of usage, ranging from the almost perfect French of Brunetto Latini, marked more often by Latinisms than by Italianisms,[56] through to the pidgin French/ Italian of some Franco-Italian *chansons de geste*. Within this spectrum there then seem to be greater and lesser degrees of consciousness in the adoption of the hybrid linguistic forms that characterize much Franco-Italian writing, though a growing body of scholars are increasingly committed to the view that in some instances at least the hybridity of Franco-Italian is a consciously and deliberately adopted feature of a literary *koinè*.[57] While realizing that 'Franco-Italian' is a problematic category, I retain it in relation to the *Devisement* for clarity, since this is how the text of BNF f.fr. 1116 is generally referred to in the scholarship.

The Franco-Italian redaction begins with a nineteen-chapter 'prologue' (XIX, 24) that in its first chapter states that the intention of the book is to enlighten 'toutes gens' ('all people') as to 'les deverses jenerasions des homes et les deversités des deverses region dou monde (I, 1: 'the diverse races of men and the great diversity of the diverse regions of the world'), based on the eye-witness account of 'meisser Marc Pol' (I, 2) before then explaining the circumstances of the composition of the text 'en le char[t]re de Jene' (I, 7: 'in the jail cell of Genoa') in 1298, and ambiguously noting the collaboration between Marco Polo and Rustichello da Pisa.[58] The remaining

---

tradition see Juliann Vitullo, *The Chivalric Epic in Medieval Italy* (Gainsville, FL: University of Florida Press, 2000).

[54] The *Tristan en prose*, the *Roman de Troie*, *Les Faits des Romains* and *L'Histoire ancienne jusqu'à César* were particularly popular in translation. The Tuscan redaction of the *Devisement* falls into this category of course. On vernacular translation in Italy, see Alison Cornish, *Vernacular Translation in Dante's Italy: Illiterate Literature* (Cambridge: Cambridge University Press, 2011).

[55] Notable authors here otherwise include Brunetto Latini, Martin da Canale and Rustichello da Pisa, though Brunetto, unlike the others, composed his major work in French outside Italy.

[56] See Max Pfister, 'Le bilinguisme de Brunetto Latini: *Le Livre du Trésor*', in Claire Kappler and Suzanne Thiolier-Méjean (eds), *Le Plurilinguisme au Moyen Âge: Orient-Occident de Babel à la langue Une* (Paris: L'Harmattan, 2009), pp. 203–16.

[57] For example, see Lorenzo Renzi, 'Il francese come lingua letteraria e il franco-lombardo: l'epica carolingia nel Veneto', in Girolamo Arnaldi and Gianfranco Folena (eds), *Storia della cultura Veneta I: delle origini al trecento* (Vicenza: Neri Pozza Editore, 1976), pp. 563–89, and Günter Holtus and Peter Wunderli, *Franco-Italien et épopée franco-italienne* (Heidelberg: Universitätsverlag Winter, 2005) (= *Grundriss der Romanischen Litteraturen des Mittelalters*, vol. 1.2, fasc. 10), pp. 20–21.

[58] It is not impossible that the text's supposed composition in a jail cell is a literary trope. See Maria Luisa Meneghetti, 'Scrivere in carcere nel medioevo', in P. Francia (ed.), *Studi di filologia e letteratura in onore di Maria Picchio Simonelli* (Alessandria: Edizioni dell' Orso,1992), pp. 185–99, and Fabrizio Cigni, 'Copisti Prigionieri (Genova, fine sec. XIII)', in Beltrami, Capusso, Cigni and Vatteroni (eds), *Studi di filologia*, I, pp. 425–39.

eighteen chapters of the prologue narrate, at a cracking pace and largely in the third person, first the journey of the elder Polo brothers to Asia in the 1260s, then their second and longer absence from Europe of twenty-four years. Most of the details given earlier about the circumstances that led to the Polo brothers' ending up at Kublai Khan's court, or about the three Polos and the new Pope in 1271 or their relation to Kublai Khan during their extended period abroad derive from the 'prologue'.

The prologue is followed in the Franco-Italian redaction by over 200 chapters (there are 233 chapters in total). These are largely descriptive, it is suggested in the 'prolegue', of the cities and provinces through which the Polos passed on their way to and from China and then those they visited while working for Kublai Khan: 'Et ce que il trovent en la voie ne voç firon mencion [or], por ce que noç le voç conteron en notre livre, avant, tout per ordre' (XIV, 2: 'And what they find on the way we will not mention now, because we will relate it to you in our book further on, all in order'). These chapters each begin with a heading and occur in an order that makes it possible to reconstruct (more or less) a trajectory east and then a return to Europe, initially by sea around the Indian subcontinent. Most of these chapters merely give the details of what is traded, of the religions practised, of whether or not tribute is paid to the Great Khan and, sometimes, of whether or not the city or province has its own language and what currency is used; some chapters are quite cursory, with formulaic descriptions that make it difficult to individuate the places other than by the proliferation of names. This said, the text does seem to have a marked interest in certain ethnographic and cultural details (more of which in Chapters 3 and 4).

This catalogue of cities and provinces is punctuated, however, with narrative episodes or interludes recounting events as various as wars, religious and political disputes, miracles or the life of the Buddha, and a substantial section is also devoted to a description of Kublai Khan, his person, his court and its activities, and his government. In the most thorough study of the *Devisement*'s narrative episodes to date, Alvaro Barbieri catalogues and classifies twenty-one (apart from the prologue itself), ranging in length from a few lines to substantial sequences of chapters: ten episodes concerning Mongol history (including the story of Genghis Khan's rise to power and his war with the rebellious Christian prince Prester John), seven edifying stories (mainly Christian such as the narratives of the moving mountain, St Thomas and the Magi) and four miscellaneous stories usually deployed to give local colour.[59]

After the prologue, the text alternates between an impersonal mode ('En Turcomanie ha trois jenerasion de jens' (XXI, 1: 'In the land of the Turks there are three races of people')) and first-person narration that addresses

---

[59] See Alvaro Barbieri, 'Il "narrativo" nel *Devisement dou Monde*: tipologia, fonti, funzioni', in Conte (ed.), *I viaggi del* Milione, pp. 54–6.

an audience or readership directly ('Or laison de la grant Harmenie et voç conteron de la provence de Jo<r>gie<n>s', (XXII, 13: 'now let's leave greater Armenia and we will tell you about the province of the Georgians')). However, not infrequently Marco Polo is named in the third person in such a way that he is clearly distinguished from a first-person-singular narrator, who in these instances identifies himself as 'je'. Elsewhere when 'je' is used, it either designates Marco himself (e.g. 'je meser Marc' (XLI, 2)), or the identity of the 'je' is unclear: the ambiguous first person of the Franco-Italian redaction will be the main focus of Chapter 1. The text concludes with twenty-odd chapters that narrate wars in the Middle East that may have affected the Polos' return to Europe. It is generally agreed that these chapters represent a modal shift in the text and that they are aesthetically the least successful and interesting part of the surviving work.

Both the French and the Tuscan redactions, which transpose the *Devisement* into more standard literary idioms, are shorter than the Franco-Italian redaction, with the latter abridging more substantially, perhaps with a view to focusing on commerce and matters of interest to a primarily mercantile Italian readership, but also adding an almost certainly apocryphal epilogue in which the Polos apparently narrate their homecoming in the first-person plural.[60] The French redaction, on the other hand, is thought to have been destined primarily for a courtly audience of the highest rank,[61] though this supposition is based largely on the luxurious nature of just a few of the eighteen surviving manuscripts and does not account for the variation found within this corpus of manuscripts. Whereas the Tuscan redaction retains the ambiguity evident in the Franco-Italian redaction in relation to narrative voice, the French redaction eliminates it, as we will see in Chapter 1, always referring to Marco Polo in the third person, and this is one of a number of elements that contribute to giving the French redaction a different feel from the Franco-Italian, Tuscan and indeed early Venetian redactions, an argument that will be taken further in Chapter 2.

The rough edges of the Franco-Italian redaction have led some scholars to wonder whether it in fact records an early draft, perhaps based on notes Marco had brought from Venice when he was working with Rustichello while held for ransom in Genoa, or alternatively whether Marco went on revising the text after his initial collaboration with Rustichello.[62] Further speculation

---

[60] For example, see Bertolucci Pizzorusso, 'Le versioni storiche', p. 204, and Dutschke, 'Francesco Pipino', pp. 12 and 29, on the Tuscan redaction's mercantile readership. The epilogue follows Chapter 209 of the Tuscan redaction; an English translation may be found in *The Travels* (trans. Latham), pp. 344–5.

[61] See Dutschke, 'Francesco Pipino', p. 11.

[62] See above, n. 36, on hypotheses concerning the existence of notes. On subsequent revisions see, for example, Ménard, 'Intérêt et importance', p. 196: 'Fatalement il [le voyageur vénitien] a dû procéder ultérieurement à des additions.'

is aroused by a second prologue that survives in three manuscripts of the French redaction (though in one manuscript it is copied at the end of the text), claiming that one Thibaut de Chepoy, a French nobleman who visited Venice in 1307, was given a copy of the text by Marco himself, a copy of which was then given to Charles de Valois by Thibaut's son, perhaps in 1311–12, which is to say at more or less the same time as the production of the French redaction.[63] Does this suggest that the French redaction derives, then, from a later, corrected and more authoritative version of the text than BNF f.fr. 1116? As we will see, it may iron out some of the Franco-Italian redaction's textual and linguistic creases, but I will argue that the French redaction, far from being a better 'authorial' revision, is rather an attempt to remodel a source that was found in some respects to be baffling and outlandish.

Although most scholarship has focused on the early vernacular versions of the *Devisement*, by far the most widely disseminated version is the Latin translation by the Dominican Fra Pipino, which survives in more than seventy manuscripts as well as being the source of several later vernacular translations. Fra Pipino's source was a version of the abbreviated first Venetian redaction: the earliest Venetian text has 155, as opposed to the 233 chapters of the Franco-Italian redaction, 194 in the French and 209 in the Tuscan redaction.[64] Pipino radically changed the nature of his source. He retained the subdivision into chapters and their headings, but also divided his translation into three books, corresponding to the way out (the Middle East and Central Asia), the Mongol empire in the Far East (Mongolia, China, Indo-China) and the way back (mainly the Indian subcontinent); he eliminated all references to Rustichello da Pisa; and finally, he introduced an anti-Islamic and pro-Christian tone to the whole text that is not consonant with the generally more open-minded tone of the Franco-Italian redaction, where Islamophobic remarks are limited in number and confined to descriptions of the Near East.[65] Fra Pipino's version, disseminated throughout Europe, is clearly destined for a clerical, learned audience, who often annotated and glossed the text liberally in Latin, but occasionally also in French, German, Italian and Spanish.[66] It seems to have been used primarily as a source of knowledge about Asia and

---

[63] See Ménard, 'Intérêt et importance', p. 187; for the text see ed. Ménard, I, pp. 115–16.

[64] The chapter divisions vary in parts, so there is not always a direct equivalence of chapters between different versions.

[65] For example, his prologue reorients the focus on diversity towards an acknowledgement of the rich abundance of God's creation, while suggesting that the book will also show the extent to which infidels live in darkness (pp. 1–2). As soon as the Pipino version begins its description of the world, negative adjectives are appended frequently to any mention of peoples of other religions: e.g. 'Turchi linguam propriam habent et Machometi abhominabilis legem' (p. 17).

[66] On the annotations, see Dutschke's detailed analysis ('Francesco Pipino', pp. 63–99).

to have circulated mainly among orders that had missions in Asia.[67] There is still, unfortunately, no modern critical edition of Pipino's text, so it is virtually inaccessible to the modern reader.

Three other, less widely disseminated Latin translations, one now lost, are vital for our understanding of the textual tradition of the *Devisement*. The sole manuscript of the *Z* redaction is a fifteenth-century copy of an early fourteenth-century source and shows traces of Venetian dialect.[68] The first third of the text is severely truncated compared with other early redactions (without any reference to Rustichello da Pisa), and it also lacks some key passages, such as the history of Genghis Khan or much of the material describing the court of Kublai Khan. However, *Z* contains numerous short and some more extensive passages (c. 200) that do not occur in the Franco-Italian or other early redactions, many of which also survive in Ramusio's early modern Italian translation, which drew on a lost Latin manuscript as well as Pipino. Furthermore, *Z* is thought to transcribe Oriental place-names more accurately and therefore to derive from a better source than BNF f.fr. 1116.[69] Where *Z* and Ramusio agree on the passages that are not found in the Franco-Italian redaction, it is argued that these passages are authentic and must therefore either have been part of Marco Polo's original text or been added by him subsequently.[70] These passages are included in many modern published translations, some of which have the explicit aim of including as much material as possible, and which do not, therefore, reflect any medieval witness.

The unedited *L* text, on the other hand, stays much closer to a source like BNF f.fr. 1116, with traces of hybrid linguistic forms that are characteristic of the Franco-Italian redaction. *L* does not abridge the text substantively but often omits sentences that might be read as value judgements, seeking to retain above all the text's encyclopaedic characteristics.[71] Like *Z*, Ramusio and Pipino, *L* offers evidence that the *Devisement* was adapted from the vernacular into Latin for a clerical, more learned, milieu than the one for which the vernacular redactions would seem to have been intended – indeed that it quickly circulated among the mendicant orders, particularly among the Dominicans, who used it as a source of information for missions to Asia.

---

[67] Though interestingly not necessarily among the Dominicans, Pipino's own order; see Dutschke, 'Francesco Pipino', pp. 224–7.

[68] See Burgio and Mascherpa, '«Milione» latino', pp. 125–32, and their 'Schede lessicografiche', pp. 156–8.

[69] See ed. Benedetto, p. CLXV, where it is remarked of *Z* that 'la letteralità non potrebbe essere più minuta' and that 'il pensiero di Marco è reso quasi sempre con piena esattezza'. This attachment to 'il pensiero di Marco' reflects an attachment to an idea of authorial intentionality that seems quaint today, but which is nonetheless common in Polo scholarship.

[70] For example, see Burgio and Eusebi, 'Per una nuova edizione', pp. 20–21.

[71] See Burgio and Mascherpa, '«Milione» latino', pp. 132–54, on *L*, particularly 137–47, for detailed analysis of *L*'s treatment of its source.

But *L* also offers oblique evidence of another important point, which is that a fair few copies of the Franco-Italian redaction apart from BNF f.fr. 1116 were in circulation in the early fourteenth century: the sources respectively of the French, Tuscan and Venetian redactions, and then the two Latin translations, *Z* and *L*, none of which seems to derive from an identical source. Thus, whereas it might seem on the basis of BNF f.fr. 1116 that the Franco-Italian redaction is a strange *unicum*, marginal in the tradition compared with the French redaction with its eighteen manuscripts, or indeed to Pipino with its pan-European dissemination, we in fact have evidence that it enjoyed some initial success, at least in Italy, after which it was displaced by versions in more standard forms of the vernacular, and in Latin.

The privileged position Benedetto accorded BNF f.fr. 1116 has not quite been universally accepted. Notably, Barbara Wehr controversially argued in 1993 for a lost original in Venetian (close but not identical to the existing early Venetian translation), of which Pipino's version, she asserted, is a relatively accurate translation.[72] The presence of Venetian forms in Pipino's Latin offers, she suggests, evidence in support of this, but she also somewhat ingeniously argues that Rustichello misappropriated this Venetian original with its three neatly organized books for a francophone courtly public, violating its clear and more streamlined structure, inserting himself into the prologue in a self-aggrandizing move and revising the style throughout to give it a chivalric and French courtly veneer. Wehr's hypothesis, however, has found no support among subsequent scholars (even among those who articulate scepticism about Benedetto's proposed stemma), and there are compelling reasons for rejecting it.[73] First, Rustichello's presence in branches of the tradition that clearly pre-date Pipino (including in the Venetian redaction thought to be Pipino's source) is undoubted, as are the stylistic features that scholars associate with him (rightly or wrongly), so Wehr's hypothesis requires the postulation of a lost vernacular source that looks nothing like any of the earlier or contemporary surviving vernacular redactions. Secondly, her hypothesis does not account for the hybridized linguistic forms of surviving texts. Thirdly, the tradition as a whole contains a good deal of material that is not found in the Venetian redaction or in Pipino, but there is no compelling reason for doubting the authenticity of much of this material.

More recently, in 2008, Eugenio Burgio and Mario Eusebi published a preliminary but nonetheless detailed re-examination of the manuscript tradi-

---

[72] Barbara Wehr, 'A propos de la genèse du "Devisement dou monde" de Marco Polo', in Maria Selig, Barbara Frank and Jörg Hartmann (eds), *Le Passage à l'écrit des langues romanes* (Tübingen: Gunter Narr Verlag, 1993), pp. 299–326.

[73] See, for example: Barbieri, *Dal viaggio*, pp. 66–7; Larner, *Marco Polo*, pp. 52–5; Philippe Ménard, 'Le problème de la version originale du "Devisement du Monde" de Marco Polo', in François Livi (ed.), *De Marco Polo à Savinio, écrivains italiens en langue française* (Paris: Presses de l'Université de Paris-Sorbonne, 2003), pp. 7–19 (pp. 8–12).

tion in which they offer a cogent re-reassessment of Benedetto's findings through an analysis of common errors in selected parts of the text that all sources share.[74] Their resulting working hypothesis is a stemma in which the French redaction is placed closer to the original than the Franco-Italian redaction as preserved in BNF f.fr. 1116, and which accords particular authority to Z as well as to an unedited manuscript (of a virtually unknown and largely independent redaction of the text) in Venetian (Berlin, Staatsbibliothek, Hamilton 424).[75] They nonetheless agree with Benedetto and all previous scholarship (apart from Wehr) that BNF f.fr. 1116 preserves the '*silhouette* formale meno distante dall' originale' (p. 47: 'the formal *silhouette* that is least distant from the original'), by which they seem to mean the hybrid language of BNF f.fr. 1116, as well as the form and content of the extensive 'prologue' and main body of the text. The *Devisement* poses, then, an insuperable problem for an editor whose project is the production of a single authorial text since, apart from BNF f.fr. 1116, all surviving witnesses are either distant from the original in terms of language or translations into different languages, some of which are not only much later but may in fact have been mediated through more than one language.[76] Furthermore, whereas all versions are apparently incomplete or abbreviated, BNF f.fr. 1116 is by some margins the most complete. Thus, quite apart from the question of language, I am less convinced than Burgio and Eusebi that the French redaction and Z deserve to be placed higher in any putative stemma of the text than Benedetto's analysis suggested: both lack significant portions of the *Devisement* as found in BNF f.fr. 1116, and, as we will see, the authenticity of passages found only in Z and Ramusio (if by 'authenticity' one means 'belonging to the earliest version in circulation) is often questionable. Some at least of these passages in Z, I will argue in Chapter 3, are the work of a skilful adaptor who buys effectively into, but elaborates on, some of the *Devisement*'s conceits concerning the Polos' role in the Orient.

Although Burgio and Eusebi give greater credence to the authority of the French redaction than Benedetto and are critical of Benedetto's classification of the manuscripts, they nonetheless, in their conclusion, take Philippe Ménard, who headed the team that has produced the recent six-volume re-edition of the French redaction, to task. Ménard has been an insistent advocate for the quality (and authority) of the French redaction in recent years, of which more shortly. In the introduction to his edition Ménard criticizes Benedetto's methodology as well as the many composite translations of the text that draw on more than one source: the desire to identify, and recon-

---

[74] 'Per una edizione'; for their stemma see p. 45.
[75] On this fifteenth-century manuscript, see Dutschke, 'Francesco Pipino', pp. 288–91; this version is quite distinct from the Venetian redaction edited by Barbieri and Andreose.
[76] This is the case with Ramusio, who says his source was in Latin, which means it was probably already a translation.

struct where possible, an original leads, he suggests, to a series of *partis pris* and arbitrary conjectures: first and foremost, that a medieval text must always be subject to fragmentation and corruption in transmission. For Ménard, in the tradition of the *Devisement* 'toutes les versions ont des fautes, des omissions (petites ou grandes), des changements (plus ou moins importants)' ('all versions have mistakes, omissions (minor and major), revisions (of greater or lesser scale)'), and by the same token 'elles méritent toutes intérêt, estime et considération' ('they are all worthy of interest, respect and consideration').[77] Not so, say Burgio and Eusebi. Their analysis of the manuscripts, they argue, confirms Benedetto's conviction that the *Devisement* undergoes in transmission 'un progressivo degradarsi e impoverirsi della tessitura orginaria, a partire da un testimone, molto vicino all' originale, già segnato da guasti' (p. 45: 'a progressive disintegration and impoverishment of the original framework, beginning with a witness that was very close to the original, but already marked by errors'). What is needed now, in addition presumably to separate editions of all the different versions, is a 'nuova edizione "integrale"' (p. 47: 'new "integral" edition'), one that will place alongside the text from BNF f.fr. 1116 the material it has supposedly lost, thereby offering a better view of the original than editing BNF f.fr. 1116 alone could possibly allow. We have here a common difference of opinion that illustrates eloquently the divergent approaches between, on the one hand, the neo-Lachmannian, largely Italian school of textual editors, who seek to reconstruct an original from what they believe to be a mass of surviving corrupt witnesses, and, on the other, the neo-Bédieriste French school of textual editors, who privilege a single version of a text (often a single manuscript) as representing at least an authentic medieval witness rather than a modern hypothesis.[78]

As we have seen, the *Devisement* is an interesting limit case in relation to this methodological controversy since a whole extra dimension comes into play, namely that of language. Modern translations of the *Devisement* that supply material deemed 'missing' in BNF f.fr. 1116 (for example, from Z) can mask the extent to which they are offering a composite text because the fact that their various sources are in different languages may be rendered to all intents and purposes invisible. But if the language of BNF f.fr. 1116 is retained (or that of any other manuscript, for that matter), splicing in 'missing' material becomes much more problematic, as Burgio and Eusebi clearly realize when they say that extra material would need to be placed alongside ('*accanto* a') BNF f.fr. 1116: reconstructing a hypothetical original

---

[77] Ed. Ménard, I, p. 13. See also his 'Intérêt et importance', pp. 188–91.

[78] For a recent *mise au point* and intervention in the debate see Lino Leonardi, 'Il testo come ipotesi (critica del manoscritto-base)', *Medioevo Romanzo*, 35 (2011), 5–34. The Bédiériste approach is perhaps best illustrated by many (though by no means all) editions published in the *Classiques français du Moyen Age* series.

as a single readable text on the basis of surviving manuscripts is impossible for the *Devisement*, at least in any medieval language.

Language is thus a major conundrum for editors of the *Devisement* and scholars of its textual tradition, though this is often occluded in the majority of scholarship and popular writing on Marco Polo, which reads the text largely for its contents. My own approach aims to put language at the centre of my analysis of the *Devisement*, which is to say that I wish to consider how its hybrid French signifies in relation to other aspects of the text. And what, then, are the implications of this hybridity being eliminated, either through a process of linguistic standardization or through translation? I also wish to consider what other textual transformations are effected when the text undergoes linguistic retooling and the relation between the two processes. If I have engaged here at some length with the scholarship on the textual tradition of the *Devisement*, it is not because I wish to affirm a stemmatic approach, but rather in order to explain for interested readers the most likely relation of the different versions before undertaking comparative readings that seek to draw out the significance of a movement between languages that starts out from a point of origin that is outside (or confounds) the usual boundaries of modern national philologies and literary histories. It is to this topic that I now turn.

When it is acknowledged that the *Devisement* was first composed in some form of French, the standard reason given, as Ménard puts it in the introduction to his edition, is that it was a 'langue réputée supérieure' (I, p. 21: 'language reputed to be superior'). Or, as he puts it elsewhere, 'Le texte de Marco Polo a été écrit par Rustichello en français, langue qui jouissait alors d'un grand prestige international. C'était la langue noble à ce moment de l'histoire' ('Marco Polo's text was written by Rustichello in French, a language that enjoyed great international prestige then. It was the noble language at this point in history').[79]

The problem for Ménard, however, is that the French in which the *Devisement* was apparently originally composed is not by his lights correct French at all. In a swathe of publications leading up to his new critical edition of the French redaction, Ménard sought to establish the merits of this text at the expense of the earlier Franco-Italian redaction. Whereas the Franco-Italian text is 'déformé par de nombreux italianismes' ('deformed by many italianisms'),[80] so that its language is 'satisfaisante ni aux yeux d'un lecteur italien, ni à ceux d'un lecteur français' ('satisfying neither in the eyes of an Italian reader, nor in those of a French reader'),[81] the French redaction is 'remarquable [...] écrite dans une langue dépourvue des graves incorrections et des confusions verbales qui déparent la rédaction franco-italienne. Elle est

---

[79] 'Le problème', p. 19.

[80] Philippe Ménard, *Marco Polo: à la découverte du monde* (Paris: Glénat, 2007), p. 9.

[81] 'Le problème', p. 13.

donc beaucoup plus agréable à lire' ('remarkable [...] written in a language without any of the serious errors and verbal confusions that spoil the Franco-Italian redaction. It is consequently much more pleasant to read').[82] His special pleading sometimes verges on proselytising fervour. The French redaction

> se trouve rédigée en un français plus correct que la langue hybride du ms. fr. 1116. où assez souvent les mots sont estropiés, les règles de la déclinaison et de la conjugaison bafouées. Un progrès manifeste apparaît au plan de la morphologie et de la syntaxe. Elle donne un texte assez fidèle (proche de la rédaction franco-italienne), sous son habillage français.[83]
>
> (is written in a more correct form of French than the hybrid language of MS fr. 1116, where frequently words are garbled, the rules of declension and conjugation muddled. There is manifest progress in morphology and syntax. It offers a rather faithful text (close to the Franco-Italian redaction) underneath its French clothing.)

Thus:

> Il faut redonner à la version française toute son importance [...] Elle n'est pas une traduction et une adaption dans une langue étrangère: son rédacteur a surtout opéré une toilette linguistique sur le texte franco-italien, qui déformait assez souvent la langue française. Enfin parce qu'elle ne pratique pas d'abrègements systématiques comme la plupart des autres rédactions, et qu'elle s'accorde habituellement avec le ms. franco-italien [...] elle mérite beaucoup de considération et de respect.[84]
>
> (We need to reinstate the French version as crucially important [...] It isn't a translation or an adaptation in a foreign language: its redactor has above all given the Franco-Italian text a linguistic make-over, since it often disfigured the French language. Finally, because unlike most of the other redactions it does not systematically abridge the text and because it usually agrees with the Franco-Italian manuscript, it deserves to be treated with the greatest of consideration and respect.)

Ménard's critical vocabulary here typifies attitudes towards language that are prevalent in the field, but it is paradoxical. Thus the notion of 'une toilette linguistique' has connotations of washing and therefore of purification, but also of dressing up ('habillage') and make-up. On the one hand, the grime of all those Italianisms is washed away. On the other, is to 'Frenchify' a text in fact to apply a beautifying but superficial layer to an imperfect but nonetheless authoritative base? It is interesting, then, that the authority Ménard attributes to the French redaction apparently derives in part at least from the fact that

---

[82] Ménard, *Marco Polo*, p. 10.
[83] Ménard, 'Intérêt et importance', p. 195.
[84] Ménard, 'Intérêt et importance', p. 197.

it often agrees with the Franco-Italian, as if – in Derridean terms – the latter supplements the former, thereby undermining the importance of the very text he is defending. In any event, the metaphors of clothing and make-up mean we need to look beneath the surface of the French redaction to get to the model to which it is apparently so faithful apart from its schoolmasterly proclivity for linguistic correctness.

Ménard's defence of the French redaction is thus riddled with contradiction. The problem, in my view, stems from an anachronistic investment in an idea of linguistic correctness that is in turn bound up with an investment in a particular model of French literary culture, according to which medieval French literature is imitated throughout Europe because it is associated with nobility and high culture.[85] This vision of medieval French literature sees it as the fitting precursor to the rigid stylistic and linguistic codification of French humanism and classicism. While it is good that the *Devisement* was composed in French, from Ménard's point of view, since it points to the language's international prestige, its French is nonetheless simply not good enough because it is too tainted by Italian.

On the other hand, the French of the *Devisement* sometimes also proves problematic for Italian literary history. Consider the following footnote to Alberto Varvaro's essay on 'Language and Culture' in *The Short Oxford History of Italy*:

> The most significant literary production of mercantile culture at the end of the thirteenth century was Marco Polo's *Milione*, dictated by the author to Rustichello da Pisa while in prison in Genoa, and subsequently written down in French. Produced in innumerable versions and adaptations, the work would remain one of the most important texts of the later Middle Ages. Another work in French by an Italian author which was successful in the thirteenth century was an encyclopaedia by Brunetto Latini, Dante's teacher. It was entitled *Tresor*, and was translated in both Italy and Spain.[86]

Thus we find tucked away, indeed one might say dismissed, in this footnote to rising literary rates in Tuscany 'and certain restricted areas' owing to 'the beginnings of commerce and finance' the only mention in this chapter of two of the most widely disseminated, and presumably therefore most successful, texts of the Italian Middle Ages. It is also noteworthy that the *Devisement* is given its Italian title here (*Il Milione*) and that since 'it was dictated by the author [...] and subsequently written down in French', this seems to imply that for Varvaro the original and authorial language had been a form

---

[85] For further examples, see Heers, *Marco Polo*, pp. 297–305, where French is described as the 'langue de cour, langue d'un premier humanisme'.

[86] In David Abulafia (ed.), *Short Oxford History of the Middle Ages: Italy in the Central Middle Ages* (Oxford: Oxford University Press, 2004), pp. 195–211 (p. 203).

of Italian, presumably Venetian. Meanwhile coupling Brunetto Latini (whose other main claim to fame here is that he was Dante's teacher) with Marco Polo in this footnote because both apparently wrote in French occludes rather than displays information in the context of the chapter as a whole, since Brunetto Latini wrote his *Tresor* while living in exile in France and in largely correct French. The chapter culminates, naturally enough, with Dante's *Commedia*, the success of which is beyond doubt: it remains by far the most widely disseminated vernacular text of the Middle Ages in any language. But tellingly, apart from the footnote I have just cited, there is only one other reference to literary texts in French in Varvaro's chapter: 'the decasyllabic *Ritmo bellunese* seems to have some of the characteristics of French epic poetry, a form that spread quite early in Northern Italy and gave rise to a hybrid linguistic form, Franco-Italian. Among other works, there is a version of the *Song of Roland* in this hybrid language' (p. 207). This brief remark, which gives way to two full pages on the troubadour lyric in Italy as a precursor to Italian lyric poetry, fails to convey the richness of the so-called Franco-Italian tradition to which it alludes, which includes as many as sixty-five texts in French (including the *Devisement*) that modern scholars have identified as emanating from Italy, in addition to numerous Italian manuscripts of other texts in French.[87] Varvaro's concern in his chapter is the rise of vernacular literature in Italy, and it is perhaps quite natural that he should focus on material in Italian and look forward to the extraordinary literary event that Dante's oeuvre was to be. But the risk is then that Italian literary history before Dante is presented as a teleological movement towards Dante and the Italianization (or perhaps more accurately Tuscanization) of literary culture that his work represents, but without proper acknowledgement of the extent to which literary texts in French were circulating, and indeed being composed, in Italy throughout the Middle Ages.[88] The Occitan troubadours are included as worthy precursors of the sophisticated high lyric style that Dante was to perfect, an inspiration he himself acknowledged and wrote about. But literature in French is relegated to the margins, buried in the footnotes and, in the case of Marco Polo, barely even acknowledged as having much to do with the French language at all,

---

[87] See Holtus and Wunderli, *Franco-Italien et épopée franco-italien*, for further details.

[88] On the Franco-Italian and Franco-Venetan tradition, in addition to Holtus and Wunderli (*Franco-Italien*), see: Fabrizio Cigni, 'La ricezione della letteratura francese nella Toscana nord-occidentale', in Edeltraud Werner and Sabine Schwarze (eds), *Fra toscanità e italianità* (Tübingen and Basel: Francke, 2000), pp. 71–108; Alison Cornish, 'Translatio Galliae: Effects of Early Franco-Italian Exchange', *Romanic Review*, 97 (2006), 309–30; Delcorno Branca, *Tristano e Lancillotto in Italia*; Renzi, 'Il francese come lingua letteraria'; and Peter Wunderli, 'Un luogo di "interferenze": il franco-italiano', in Luigina Morini (ed.), *La cultura dell'Italia padana e la presenza francese nei secoli XII–XV* (Alessandria: Edizioni dell'Orso, 2001), pp. 55–66.

because what matters is the emergence of Italian as the language of high culture and literature in the Italian peninsula.

Of course, the dissemination and production of francophone texts in Italy are hardly an unknown phenomenon among medievalists, but the status of these texts nonetheless remains under-researched and controversial because of all that is invested in modern national literary histories and linguistic identities. What if the French language is less 'French' than the French themselves like to think? And what if some of the high points of medieval 'Italian' literature were actually written in French? One of my main premises in this book is thus that we need to try to set aside post-medieval literary historical and cultural turf wars in order to understand fully how a text like the *Devisement* works across national and linguistic boundaries that were not so firmly in place, if in place at all, in the Middle Ages. Another is that historical and post-colonial approaches to a text like the *Devisement* need to be informed by the tools of literary criticism and, perhaps even more importantly, philology for the information and ideas for which it is a vehicle to be properly evaluated: language cannot simply be regarded as a neutral vehicle for content; it bears its own ideological and cultural freight.

What we see here is the extent to which language makes Marco Polo and the *Devisement* difficult to position in literary and cultural history. Considered neither a French nor an Italian text at some points, the *Devisement* can then morph into a French or an Italian text as the occasion demands.[89] Nonetheless, by and large the tendency among many literary scholars and historians has been to ignore it: to give but one telling example, there is no entry for the *Devisement* or Marco Polo in *The New Oxford Companion to Literature in French*.[90] Is the *Devisement* not then literature? I will return in more detail to the question of language in Chapter 2: suffice it to say for the time being that the *Devisement*'s language makes it an awkward text for modern scholarly paradigms and that the language of its earliest articulations, even when the text is adapted into more standard forms of French or Italian (or indeed Latin), is thought to be hybrid, or at the very least to show traces of hybridity. But for now let me turn to the question of genre.

The genre of the *Devisement*

The genre of the *Devisement* has proved controversial. It has been variously argued that it either is, or should be seen as related to, or as borrowing from,

---

[89] We find a rare acknowledgement of this in Heers, *Marco Polo*, p. 288: 'Le *Devisement* de Rusticello serait une oeuvre de tradition et d'esprit français; le même livre, appelé *Milione* et attribué uniquement à Marco Polo, appartient tout entier au patrimoine italien.'

[90] Ed. Peter France (Oxford: Clarendon Press, 1995).

one (or more) of the following existing, emerging or future modes of Western writing:[91]

the merchant's manual[92]
the crusading tract[93]
the encyclopaedia[94]
the missionary manual[95]
ethnography and/ or geography[96]
the wonder book[97]
vernacular writing about the Orient (e.g. the *Roman d'Alexandre*)[98]
Old French romance and/ or the Old French *chanson de geste*[99]
travel writing[100]

Whereas some scholars have argued that the *Devisement* belongs purely in just *one* of these categories and should be read accordingly, most recognize that it borrows thematically and stylistically from a range of different modes of writing. And the list could be expanded further: as I will suggest in

---

[91] Quite apart from attempts to demonstrate Oriental sources and/or influences for some sections of the text. For example, see Gang Zhou, 'Small Talk: A New Reading of Marco Polo's *Il Milione*', *Modern Language Notes*, 124 (2009), 1–22.

[92] See the frequently cited Borlandini, 'Alle origini del libro'.

[93] See Espada, *Marco Polo*.

[94] Many scholars evoke this parallel. For a stimulating analysis, see Katherine Park, 'The Meaning of Natural Diversity: Marco Polo on the "Division" of the World', in Edith Sylla and Michael McVaugh (eds), *Texts and Contexts in Ancient and Medieval Science: Studies on the Occasion of John E. Murdoch's Seventieth Birthday* (Leiden and New York: Brill, 1997), pp. 134–47.

[95] The clearest articulation of this thesis is Ruggero Ruggieri, *Marco Polo e l'oriente francescano* (Rome: Edizioni Porziuncola, 1984).

[96] Barbieri sub-titles a subsection of his book 'Etnografia poliana', *Dal viaggio al libro*, pp. 155–251; see also Marianne O'Doherty, '"They Are Like Beasts, For They Have No Law": Ethnography and the Construction of Human Difference in Late Medieval Translations of Marco Polo's *Book*', in Jean-François Kosta-Théfaine (ed.), *Travels and Travelogues in the Middle Ages* (Brooklyn: AMS Press, 2009), pp. 59–93. Larner's position in his *Marco Polo* is that the *Devisement* is a work of geography.

[97] The *Devisement*'s inclusion in the richly illustrated and famous 'livre des merveilles', BNF f.fr. 2810, speaks for itself. For a consideration of Marco Polo specifically in the context of 'wonder' books, see Lorraine Daston and Katherine Park, *Wonders and the Order of Nature, 1150–1700* (New York: Zone Books, 1998), pp. 24–34.

[98] Heers in particular (*Marco Polo*, pp. 317–31) stresses the *Devisement*'s debt to previous vernacular writing on this score.

[99] See Bertolucci Pizzorusso's nuanced remarks in 'Lingue e stili', pp. 66–7.

[100] Campbell, *Witness and the Other World*, pp. 87–121; Islam, *Ethics of Travel*. Racine's suggestion that the *Devisement* is reportage (*Marco Polo*) also aligns it with travel writing. On medieval travel writing generally, see Paul Zumthor, 'The Medieval Travel Narrative', *New Literary History*, 25 (1994), 809–24, who cautions against considering medieval travel narrative as a discrete genre (p. 811).

Chapter 1, there are also similarities in terms of narrative voice between the *Devisement* and earlier Old French chronicles.

The fact that many of the types of writing I have just listed would not be recognized by modern critics as 'literary' is perhaps a factor in the sparse attention the *Devisement* has received from literary scholars. But the category of the 'literary' is a modern one, and in saying that I will read the *Devisement* foregrounding its literary qualities, I mean primarily that I subject it to the tools of literary analysis, considering style, narrative voice, modes of representation and so on. Clearly the text does not belong to any of the canonical genres of high medieval literature (epic, romance, lyric, allegory etc.). But it is by no means clear that medieval writers, transmitters or readers distinguished different modes of writing as we do, while some distinctions that we might assume (for example, the difference between fiction and history) were in fact more fluid for medieval writers and readers.

What matters most here is that the *Devisement* consciously recalls different modes of writing without replicating them. Thus the stress in the prologue on the *devisement/divisement* of the world, meaning both its description and its division into different parts, and on the world's diversity, recalls encyclopaedic writing on the same topic. Compare the opening rubric of the *Devisement* with that of the section of Brunetto Latini's *Tresor* devoted to the description of the world:

> Ci comancent le lobrique de cest livre qui est appelé le Divis[a]ment dou Monde (I)
>
> Ci [comenc]e le devissement de mappemonde, c'est coment la terre est ordenee.[101]

Whether or not these rubrics are authorial, the parallel is clear, and throughout the *Devisement* in the Franco-Italian redaction the numerous rubrics that begin 'Ci devise de ...' suggest the format of the textual 'mappamundi' that is frequently incorporated into encyclopaedias. On the other hand, some of the details that are given for each place (for example, what is produced and traded there), attention to distances and the way sequences of places suggest an itinerary are also strongly reminiscent of the so-called merchant's manual, composed for purely practical purposes, examples of which survive, but not from before the fourteenth century.[102] Yet the *Devisement* is clearly neither an encyclopaedia nor a merchant's manual: it is not an encyclopaedia because it does not aim to be comprehensive (it has nothing to say about Europe, for example), and it is not a merchant's manual because it gives few practical details about travel or trade (pilots' fees, port taxes, modes of transport etc.).

---

[101] Cited from Brunetto Latini, *Tresor*, ed. Beltrami *et al.*, I, 121.
[102] See Borlandi, 'Alle origini del libro'.

As Ugo Tucci astutely observes, modes of writing such as the encyclopaedia and the merchant's manual provide a framework that allows for the organization of material in the *Devisement*, but without transforming the text into a simple vehicle for information and knowledge.[103] On the other hand, there can be no doubt that playing on modes of writing that do impart information and knowledge enhances subliminally the text's claim to authenticity and truth.

The *Devisement* is haunted by other modes of writing – and indeed by literary tradition – in other ways. For example, one main source of information for medieval readers about the Orient were narrative texts – in Latin and in the vernacular – about Alexander the Great, of which there was an extensive tradition in French.[104] The *Devisement* is careful to index Alexander's exploits in Asia as a point of comparison in its own account. Thus early in the Franco-Italian redaction we read, in a chapter entitled 'Ci devise dou roi des Giorgiens e de lor affer':

> Et <est> cest la provence ke Alexandre ne poit paser quant il vost aler au ponent por ce que la vie est estroit et dotose: car de l'un les est la mer et de l'autre est gran montagne que ne se poent cavaucher. La vie est mout estroit entre la montagne et la mer; et dure cest estroit vie plus de quatre liegues, si ke pou homes tendront le pas a tout le monde. Et ce fo la caxon por coi Alexandre ne poet passere. Et voç di ke Alexandre hi fist fermer una tore et hi fist une forteçe por coi celle jens ne poesent pasere por venir sor lui et fu appelé la port dou fer et ce est le leu que le livre Alexandre conte comant il enclouse les Tartarç dedenç deus montagnes. Et ce ne fu pas voir qu'il fuissent Tartar, mes furent une jens qui estoient apellés Comain et autres jenerasion asseç, car Tartarç n'estoient a celui tens. (XXIII, 6–11)

> (And this is the province where Alexander could go no further when he wanted to travel West because the road was so narrow and difficult: for it is hemmed in by the sea and high mountains over which it is not possible to ride. The road is so narrow between the mountain and sea, and this narrow road lasts for more than four leagues, so that a few men can hold the pass against many. This is why Alexander could not pass. And I tell you that Alexander had a tower built and a fortress so that the people could not attack him, and it was called the Iron Gate. And this is the place where the book of Alexander relates how he enclosed Tartars between two mountains. And it is not true that they were Tartars, rather they were a people called Comanians, and other races besides, for there were no Tartars in those days.)

---

[103] Ugo Tucci, 'I primi viaggiatori e l'opera di Marco Polo', in Arnaldi and Folena (eds), *Storia della cultura veneta*, I, pp. 633–70 (pp. 654–5); see also Barbieri, *Dal viaggio al libro*, pp. 135–6.

[104] See Martin Gosman, *La Légende d'Alexandre le Grand dans la littérature française du 12e siècle* (Amsterdam: Rodopi, 1997).

This first of several explicit references to Alexander is interesting on a number of counts. First, it is noted, almost in passing and towards the beginning of the book, how Alexander's journeys are constrained by physical obstacles. Here Alexander is halted, but not so, implicitly, Marco Polo, since the book moves on seamlessly to describe another province. True, it is not stated that Marco actually passed along the narrow road that defeated Alexander here: we are being told rather about 'les confin d'Armenie dever tramontane' (XXIII, 19: 'the limits of Armenia to the north'), while the next chapter concerns 'le autre confin que sunt entre midi et levant' (XXIII, 20: 'the other border, to the south and east'). But this part of the world nonetheless represents the very beginning of Marco's journey. The text also seems (with the Iron Gate that holds back barbarian peoples) to be evoking the biblical Gog and Magog, which is in addition the mythical place traditionally sited in the Caucasus (i.e. on the borders of Armenia) where Alexander is said to have erected a barrier to keep barbarians away from civilized peoples. Gog Magog is often considered the edge of the known world (Alexander travelled south-eastward round the Caspian Sea from here towards Persia and India, but not north-eastward towards central Asia). Marco Polo, however, just bowls past to reveal to his readers a host of hitherto unimagined lands precisely on the route that Alexander failed to follow. The second noteworthy point here is that previous written accounts of Asia, here quite explicitly *le livre Alexandre*, are corrected in the *Devisement*, and in this instance from both an ethnographic and an historical point of view. Indeed, there may be a further implicit correction to received wisdom here: we realize, some thirty chapters later (LXXIV, 11–12), that Marco locates Gog and Magog in Mongolia and associates it with the legendary Prester John. Don't believe what you have read in books before this one about the rest of the world, the *Devisement* seems to be saying: trust instead the account of someone who has actually been to the lands of which you read.

Having said this, there are plenty of passages in the *Devisement* where description and narration are embellished by 'literary' technique. Consider the following extract from the account of Kublai Khan's civil war with his rebellious (and treacherous) uncle Nayan, who is a Christian:

> Et que voç en diroie? Il comancent la meslee mout cruele et felones[c]: or poit l'en veoir voler sagites, car toit l'air n'estoit plien, come [s]e il fuist pluie; or poit bien veoir chevaliers et chevaus mort caoir a la tere; il hi estoit si grant la grié et <la> remoute que l'en ne o[is]t le dieu tonant. Et sachiés que Naian estoit cristienz bateiçiéç et a ceste bataille avoit il la crois de Crist sor la enseigne.
>
> Et porcoi voç firoie je lonc conte? Sachiés tout voirement que cele fu la plus perilieuse bataile et la plus dotouse que jamés fust veue: ne a nostre tens ne furent tantes jens en un canp a bataille et propremant homes a chevaus. Il hi morurent tant homes et d'une part et d'autre que ce estoit mervoille a veoir. (LXXIX, 10–13)

(And what more can I tell you? They begin a most terrible and cruel battle: now one can see arrows flying through the air, for the sky was full of them as if it were raining; now one can see knights and horses falling dead to the ground; the fighting and noise were so great that it was like hearing God raging. And you should know that Nayan was a baptized Christian and that in this battle he had Christ's cross on his banner.

And why should I make this into a long story? You should know truly that this was one of the harshest and most fearful battles that has ever been seen; neither in our time or earlier have there been so many armies on a battlefield, so many men or horses. So many men died there on both sides that it was a marvel to behold.)

Readers familiar with Old French verse and prose romance or with Old French *chansons de geste* and chronicles would recognize here a range of common stylistic devices (the use of the rhetorical question about pressing ahead with the story, the patterns of repetition created by these questions) and motifs (arrows falling like rain, the battlefield strewn with the bodies of men and horses, the hyperbolic claim that this was the greatest battle ever fought). Such passages have bolstered the view held by some scholars that, whereas the substance of the *Devisement* was supplied by Marco Polo, the style was Rustichello da Pisa's. I will say a little more in the next section about why I think this approach is too simplistic and explore the issue in more detail in Chapter 1, but one thing is clear: the stylistic devices used here are deployed to help make the unfamiliar more legible for European readers (an Oriental war between a Christian prince who is in the wrong and his pagan overlord, who is being represented as in the right) by casting it in terms they will recognize.

What emerges from this is a protean text that borrows at will from other modes of writing. But this is also a chameleon text that can seem more like an encyclopaedia, a romance or epic narrative, a crusading tract, a wonder book, or a personal travel narrative depending on the manuscript and form in which it is transmitted. To stick just to examples of the French redaction:

- BNF f.fr. 5649 is one of several manuscripts in which the presentation is similar to that of contemporary vernacular encyclopaedias, with a numbered table of rubrics in red at the beginning of the volume that is keyed to the rubrics of individual chapters. This table could be used in a manner similar to an index in a modern book, making it easy to consult the manuscript in order to retrieve information quickly.
- The exquisite and richly illustrated Oxford Bodley 264 is a composite manuscript made up of a Flemish copy of parts of the *Roman d'Alexandre*, dated by the scribe 1338 and by the artist 1344, which is then bound together in England c. 1400–10 with a short extract of an English *Alexander* and a copy of the *Devisement* by the same scribe as

the English *Alexander*.[105] Placing the *Devisement* second in the volume with the *Alexandre* suggests the former may be read through the prism of the latter, particularly since the two texts are bound together by a programme of illustrations that invite comparison.[106]

- British Library Royal 19 D 1 was almost certainly Bodley 264's source for the text of the *Devisement*. Made in Paris, almost certainly in the workshop of Richard and Jeanne Montbaston in the 1330s, it was probably taken to England shortly afterwards. Its numerous illustrations, deemed by art historians to be of poor quality, nonetheless have much to say about how the texts it contains were understood. These include, apart from the *Devisement*: various texts from the French *Alexandre* tradition, Jean de Vignay's French translation of Odoric of Pordenone, a French translation of chapters from Vincent of Beauvais's *Speculum* about Asia (including the abridgement therein of John of Plano Carpini's account of his mission to Asia), various French translations of crusading texts. According to a number of scholars, this MS can be read as propaganda for a renewed crusade in the Middle East.[107]

- The famous and much-studied *Livre des Merveilles*, BNF f.fr. 2810, made c. 1400 and given in 1413 by Jean sans Peur, Duke of Burgundy, to the consummate bibliophile Jean de Berry, who in turn passed it to Jacques d'Armagnac, opens with the *Devisement* and, like Royal 19 D 1, includes a series of texts about Asia, all in French and including: Odoric of Pordenone again, Mandeville, William of Boldensale, Hayton. The text occurs here without a table of rubrics and with no chapter numbers, its main organizational feature – and indeed that of the manuscript as a whole – being a sequence of remarkable illustrations: there are eighty-four miniatures in the *Devisement* and 265 in the volume as a whole. Scholars have long remarked upon the extraordinary visual conception of this book, which draws the reader not just to read the book in a linear manner, but also (and perhaps instead) to move back and forth between texts because of visual parallels between illustrations to distant places in different texts in the compilation. Indeed, it is quite possible to imagine this exceptionally handsome volume being used primarily as a picture book. The focus of the illustrations is primarily on exotic

---

[105] On this manuscript, see Consuelo W. Dutschke's brilliant article 'The Truth in the Book: The Marco Polo Texts in Royal 19 D1 and Bodley 264', *Scriptorium*, 52 (1998), 278–300.

[106] On the *Alexandre* portion of this MS, see Mark Cruse, *Illuminating the Roman d'Alexandre: Oxford, Bodleian Library, MS Bodley 264: The Manuscript as Monument* (Cambridge: D.S. Brewer, 2011).

[107] See: Dutschke, 'The Truth in the Book'; Ross, 'Methods of Book Production'; Richard H. and Mary A. Rouse, *Manuscripts and Their Makers: Commercial Book Producers in Medieval Paris, 1200–1500*, 2 vols (London: Harvey Miller, 2000), pp. 244–7.

locations and exotic phenomenon, hence its early sobriquet as the *Book of Wonders*.[108]

- Finally Paris Arsenal 5219, which dates from the early sixteenth century, has an equally remarkable, if considerably less sumptuous, programme of illustrations. Here the text occurs with no table, but has chapter headings/ rubrics that initially are run together with the preceding chapter, but which after a certain point follow the miniatures that head every chapter. Although some of these could be generic representations of travel and distant lands, most illustrate precisely the content of the relevant chapter. Their quality is indifferent, though they do have a certain elegant simplicity. In any event, it is clear that someone went to a lot of trouble to make this book and to ensure that its programme of illustrations reflected very closely its textual contents. This greatly enhances the sense that the text represents a journey and consequently gives this book the aura of a personal travel narrative.

What emerges from this brief survey is the extent to which the *Devisement* is malleable in reception, a quality I would wish to relate to its generic hybridity.

This Book

This book has four chapters. Chapters 1 and 2 will look in more detail respectively at the ambiguous narrative voice of the *Devisement* and at its hybrid language. The focus here, indeed throughout this book, will be the Franco-Italian redaction, but I will also make frequent reference throughout to other early versions of the text, particularly the French, Tuscan and Z redactions, with occasional reference to the earliest Venetian redaction and to Pipino. Chapter 1 will first examine the ambiguous identities of 'je' and 'nous' in the Franco-Italian redaction and how they are treated by other versions; secondly, it will show how this maps on to the treatment of time and space; and finally, it will suggest how we might read the presentation of Marco Polo as storyteller extraordinaire. Chapter 2 will first examine the hybrid nature of the Franco-Italian redaction's language and how this is treated in other redactions; secondly, it will offer a case study of how one episode is adapted from its source in the French redaction; and finally, it will consider the *Devisement*'s own representation of linguistic difference.

The premise behind these two chapters is that, rather than speculating on the circumstances that led to the *Devisement* being written in the language

---

[108] There is a great deal of scholarship on this MS, but see principally Avril, Gousset, Monfrin, Richard and Tesnière (eds), *Das Buch der Wunder*, and Meneghetti, 'Quando l'immagine dice di più'.

and form that it takes in BNF f.fr. 1116, we should seek instead to consider the *effects* of the text as it is. Rather than seeking to identify the 'je' or 'nous' speaking at any given point, the question would then rather become: how are we to read a text where the narrative voice at times disappears, at times identifies itself and at times seems deliberately to create ambiguity as to its precise identity? In this approach 'Marco Polo' and 'Rustichello da Pisa' become first and foremost figures within the text – author, narrator, if you will – as much as they are the historical collaborators many Marco Polo scholars have imagined at work in their prison cell in Genoa. As for the *Devisement*'s language and style, rather than attributing some features to Marco and others to Rustichello, I want again to ask what are the *effects* of an ambiguous narrative voice, and of linguistic or indeed generic hybridity? And here I wish to contextualize the language and style of the *Devisement* by insisting both on its use of French and on its Italian origin, but in doing so I want also to suggest a different interpretation of the phenomenon of the use of French as a literary language in Italy from the one often suggested in much medieval French scholarship: rather than seeing 'French' as something that belongs to 'France' and 'French' high culture, I prefer to see French as the vernacular of choice when a writer wishes to address an international audience, and thus as an index of cultural mobility rather than as a sign of the prestige of one culture in particular.[109] Of course, if the information the *Devisement* gives us about how it came to be composed is correct, all kinds of scenarios are possible as to who was responsible for which aspects of the text, and whether or not it was revised after the initial collaboration. But unless new documents concerning the collaboration of Marco Polo and Rustichello da Pisa come to light, answers to questions concerning the circumstances of composition of the text and the specific input of its supposed authors will always ultimately be hypothetical. My premise, therefore, is that even to ask these questions is in some ways to miss the point, which is that the questions themselves are generated by the *Devisement*'s framing of itself in most of the earliest versions as a joint composition and by its own subsequent articulation (linguistically and narratologically). Of course, this is not necessarily intentional, and there is a possibility that some of the features of the Franco-Italian text in BNF f.fr. 1116 and the other early redactions that interest me are accidental, owing to inattention or oversight. However, the fact remains that the *Devisement* is a text that in its earliest incarnation seeks to convey empirical knowledge about the world in a language it flags as 'foreign' to its two authors (in that it is neither's mother tongue) and which it seems deliberately to mix with another, only then to occlude knowledge about itself. Furthermore, it establishes as the authority for all the information

---

[109] In this I follow Bertolucci Pizzorusso; see, most notably, 'Lingue e stili', pp. 62–3.

it imparts an eye-witness whose presence is then elusive and slippery. I wish to investigate the effects of this.

Whereas Chapters 1 and 2 focus on stylistic and linguistic detail, Chapters 3 and 4 take a broader and more thematically oriented approach. They will focus on knowledge and difference respectively. If the *Devisement* imparts a great deal of information about the world, how straightforward is the knowledge of the world the text imparts, once we factor in the narrative, stylistic and linguistic hybridity I discuss in Chapters 1 and 2? Chapter 3 will look first at how the *Devisement* plays on, yet rehandles, the trope of the marvel or wonder, which is at one and the same time a literary motif, a phenomenon and an ontological category, and it will explore further how it seeks to correct traditional knowledge about the world. It will then consider the portrayal of Kublai Khan. I shall argue here that the *Devisement* can usefully be read through the optic of Freud's idea of the uncanny, which is to say that one of the effects of the text is to render the strange familiar and the familiar strange. The *Devisement*'s representation of other religions, which is the focus of the third section of Chapter 3, also offers the reader an uncanny mirror of Christian practices. The agent in this is Marco Polo himself, the narrator, the traveller within the text, and how he is positioned: one key passage in Z, not found in other early sources, is particularly interesting for the way in which it plays up Marco's role as a mediator (but also a recuperator) of foreignness.

This will lead onto an analysis of diversity and categories of difference in Chapter 4. Diversity is both a category and a phenomenon on which the *Devisement* insists ('les deversités des deverses region dou monde', I, 1), and I wish in turn to insist upon it to counter the claim made by some critics that 'Marco Polo [...] sets out to represent the exorbitant otherness of an "outlandish" world'.[110] The *Devisement* belies any stereotype of the medieval world as uniformly given to the crude 'othering' of other cultures, seen first and foremost in binary opposition to Christian, western European (and implicitly white) culture. In fact, Marco Polo's view of the world turns out to be quite the opposite of what we now call Eurocentric: the *Devisement* portrays distant lands and cultures as significantly more sophisticated, powerful and opulent than Europe and lays out a world of graduated differences and infinite variety, with Europe on its margins rather than at its centre. The second and third sections of Chapter 4 are devoted to phenomena to which the *Devisement* returns repeatedly: money and cannibalism. My aim here is to illustrate how the text promotes diversity, rather than alterity, as its main category for representing the world and how its different parts relate to each other.

In my conclusion I will return to the question of genre and set the *Devisement* briefly alongside other medieval texts about travel and the rest of the

[110] Islam, *Ethics of Travel*, p. 149.

world, the most famous of which is Mandeville's *Le Livre des Merveilles*, to which it is often compared. I will also suggest how the *Devisement* may be read through the lens of a famous modern fictional engagement with travel writing that is quite explicitly inspired by the Tuscan redaction of Marco Polo's text, Calvino's *Le città invisibili*. Travel literature occupies an important position in post-colonial criticism and theory, but medieval texts are frequently either neglected or mentioned only as precursors to modern traditions, the assumption being that the world changes radically once Columbus 'discovers' America and colonialism rears its head. It is too simplistic simply to insist on the fact that Columbus, like Marco Polo, was a medieval Italian merchant and that he was in part at least inspired by Marco's book, since the effects of their actions and intentions were so different. We need also to distinguish between the *Devisement* as it seems originally to have been conceived and as it may have circulated in the early fourteenth century, and then the form it took on in transmission in the later Middle Ages. But the point concerning Columbus's debt to Marco Polo does illustrate the extent to which modern views of the world are rooted in medieval views of the world. One contention in my conclusion is that we need to do more to understand how medieval views of the world had a hand in structuring our own.

This is not a theory-heavy book, but it does have a theoretical underpinning that I will bring to the fore when necessary. The theoretical starting point for my investigation of Marco Polo's text is Jacques Derrida's inspiring and moving book *Le Monolinguisme de l'autre*, which is initially a meditation on his youthful relation to French as a monolingual, francophone Algerian Jew in the Second World War, but which becomes a meditation on language more generally.[111] The young Jacques grows up in a multilingual society but finds that the only language he speaks, on which he relies to mediate his view of the world, is increasingly marked as belonging to others, and ultimately he is stripped of the citizenship this language symbolizes. This underscores, for Derrida, the extent to which we are all condemned, though often without realizing it, to speak the language of the Other, a foreign language, a language over which we can never exert any form of mastery,[112] and into which we translate constantly, thereby giving ourselves over to and placing ourselves inside a strange and estranging discursive frame. This monolingual mode of 'translation' – Derrida calls it 'absolute translation' – can, I suggest, provide new insights on the *Devisement*'s use of French and on the forms of French it uses.[113]

---

[111] Jacques Derrida, *Le Monolinguisme de l'autre ou la prothèse d'origine* (Paris: Galilée, 1996).

[112] "*Je n'ai qu'une langue, or ce n'est pas la mienne*" (*Monolinguisme*, p. 15: '*I only have one language, yet it is not mine*', original emphasis).

[113] *Monolinguisme*, p. 117.

A second theoretical building block for my argument, already mentioned, is the Freudian notion of the uncanny, which serves to collapse perpetually the familiar and the foreign into each other, so as to contain one in the other. My own use of the idea of the uncanny is strongly inflected by Homi Bhabha's influential *The Location of Culture*, which offers a Derridean and psychoanalytic perspective on post-colonial theory. In his introduction Bhabha explores the interest of 'a hybridity, a difference "within", a subject that inhabits the rim of an "in between" reality'.[114] Marco Polo and the *Devisement* might seem a world (and 700 years) away from the coloured South African subjectivity that this clause qualifies, but it is Marco Polo's situation of himself 'in between' West and East that makes the *Devisement* such a compelling text, while he himself, whether telling stories at the court of the Great Khan in China (on which see Chapter 1, section 3), or back ('home'?) in Italy writing about the marvels he has seen, might easily be described as a 'difference "within"'.

---

[114] Homi K. Bhabha, *The Location of Culture* (London and New York: Routledge, 1994), p. 13.

1
Narrative voice and style: 'ego Marcus Paulo'

The aim of this chapter is to examine the ambiguous narrative voice(s) of the *Devisement*. The ambivalence of first-person pronouns in the text has not escaped remark before, and my own analysis is indebted, in particular, to articles by Valeria Bertolucci Pizzorusso, Dietmar Rieger and Cesare Segre.[1] I hope, however, that my own discussion can go further than previous studies by relating the fundamental ambivalence of first-person pronouns to broader issues of storytelling and reader response as they emerge not only in the narrative frame of the *Devisement* itself but also in the text's reception. This chapter has three sections. In the first I will examine the text's striking and insistent use of first-person forms, consider how this relates to the equally striking and insistent references by name to Marco Polo himself and then how different versions handle and rework their source's narrative voice. In the second I will look at how narrative voice impacts upon and relates to the representation of space and time both in the reader's apprehension of the world the text describes and in his or her engagement with the text itself. In the final section I will consider how the text's insistence on Marco Polo's role, not just as an observer but as a teller of tales about the world, affects how readers respond to Marco Polo as a figure in the text, as the text's author and as a real-life, or possibly fictional, traveller, something that in turn impacts upon the text's role as a purveyor of knowledge about the world.

---

[1] Valeria Bertolucci Pizzorusso, 'Enunciazione e produzione del testo nel *Milione*', *Studi Mediolatini e Volgari*, 25 (1977), 5–43; Dietmar Rieger, 'Marco Polo und Rustichello da Pisa: der Reisende und sein Erzähler', in Xenia von Ertzdorff (ed.), *Reisen und Reiseliteratur im Mittelalter und in der Frühen Neuzeit* (Amsterdam: Rodopi, 1992), pp. 289–312; Cesare Segre, 'Marco Polo: filologia e industria culturale', in Gabriella Ronchi, Marica Milanesi and Cesare Segre (eds), *Avventure del 'Milione'* (Parma: Zara, 1983), pp. 9–20, and 'Chi ha scritto il *Milione* di Marco Polo?', in Silvia Conte (ed.), *I viaggi del 'Milione': itinerari testuali, vettori di trasmissione e metamorfosi del Devisement du monde di Marco Polo e Rustichello da Pisa nella pluralità delle attestazioni. Convegno internazionale Venezia, 6–8 ottobre 2005* (Rome: Tiellemedia, 2008), pp. 5–16.

First-person forms: 'I', 'we'; Rustichello, Marco

The presence of a narrative voice in the Franco-Italian redaction makes itself felt in the very first chapter of the 'prologue', which is also marked by the interpellation of both specific and non-specific addressees:

> I CI COMANCENT LE LOBRIQUE DE CEST LIVRE QUI EST APPELÉ LE DIVIS[A]MENT DOU MONDE
> Seignors enperaor et rois, dux et marquois, cuens, chevaliers et b[o]rgio[i]s, et toutes gens que volés savoir les deverses jenerasions des homes et les deversités des deverses region dou monde, si prennés cestui livre et le feites lire. Et qui trovererés toutes les grandismes mervoilles et les grant diversités de la grande Harminie et de Persie et des Tartars et <de> Indie, et de maintes autres provinces, sicom notre livre voç contera por ordre apertemant, sicome meisser Marc Pol, sajes et noble citaiens de Venece, raconte por ce que a seç iaus meisme il le voit. Mes auques hi n'i a qu'il ne vit pas, mes il l'entendi da homes citables et de verité; et por ce metreron les chouse veue por veue et l'entendue por entandue, por ce que notre livre soit droit et vertables sanç nulle ma<n>songe. (I, 1–3)

> (I HERE BEGINS THE RUBRIC TO THIS BOOK, WHICH IS CALLED THE DESCRIPTION OF THE WORLD
> My lords, emperor and kings, dukes and marquises, counts, knights and townsfolk, and all you people who wish to know about the diverse races of men and the diversity of the diverse regions of the world, take this book and have it read. And here you will find all the greatest marvels and great diversity of Great Armenia and of Persia and of the Tartars and of India, and of many other provinces, just as our book will relate in order and openly, as Mr Marco Polo, wise and noble citizen of Venice, relates, for he saw it with his own eyes. But some things he did not see, but rather he heard about them from reliable and truthful men; and for this reason we will stipulate what he saw and what he heard about, so that our book might be straightforward and truthful, without any lies.)

There is much to say also about the language of this opening, but I will postpone any comment on language until Chapter 2. For now, let me start by pointing out that a narrative voice speaks here in the first-person plural (*notre livre*, *metreron*, *notre livre*) about a Marco Polo who is clearly designated in the third person (*meisser Marc Pol*). As Valeria Bertolucci Pizzorusso suggests, this 'we' might initially seem to be simply what she calls the 'academic' we, used in many kinds of neutral, factual discourse and generally considered impersonal.[2] However, the short paragraph at the end of the chapter about the genesis of *notre livre* encourages the attentive reader to think again:

---

[2] 'Enunciazione e produzione', pp. 12–13.

> Le quel puis, demourant en le char[t]re de Jene, fist retraire toutes cestes chouses a messire Rust[i]ciaus de Pise, que en celle meisme chartre estout, au tens qu'il avoit MCCXCVIII anç que Jesucrit nesqui. (I, 7)

> (Then this man [Marco], staying as he was in prison in Genoa, had all these things written down by Mister Rustichello da Pisa, who was in the same prison, in the year 1298 after the birth of Jesus Christ.)

This clearly (though retrospectively) raises the possibility that the first-person plural is not an unspecified and neutral academic 'we', but rather much more specifically Marco Polo and Rustichello da Pisa. 'Our book', which already in Chapter 1 seems to have its own ontological reality as a finished work,[3] is, it is underlined here, the work of two people, a point already hinted at in the intervening paragraph:

> Et chascuns que cest livre liroie ou oiront le doient croire, por ce que toutes sunt chouses vertables; car je voç fais savoir que, puis que notre sire Dieu pasme de seç mainç Adam notre primer pere jusque a cestui point, ne fu cristienç, ne paiens, ne tartar, ne yndiens, ne nulç homes de nulle generasion, que tant seust ne cherchast de les deverses partie dou monde et de les grant mervoilles come cestui messire Marc en cherche et soi. Et por ce dit il a soi meisme que tropo seroit grant maus se il ne feist metre en ecriture toutes les granç mervoilles qu'il vit et qu'il oi por verités, por ce que les autres jens que ne le virent ne <ne> sevent, le sachent por cest livre. Et si voç di qu'il demora a ce savoir en celles deverses parties et provences bien XXVI anç. (I, 4–6)

> (And anyone who reads or hears this book should believe it, since everything in it is true; for I would have you know that to this day since the time when our lord God formed with his own hands Adam, our first ancestor, there has been no man – Christian, pagan, Tartar, Indian or of any race – who knew so much about nor sought to see so many of the various parts of the world and so many of its wonders as Marco did. And for this reason he said to himself that it would be a great shame if he didn't have all the truly marvellous things he saw and the true things he heard about written down, so that other people, who did not see them or know about them, might know about them through this book. And I tell you, he stayed in these various places and provinces some twenty-six years in order to acquire this knowledge.)

Marco did not write down all the things he saw himself, but rather he had them written down by someone else ('se il ne feist metre en ecriture', 'fist retraire'). Now while it is in some sense true that any medieval author has things written down, in that works have to be copied by hand, a more specific (if nonetheless not entirely clear) form of collaboration between two people

---

[3] On this point, see also Bertolucci Pizzorusso, 'Enunciazione e produzione', p. 11.

(two authors?) is explicitly signalled here. We can also see a movement from what Bertolucci Pizzorusso calls 'una *voluntà* di libro' ('a desire for a book'), to 'il patto del libro' ('the pact of the book'), the desire for a book being Marco's ('dit il a soi meisme que tropo seroit grant maus se il ne feist metre en ecriture'), but the pact, hatched in a Genoese prison, being Marco's and Rustichello's, making the book truly 'ours'.[4]

The first-person plural forms here are all the more striking given that a first-person singular voice also (surreptitiously?) makes its mark in the second paragraph (4: 'je voç fais savoir'; 6: 'Et si voç di'). This 'I', by implication, can only be Rustichello, making the grammatical structure of enunciation in this chapter: 'I' (Rustichello) will tell 'you' (kings, dukes etc.) about what 'he' (Marco Polo) saw on his travels in order to make 'our' (Rustichello and Marco's) book.

Throughout the nineteen-chapter 'prolegue' Marco continues to be referred to in the third person as his father and uncle's first trip to Asia is narrated, then their return to Europe and then their more extended journey and stay in Asia with Marco. The 'I' telling the story remains discreetly in the background, only occasionally making his presence felt with stock formula such as 'Et que voç en diroie?', 'Et voç di que', 'come voç ai contés' and 'Et encore voç di un autre chouse' etc. (see III, 2; IX, 5 and 6; XII, 6; XIV, 4; XV, 1; XVI, 1; XVII, 2 and 4; XVIII, 13; XIX, 5, 14, 17, 19, 21, 23 and 24). First-person plural forms seem, initially at least, associated in some way with 'our book' (V, 2; XIV, 2) and/or with the narration to come (V, 2; XIV, 2; XIX, 22), but one, at least, of these passages with first-person plural forms in the 'prolegue' already hints at the ambivalence concerning first-person forms to come:

> Et atant se mestrent a la voie con cest mesajes et alerent un an por tramontane et por grec avant que il fussent la venu; e trovent grant mervoilles et diverses coses les quelç ne voç conteron ci por ce que messier Marc, fil de meser Nicolau, que toutes cestes choses vit ausint, le voç contera en ceste livre avant apertemant. (V, 2)

> (And on this they went on their way with this messenger and travelled for a year north and eastwards before they reached their destination; and they found great marvels and many different things that we will not relate to you now, since Mister Marco, the son of Mister Nicholas, who saw all these things thus, will relate them to you in due course quite openly in this book.)

When the story gets going, then, will Marco be narrating his traveller's tales directly, superficially at least without the intermediary of Rustichello?[5]

---

[4] 'Enunciazione e produzione', pp. 9–10. On the 'patto del libro', see also Alvaro Barbieri, *Dal viaggio al libro. Studi sul 'Milione'* (Verona: Fiorini, 2004), pp. 129–54.

[5] Segre ('Chi ha scritto?', p. 12) finds this remark particularly significant.

After the prologue (and indeed throughout much of the text), the use of first-person forms, plural and singular, is remarkably insistent, far more insistent than is the case in prose romance, the other genre in which Rustichello is known to have composed.[6] To give a measure of this, in the first ten chapters after the prologue in the Franco-Italian redaction (XX–XXIX), there are thirty-seven first-person-singular or -plural verb forms, excluding those found in direct speech (e.g. 'si voç di', 'les qualz ne voç conterai', 'Or laison de cest provençe', 'Et encore voç di', 'des quelz voç en parlerai encore avant' etc.). It is instructive to compare these chapters with the Tuscan and French redactions, where the equivalent chapters have fifteen and twenty-four first-person forms respectively, while conveying more or less the identical content, with the former abridging slightly and the latter hardly at all.[7] Granted, the difference between thirty-seven and fifteen first-person forms reflects the tendency of the Tuscan redaction to a terser style and to dropping detail, but in this instance it is hard not to suspect that the Tuscan redactor was consciously removing phrases that might be regarded as redundant as far as content was concerned. Given the French redaction also has notably fewer first-person forms, this may suggest that some early readers of the *Devisement* identified the overuse of the first-person as a stylistic flaw and sought not necessarily to eliminate the linguistic tic altogether but certainly to temper it. Thus, if the first person in the French redaction is often maintained, compare nonetheless 'Et si voç di ke toit les cristians' in the Franco-Italian redaction (XXIV, 5) with 'car sachiez que touz les Crestiens' in the French (23, 12–13), or likewise 'Et encore voç di ke sor cel flum ' (XXV, 5) with 'Encore y a sur le flun' (24, 9). On the one hand, the insistent use of the first person in the Franco-Italian redaction, indeed one might say its overuse, is part of the text's stylistic roughness; on the other, its effects are perhaps worthy of consideration.

I should make clear that, although in the ensuing discussion I am going to refer to 'Rustichello' and 'Marco', I do so primarily in order to identify implicit voices *within* the text and not to attribute specific utterances to flesh-and-blood authors or collaborators *outside* the text. As Valeria Bertolucci Pizzorusso suggests, the narrative voice of the *Devisement* is always double,

---

[6] For discussion of the use of the first person in prose romance see Sophie Marnette, *Narrateurs et points de vue dans la littérature française médiévale: une approche linguistique* (Bern: Peter Lang, 1998), pp. 43–51. Interestingly, Marnette shows that the textual tradition in which the first person is used most insistently in prose romance is the *Tristan*, a tradition in which Rustichello participated.

[7] Tuscan redaction, 19–29; French redaction 19–28. The Latin text, Z, is heavily abbreviated and lacunary in this opening section of this text, so most of chapters XX–XXIX are missing. There are, however, few first-person forms in the early part of this version. See 1, 15 and 27 for 'academic' first-person plural foms ('ut ad alia necesaria transeamus' and 'dicamus de Turcomania'), but compare 3, 6, and 4, 13, where passive third-person forms are used ('de quibus infra dicetur' and 'dicitur').

which means, as Cesare Segre notes, that the status of the 'I' who speaks is often 'in crisis', an effect Dietmar Rieger considers quite deliberate.[8] To borrow a thought from a famous essay by Michel Foucault, I am indifferent to the question of who said what in reality; I wish to consider rather how the text performs its act of enunciation through a 'double' and indeterminate narrative voice, and how this impacts upon what Foucault calls the author function here,[9] in other words, how the text both instantiates and confuses an account of its own genesis and authorship.

In some instances, because Marco Polo is referred to in the third person and by name in close proximity to a first-person verb form or pronoun that denotes narration, the speaking subject is implicitly, but nonetheless clearly, Rustichello da Pisa:[10]

> Or voç ai contés de ceste plaigne et de les gens que font fer la scurité por rober; et s[i] voç di que messier Marc meesme fut el come pris da celle gens en celle oscurité. (XXXVI, 21)

> (Now I have told you about this plain and about the people who make darkness in order to rob; and I tell you that Mr Marco himself was taken by these people in that darkness.)

> Et si vos di que mesier Nicolau et mesier Mafeu et mesier Marc demorent un an en ceste cité por lor fait que ne fa a mentovoir. (LXII,15)

> (And I tell you that Mr Nicholas and Mr Matthew and Mr Marco stay a year in this town to conduct affairs of their own that there is no need to talk about.)

Most notably, one narrative episode describes at some length how Marco, his uncle and father construct a trebuchet in order to help the Mongols raise the siege of Sanyanfu (Xiangyangfu, see CXLVI and also pp. 123–5, on this episode). The Polos' exploits are narrated by a first person who makes his presence felt repeatedly (see CXLVI 4, 6, 15, 21, for the familiar formulae and fillers 'Et si voç di', 'que je vos dirai', 'E que voç en diroie?'), so at this point, as Dietmar Rieger has argued, Marco is stripped of authorial authority and becomes simply one of the text's protagonists.[11]

The naming of the presumed author of a text in the third person is not uncommon in medieval literature, but the practice here most closely recalls in some respects earlier Old French chronicles of the Fourth Crusade (1202–4),

---

[8] Bertolucci Pizzorusso, 'Enunciazione e produzione', p. 15; Segre, 'Chi ha scritto?', p. 12; Rieger, 'Marco Polo', pp. 304–5.

[9] Michel Foucault, 'Qu'est-ce qu'un auteur?', *Bulletin de la Société Française de Philosophie*, 63 (1969), 73–104.

[10] For other examples see: XXXI, 5–6, and CV, 1–2.

[11] 'Marco Polo', pp. 301–2.

such as those of Robert de Clari and Geoffroi de Villehardouin, where, as in the *Devisement*, the supposed authors are also protagonists:[12]

> Ore avez oï la verité, comme faitement Constantinople fu conquise; et comme li cuens de Flandres Baudouins en fu empereres, et messire Henri ses frères après; que cil qui y fu et qui le vit, et qui l'oï, le tesmoigne, ROBERS DE CLARI li chevaliers, et a fait metre en escrit la verité si comme ele fu conquise.
> (Robert de Clari, *La Conquête de Constantinople*, CXX)

> (Now you have heard the truth about how Constantinople was conquered; and how Baldwin, Count of Flanders, became emperor, and Sir Henry his brother afterwards; for the one who was there, who saw it and heard it, bears witness to this, Robert de Clari, knight, and he had the truth written down about how it was conquered.)

> Lors veissiez assaut grant et merveilleus; et ce tesmoigne Joffrois de Ville-Harduin, li mareschaus de Champaigne, qui ceste ovre traita, que plus de quarante li distrent por verité que il virent le gonfanon Saint Marc de Venise en une des tors, et mie ne surent qui l'i porta.
> (Geoffroi de Villehardouin, *La Conquête de Constantinople*, XXXVI)

> (Then you would have seen a powerful and marvellous attack; and Geoffroi de Villehardouin, Marshal of Champagne, who dictated this work, bears witness to this, for more than forty men told him in truth that they saw the banner of St Mark of Venice above one of the towers, though they knew not who carried it there.)

> Et bien tesmoigne Joffrois de Vile-Hardoin, le mareschaus de Champaigne, à son escient par vérité, que puis que li siecles fu estorez, ne fu tant gaaignié en une ville. (Villehardouin, *Conquête*, LV)

> (And Geoffroi de Villehardouin, Marshal of Champagne, indeed testifies, truthfully to the best of his knowledge, that since the world began such wealth has never been conquered in a single town.)

Further striking stylistic similarities between these texts and the *Devisement* are the insistence on the truthfulness of the text because its author was an eye-witness to the events recounted (Villehardouin's text, in particular, reminds us frequently that he was there, close to the action), the distinction that is made between what the author actually saw and what he was told,

---

[12] Both texts cited from *Historiens et chroniqueurs du moyen âge: Robert de Clari, Villehardouin, Joinville, Froissart, Commynes*, ed. Albert Pauphilet (Paris: Gallimard, 1952). Cf. also Villehardouin, 'Cil qui ceste hystoire traita ne sot s'il fu à tort ou à droit, mais il en oï un chevalier blamer' (CXII: 'The one who dictated this story did not know whether it was rightly or wrongly, but he did hear a knight blamed').

and the possibility that both texts were dictated.[13] As Sophie Marnette puts it: 'c'est en référant à eux mêmes à la 3ᵉ pers. que Villehardouin et Clari se présentent comme témoins des événements racontés et cherchent ainsi à garantir la vérité du récit dont ils sont les auteurs' ('It is in referring to themselves in the third person that Villehardouin and Clari present themselves as witnesses to the events that are related and they seek thus to garantee the truth of the texts of which they are the authors').[14] It may well be that Rustichello, Marco or Rustichello and Marco together sought – whether consciously or unconsciously – to enhance their text's claim to tell the truth about what Marco saw and learned while in Asia by using a stylistic device associated with recent historical writing: Robert de Clari and Villehardouin were, it should be remembered, pioneers in seeking to relate personal experience of recent historical events in prose, a medium otherwise primarily used in the thirteenth century for Arthurian romance.[15] However, there are also crucial differences between the *Devisement* and these earlier chronicles. As Sophie Marnette has noted, Robert de Clari and Villehardouin use the first-person singular very sparingly and never to refer to themselves, yet they do use the first-person plural extensively to create a narrative voice 'pour mettre en relief la notion de narrateur [...] Grâce au pluriel, il est davantage qu'un simple individu, il perd de sa singularité et devient une autorité, et, dans le cadre des chroniques tout au moins, un historien' ('to foreground the notion of the narrator ... The plural means he is more than a simple individual: he loses his singularity and becomes an authority, and, within the framework of the chronicles at least, a historian').[16] This, then, is the 'academic' we, and these texts have a neutral, unidentified and factual narrator. The *Devisement*, on the other hand, seeks at key points to identify, whether implicitly or quite specifically, the narrating 'je' or 'nous', but at others quite deliberately to generate ambivalence as to his/their identity.

As an example of the implicit identification of the narrative voice, consider the passages in the *Devisement* in which stories about a specifically identified third-person Marco Polo are related by a first-person narrator, such as the account of the siege of Sanyanfu (Xiangyangfu). These might seem

---

[13] The verb *traita* in Villehardouin is ambiguous, but the implication is that the text was dictated. For Andrea Frisch the *Devisement* is a key medieval text for the emergence of an early modern idea of the eye-witness, but although she cites other medieval analogues, she does not mention these key historical analogues: *The Invention of the Eyewitness: Witnessing and Testimony in Early Modern France* (Chapel Hill: University of North Carolina Press, 2004), pp. 41–60.

[14] *Narrateurs et points de vue*, p. 42; see also p. 101.

[15] On the rise of prose and its association with historical writing, see Gabrielle M. Spiegel, *Romancing the Past: The Rise of Vernacular Prose Historiography in Thirteenth-Century France* (Berkeley and Oxford: University of California Press, 1993).

[16] *Narrateurs et points de vue*, p. 54; on the extensive use of the first-person plural in these chronicles, see p. 53.

to suggest that the default first-person singular voice in the *Devisement* is Rustichello's, which is also the implication of the only place in the text after the first chapter where Rustichello is referred to explicitly:

> Nos ne voç avon contés, des IX roiames dou Mangi, mes que des III; ce sunt Yangiu et Quisai et Fugiu, e de ce avés voç bien entendu; de les autres VI noç en sauronmes encore bien cont[er]; mes por ce que trop seroit loingaine matiere a mentovoir, nos en taieron atant. Car bien voç avon contés – dou Mangi et dou Catai e de maintes autres provences – et des jens e des bestes e de osiaus e de l'or e de l'arjent e de pieres e de perles e des mercandies e de maintes autres couses, ensi com vos avés oi. Et por ce que nostre livre n'estoit encore conpli de ce que nos hi volun iscrivre – car il hi faloit toutes les fais de les yndienz, que sunt bien couses de faire savoir a celz que ne le savent, car il [h]i a maintes mervelioses couses le quelz ne sunt en tout les autres mondes, e por ce fait bien et est mout buen et profitable a metre en sc<r>it en nostre livre – e<t> le mestre le y metra tout apertamant, ensin come mesier Marc Pol le devise et dit. Et si voç di toit voirmant que mesire Marc y demore tant en Indie, e tant en soit de lor afer e de lor costumes e de lor mercandies, que a pie[c]e mes ne fu homes que miaus en seuse dir la verité. E bien est il voir que il hi a de si merveliose couse que bien estront mervilliant les jens que les oirent: mes toutes foies n[o]s les m[e]teron en escrip<t> le une aprés le autre, ensint come meser Marc le disoit por verité. E començeron tout maintinant, ensi com voç porés oir en ceste livre avant. (CLVII, 16–21)

> (We have only told you about three of the nine provinces of Manzi: that is to say, Yangiu, Xingzai and Fuzhoi, as you have well understood. We could easily tell you about the other six, but because this would be too large a subject to cover, we will be silent on it. For we have told a great deal – about Manzi, about Cathay and many other provinces – about their peoples, animals and birds, about their gold, silver, precious stones and pearls, about their merchandise and many other things, just as you have heard. And because our book was not yet complete with everything we want to write in it – since it lacked everything about the Indians, which are indeed things that those who don't know should be told, and because there are many marvellous things to be found in all the other worlds, and for all these reasons, it is good and useful to write them down in our book – and the master will set them all down there, just as Marco Polo relates and says it. And I say to you that in all truth Mr Marco stays so long in India and gets to know so much about them and about their ways and what they trade, that there is no man who better knows the truth about it. And it is indeed true that there are so many marvellous things there that the people who hear about them will marvel greatly; and so we will write them down, one after the other, just as Mr Marco related them truthfully. And we will start now, just as you can hear further on in this book.)

This paragraph begins with a first-person plural that could initially be the neutral, 'academic' we, but then seems to become much more specifically

Rustichello and Marco in their joint textual entreprise. This 'we' is then split into two figures – *le mestre* (the master, whom all scholars identify with Rustichello, partly at least because this is how he refers to himself in his Arthurian prose romance compilation),[17] and 'mesier Marc Pol' – both of whom are the subject of third-person verb forms: *metra* in the case of Rustichello; *devise et dit* in the case of Marco. But this is immediately followed by that omnipresent first person, who in this instance clearly distinguishes himself from Marco: 'Et si voç di toit voirmant que mesire Marc y demore tant en Indie' (19). The subject of enunciation here is thus implicitly Rustichello.

It may then be significant, in terms of the account of its own genesis to which the text contributes here, that Marco relates and tells of India in the present, while Rustichello *will write* in the future. This suggests a clear sequence (Rustichello *will write* the part of the book we have yet to read; we are therefore reading a work in progress) and a clear division of labour (Marco speaks; Rustichello will transform his words into a written text).[18] This might seem to support the much-repeated view that the Franco-Italian redaction of the *Devisement* is not properly finished and that, whereas the substance (perhaps supplied in note form) is Marco's, the style – albeit sometimes poor and rambling – is Rustichello's.[19] But would it not be naive to assume that everything a text tells us about itself is true? The *Devisement*, like other celebrated medieval texts, effectively fictionalizes its own compo-

---

[17] See I, 3: 'Et maistre Rusticiaus de Pise, li quelz est imaginés desovre, conpilé ceste romainz, car il en treslaité toutes les tresmervillieuse novelles qu'il truevé en celui livre et totes les greingneur aventures; et traitera tot sonmeemant de toutes les granz aventures dou monde'; 5: 'Et li maistre dira [...] pour ce que li maistre le treuvé escrit eu livre dou roi d'Engleterre'; 6: 'Mes si metra li maistre un grandisme aventures tot primieremant'. See also 38, 1, and 8, and 39, 11 ('maistre Rusticiaus'). Scholars also identify linguistic and stylistic parallels between the *Devisement* and Rustichello's compilation. See, in particular: Valeria Bertolucci Pizzorusso, 'Pour commencer à raconter le voyage: le prologue de la relation de Marco Polo', in Emmanuèle Baumgartner and Laurence Harf-Lancner (eds), *Seuils de l'œuvre dans le texte médiéval* (Paris: Presses de la Sorbonne Nouvelle, 2002), pp. 115–30; and Fabrizio Cigni, '"Prima" del *Devisement dou Monde*. Osservazioni (e alcune ipotesi) sulla lingua della *Compilazione arturiana* di Rustichello da Pisa', in Conte (ed.), *I viaggi del 'Milione'*, pp. 219–31.

[18] For the text as it survives as a '*work in progress*', see Rieger, 'Marco Polo', pp. 306–7, and Segre, 'Chi ha scritto?', p. 12.

[19] See Introduction, n. 37. For another example of the traditional view of the division of labour in the production of the *Devisement*, see John Larner, *Marco Polo and the Discovery of the World* (New Haven, CT, and London: Yale University Press, 1999), p. 105: Larner conjectures how Rustichello transformed Marco's 'unpromising collection of materials' into 'a variety of amusing and edifying stories from foreign parts'. Cf. also Segre ('Chi ha scritto?', p. 12), who suggests that the *configurazione base* in the text is 'Marco che fornisce appunti o notizie a voce, e Rustichello, responsabile della scrittura'. For some fine analysis of the problems with such schemas, see Marina Münkler, *Marco Polo: vita e leggenda*, trans. Giuliana Cavallo-Guzzo (Milan: Vita e Pensiero, 2001), pp. 47–55 ('L'autore e il suo narratore').

sition by incorporating an account of the circumstances that led to its genesis into its narrative frame, both in the first chapter and here in Chapter CLVII.[20] This does not necessarily mean that the prologue is *not* telling the truth – in other words, that the *Devisement* was not composed jointly by Rustichello da Pisa and Marco Polo while both were held hostage in Genoa in 1298; it means, rather, that the text troubles any clear-cut distinction between fact and fiction in the interests of storytelling.

If this is the case, then there is an *effet de réel* in the *Devisement* designed to give the text more immediacy, to give the impression that it is being narrated in the present rather than being the retrospective account it clearly is.[21] We need to bear two points in mind here. First, the *Devisement* is a written text, even though, like many medieval prose texts in French, it often bears the traces of oral discourse: references to writing and to the *livre* are frequent, as we see in Chapter CLVII.[22] Secondly, the 'prologue' has already narrated in detail the Polos' itinerary in the preterit, so on a textual level, at least, we know that the future of their travels already lies in the past. This does not necessarily mean that the account of India and the Polos' journey back to Europe has already been written at this stage of the composition of the text, but note that, when talking about the book's incomplete state, the imperfect is used ('n'estoit encore conpli', 'il hi faloit'). As in Chapter I, 'the book' here already implicitly has ontological reality: in the diegetic present 'we want to write in it' ('nos hi volun iscrivre') in order to make it complete, but from an extra-diegetic perspective the book's incompletion already lies in the past. I will return in more detail to the implications of the *Devisement*'s treatment of time and space in the next section of this chapter. The point I wish to highlight here is that the text seems to create deliberate ambiguity about the point in time (and as we will see also the position) from which it speaks: this ambiguity is only intensified when we also do not know who is speaking, which in many instances turns out to be the case. For if Chapters I and CLVII imply that the default identification for the 'je' of the text is Rustichello, there are many passages in the *Devisement* that call this into question.

This is most notably so when the 'je' identifies himself as Marco Polo, which might suggest that in these instances the *Devisement*'s narrative dynamic is similar to that of Jean de Joinville's *Histoire de Saint Louis*, in

---

[20] Two obvious examples, which have received a good deal of critical attention, are Chrétien de Troyes's *Le Chevalier de la Charrete* and *Le Roman de la Rose*.

[21] On the idea of the *effet de réel* see Roland Barthes's famous essay 'L'effet de réel', *Communications*, 11 (1968), 84–9. Barthes's focus (realist fiction) is, of course, different from mine, but his notion of *l'illusion référentielle* is crucial to reading the *Devisement*.

[22] On how the narrative technique of Old French texts may be informed by their being mediated orally, see Suzanne Fleischman, *Tense and Narrativity: From Medieval Performance to Modern Fiction* (London: Routledge, 1990).

which an omnipresent narrative 'je' constantly reminds his readers that he was in fact present and took part in everything he recounts:[23]

> Or vos conterai tout son afer solonc que je meser Marc oi la conter a plusors homes. (XLI, 2)
>
> (Now I will tell you all about him (the old man of the mountain) just as I, Mr Marco, heard about it from many men.)
>
> Bangala est une provence ver midi que as MCCXC anz de la nativité de Crist, quant je Marc estoie a la cort dou g<r>ant kan, encore ne l'avoit pas conquisté. (CXXVI, 1)
>
> (Bengal is a province to the south which in the year 1290 of our Lord, when I, Marco, was at the Great Khan's court, he had not yet conquered.)
>
> Et selonc que en celle escripture se contenoit <...> fu verité selonc ce que je Marc Pol vit puis apertemant a mes iaux. (CLII, 6)
>
> (And according to what this writing contained [a letter written by the queen of Quinsai to Kublai Khan] it was true, according to what I, Marco Polo, saw quite clearly with my own eyes.)

These, and three further instances,[24] might suggest that the first-person voice of the *Devisment* should be understood as Rustichello's unless the text specifies otherwise, and that when it is specified that Marco is speaking, this is to underscore the authority and truthfulness of the text, grounded as it is in eye-witness account and personal experience. The fact that the composition of Joinville's *Histoire* is almost exactly contemporary with the production of the early redactions of the *Devisement* (he is thought to have begun his text in 1298 and to have completed it by 1309)[25] raises the intriguing possibility that this quasi-autobiographical use of the first-person singular in prose accounts of recent events is a stylistic innovation of the late thirteenth century that then informs the style of great historical writers of the later Middle Ages, such as Froissart and Commynes. However, Joinville never needs to specify the identity of the narrative 'je', since there is never any ambiguity as to who is speaking. And, troublingly for the hypothesis that the narrative 'je' of the *Devisement* is Rustichello unless otherwise specified, there are at least two cases where an unidentified first-person singular only makes sense if it is understood as representing Marco's voice:[26]

---

[23] Joinville is cited from *Historiens et chroniqueurs du moyen âge*, ed. Pauphilet; on the 'je' in Joinville, see Marnette, *Narrateurs et points de vue*, pp. 41-2.

[24] See CLIII, 9; CLXII, 15; CLXVII, 1.

[25] See *Historiens et chroniqueurs*, ed. Pauphilet, p. 197.

[26] The 'je' is also clearly Marco in 'ce que je en vi' at CXCI, 19 and 21. There are certainly other instances, but they are perhaps less marked. See, for example, CLXX,

Car je voç di que je ot un conpagnons, que avoit a nom Çurficar, un turs que mout estoit saje, qui demoroit trois anz por le grant can en celle provence por fair traire celle salamandre et cel undanique et cel acer et toutes couses. <Car toutes> foies hi mande seignor le grant can por trois anz por seignoreier la provence et por fer la besogne de la salamandre, et mun conpains me dist le fait et je meisme le vi. (LX, 7–8)

(For I tell you that I had a companion, whose name was Çurficar, a Turk who was very wise, who stayed there for three years on behalf of the Great Khan to export this salamander [i.e. asbestos], ondanique[27] and steel and other things. For my lord the Great Khan sends men to rule over the province for three-year stretches to take care of the salamander, and my companion told me about this and I myself saw it.)[28]

Et si voç di que ceste flun vait tant longe et por tantes pars, et tantes cités hi sunt sovre, que je voç di voirement que por ceste flun ala plus naives e con plus chieres couses et de greignor vailance que ne vont por tus le flu<n>s de cristiens, ne por tout lor mer. Car je voç di que je hi vi a cest cité bien <…> nes a une foies, que toutes najent por ceste flum. (CXLVII, 5–6)

(And I tell you that this river is so long and extensive, with so many cities upon it, that I can assure you that more ships navigate this river and with more precious things and more valuable merchandise than all the rivers of the Christians, or than all their seas. For I can tell you that I saw in this city a good […] ships at once all on the river at the same time.)[29]

This means that in any given instance 'je' may represent either of the two figures the text tells us had a hand in its composition, which might encourage an attentive reader to ask who exactly is speaking at certain points of the *Devisement*. Indeed, as Valeria Bertolucci Pizzorusso puts it, the text is marked by 'le voci di un complesso soggetto produttore' ('the voices of a complex subject–producer'), and so 'una lettura che non le ascoltasse apparirebbe,

---

6: 'et ne font meint me[n]gier de paste que moult sunt buen a mangier, car je voç di que nos meesme les provanmes aseç, car nos en menuiames plusors foies' ('and they often give copious portions of a dough that is good to eat, for I can tell you that we ourselves tried these doughs often, and ate them several times'). In this instance, the *je* is eclipsed somewhat by the *nos*, which here signifies 'we travellers' rather than Marco and Rustichello (on which see further below).

[27] *Ondanique* is high-grade Indian steel.

[28] The traditional view of the salamander as a creature that can live in fire is being consciously corrected here; see LX, 4–6. 'Salamander', in the *Devisement*, is rather an ore that can be extracted to make very fine, but tough fabric: in other words, asbestos. The appointment of Marco's companion as governor of a province for three years finds an echo later in the text when we are told that Marco himself governed the city of Yangiu (Yangzhou) for three years; see CXLIV, 5.

[29] No figure is given in the Franco-Italian redaction The French redaction reads 10,000 (146, 24), the Tuscan text 15,000 (143, 6); this passage is not in Z.

ancora una volta, troppo semplificatrice' ('a reading that does not listen to them would seem, once again, too simplifying').[30]

In the vast majority of cases where the first person is used in a formulaic manner ('et si voç di', 'com je voç ai conté', 'et que voç en diroie?', 'E voç dirai le porcoi' etc.) it makes little difference who is deemed to be speaking. But in some instances there are implications for the text's account of its own genesis that are troubling. The most striking example is the one occasion when 'the book' is referred to not as 'nostre livre' or as 'ceste livre', but as 'mon livre':[31]

> Or voç vueil come[nce]r de les contree que je voç nomerai e<n> mon livre dever tramontaine, et orés comant. (XXXVII, 28)
>
> (Now I want to begin on the countries to the north that I will name in my book, and you will hear all about them.)

Whether or not this is a lapse and whatever one thinks about how 'finished' the *Devisement* is, this one reference to 'my book' raises questions about authorship, authority and ownership that in turn impact upon the truth claims made in the first chapter and reiterated at regular intervals throughout – particularly, as we have seen, when Marco speaks in the first person. Does the book 'belong to' Marco, an eye-witness giving his readers the benefit of his vast and rich experience of the vast and richly varied world? Or does it, on the other hand, belong to 'master' Rustichello, otherwise known as a romancer, as a teller of 'adventures' designed primarily for pleasure,[32] a notion that might contrast with the aspiration expressed in the *Devisement* that it should be edifying and *profitable* (see I, 6, and CLVII, 18).

How reliable, then, is this book if we don't know who is speaking, even if Marco Polo's value as an eye-witness is repeatedly stressed? The regular claims to have forgotten something that now needs recalling and inserting (another stylistic feature that the *Devisement* shares with earlier chronicles)

---

[30] 'Enunciazione e produzione', p. 43.

[31] Bertolucci Pizzorusso logs thirty-two instances of *notre/nostre livre* and more than fifty of *ceste livre* ('Enunciazione e produzione', pp. 9–10).

[32] See Rieger ('Marco Polo', p. 294), who describes Rustichello as a 'Fiktionsspezialist' and Marco as a 'Realitätsspezialist'. In the prologue to his Arthurian compilation, which the prologue to the *Devisement* echoes closely, Rustichello underlines the pleasurable nature of listening to 'adventures': 1: 'Seingneur enperaor et rois, princes et dux, et quenz et baronz, civalier et vauvasor et borgiois, et tous le preudome de ce monde que avés talenz de delitier voz en romainz, ci prenés ceste, et le feites lire de chief an chief; si i troverés toutes les granz aventures qui avindrent entre li chevaliers herrant dou tenz li roi Huter Pandragon jusque au tenz li roi Artus, son fiz, et des conpains de la Table reonde.' On the relation between Rustichello's prologue and that of the *Devisement*, see most notably Bertolucci Pizzorusso, 'Pour commencer à raconter le voyage'.

both support and undermine assertions of reliability.[33] On the one hand, they give the impression that the text wishes to tell all and forget nothing, to be as comprehensive as possible; on the other, the reader might ask what else has been forgotten and whether the text is as 'orderly' as it claims to be (I, 2). Claims to have forgotten something occur regularly throughout the *Devisement* in the first-person singular and twice in the first-person plural.[34] Cesare Segre sees in these references to lapses of memory and late additions the traces of Marco Polo and Rustichello da Pisa's method of working together, with Marco re-reading Rustichello's work as he drafted it and pointing out things that he (Marco) had forgotten; this also explains, in part at least, why, as he puts it, the status of the 'I' is 'in crisis'. For Segre, when Marco forces Rustichello to include something he (Marco) had forgotten, 'ora è Marco che ne riprende possesso, e impone la presenza del proprio *io*. Come dire: l'autore del *Devisement* sono io!' ('now it is Marco who is taking back custody [of his book] and imposing the presence of his own "I". As if to say: *I* am the author of the *Devisement*').[35] But the 'I' who forgets is not securely identifiable with Marco: in one instance, for example, he claims to have forgotten to write something (LXX, 33), which does not make sense in Segre's scenario, which has Rustichello scrambling to write down Marco's reminiscences. Or is Rustichello rather the one who is forgetting, with an implicit reference here to the notes many assume were used in the composition of the *Devisement*? And what are we then to make of the two instances in which 'we' forget? One might argue that the 'we' here is the 'academic' we of neutral narration, but if so, then forgetting implies a much more personalized act of enunciation than this would require. Rather than seeking to identify the referent of first-person pronouns, it is perhaps more pertinent to interrogate the effects of the text's ambiguous usage. As Segre goes on to suggest, any attempt to 'attribute' the first person in the *Devisement* quickly founders because the first person is rarely specifically identified.[36] This, then, is a text that insists upon the importance of personal witness, but fails to delineate clearly the contours of the person whose testimony is being offered. One result of this indeterminacy

---

[33] On the narrators of chronicles inserting forgotten incidents and facts, see Marnette, *Narrateurs et points de vue*, pp. 101–2.

[34] For the first-person singular see: XLIII, 6 ('encore voç vuoil dir un autre chouse que je avoi laissé de lui'); LXX, 33 ('un autre merveliose usançe qu'il ont que je avoie dementiqué a scrivre'); XCVIII, 12 ('una cause que je avoit dementiqué'); CXLVII, 9 ('une couse que je avoie dementiqué'); CXCII, 13 ('aucune cose dou leofant, que je avoit dementiqué'); CCXIX, 13 ('aucune couse que je avoit dementiqué'). For first-person plural see: CXXI, 1 ('Or sachiés que nos avavames dementiqué une mout belle bataille'); and CLXXVII, 42 ('une bielle novelles que noç avon dementiqué').

[35] 'Chi ha scritto?', p. 12.

[36] 'Chi ha scritto?', p. 13.

is that it encourages the reader to invent scenarios – sometimes elaborate and romanticized – to explain which 'I' is speaking in any given instance.[37]

First-person-plural pronouns are similarly ambivalent. As I have already suggested, the information that is offered about the circumstances in which the text is said to have been composed suggests that 'we' may on occasion have a more precise referent than the neutral, 'academic' 'we' and may mean specifically in some instances Marco and Rustichello. Even so, as Segre argues, 'we' becomes indistinguishable from 'I' in many instances, so that 'we', like 'I', can in fact mean either Marco or Rustichello.[38] This is particularly the case when 'I' and 'we' alternate in rapid succession (as often happens),[39] when large amounts of information are being conveyed and when who is speaking seems to matter little. However, in some contexts 'we' does seem to have a quite specific referent. Depending on context, 'we' seems to designate (apart from Marco and Rustichello of course): 'we' Westerners; Marco and his travelling companions; or Rustichello, Marco and their readers. One example of each will suffice:

> Et encore sachiés que ceste regne, et por tout Indie, ont toutes bestes et osiaus deviséç des nostres, for solemant un oisiaus, e ce est la quaie: ceste oisiaus san faille est senblable as nostres, mes toutes autres couses ont mout deversemant deviséç des nostres. (CLXXIV, 64)

> (And know as well that this land, and indeed everywhere in India, has beasts and birds that are different from ours, except for one bird, which is the quail: this bird is without doubt similar to ours, but all other things are completely different from ours.)

> Et si voç di tout voiremant que nos en aportames de celle seme<n>se a Venese et le seminames sor la terre, si voç di qu'il n'i nasqui noiant: e ce avint por <le> leu froit. (CLXIX, 4)

> (And I tell you most truthfully that we brought some of that seed back to Venice and sowed it on the ground, but I tell you that nothing grew: this was because the ground was too cold.)

---

[37] For example, see Segre, 'Chi ha scritto?', p. 12: 'Sarebbe facile immaginare Marco Polo che legge il *Devisement* via via che Rustichello lo scrive, gli suggerisce aggiunte, o le scrive lui stesso ai margini delle pagine.' My intention here is not so much to take issue with Segre's fine analysis as to point out how the text itself invites the reader 'to imagine' how it came to be written as it is.

[38] 'Chi ha scritto?', p. 13. In these instances, the narrative 'nous' is analagous to the narrative voice described by Marnette in chronicles; see *Narrateurs et points de vue*, pp. 53–4.

[39] On which phenomenon in other texts see Marnette, *Narrateurs et points de vue*, p. 54.

> Lor costumes e les couses que hi naisent vos diron tout apertmant; e voç les porés entendre plus cleremant por ce que nos venons aprochant a plus domesces leus. (CLXXXII, 3)

> (We will tell you about their customs and about the things that grow there most openly; and you will be able to understand about these much more easily since we are approaching more familiar places.)

Again, there are analogies here with chronicles: Robert de Clari and Villehardouin repeatedly use first-person-plural possessive adjectives ('Nostre pelerin', 'nostres barons', 'noz François') to identify a first-person-plural narrative voice with the crusading French; Joinville narrates events as well as observing them in the first-person plural ('l'ariver que nous feimes devant Damiete' (II), 'nous revenimes' (III)).[40] But again the *Devisement*'s usage is both more various and more ambiguous. 'We' Westerners implies a Eurocentric perspective that the text annexes quite deliberately on some occasions, only to vacate at others: I will be examining the questions this raises further in Chapters 3 and 4. When the text uses 'we' to mean Marco and his travelling companions, this creates a similar kind of ambiguity in relation to 'we' to the one I have already discussed in relation to 'I', inviting the attentive reader thereby to question the referent of a pronoun that might otherwise be straightforward. Because 'we' often seems to designate Rustichello and Marco, it is as if Rustichello becomes incorporated into Marco's experiences as well as into the narration of the text: as Dietmar Rieger puts it, Rustichello becomes Marco's 'fictional travelling companion'.[41] The resonance of the lexis and mimetic strategy of the final example, which relates to Eli (Ely) on the Malabar coast, which is to say on the Polos' way back to Europe, will be explored in more detail in the next section of this chapter. The point I wish to make here is that, although there initially seems to be a distinction between 'we' and 'you' in this sentence ('voç les porés entendre'), it is also the case that 'we', the readers of this text, are also now approaching more familiar (*domesces* = 'domestic') places in our journey through the text, not just Marco and his travelling companions, or Marco and Rustichello in their narration.[42] The text draws us into the journey it describes as participants, and reading the text becomes an avatar for travelling to and experiencing the places it describes. One might say the text itself becomes a metaphor for the journey.

---

[40] On this point see Marnette, *Narrateurs et points de vue*, pp. 55–6.

[41] 'Fictionalen Reisebegleiter': 'Marco Polo', p. 311.

[42] Cf, also CLXI, 18: 'Or desormés ne voç conterai plus de ceste contree, ne de cestes ysles, por ce que trop <sunt> des<v>oiables et encore que nos ne i somes estés' ('Henceforth, I will not tell you any more about this country, nor about these islands because they are too forbidding and also because we have not been there').

The use of first-person pronouns, possessives and first-person verb forms in the *Devisement* instantiates, in other words, a perpetual and challenging, sometimes troubling, leakage between different positions in, and relations to, the text: between Marco and Rustichello, between author(s) and narrator(s), between narrator(s) and readers, between protagonists and readers. We will see further, in the next section, how the text's use of tenses and treatment of time and space generally enhance these effects, but I would like to conclude this section on first-person forms with a brief consideration of how other early versions treat the pronominal ambiguity I have identified in the Franco-Italian redaction from which they are all thought to derive, whether directly or indirectly.[43] Several other redactions eliminate much of this ambiguity altogether, and all tone it down.[44] What are the implications of this?

As already noted, the Tuscan redaction abbreviates substantially, which is also the case with the Venetian redaction. Both maintain the reference to Rustichello da Pisa in the first chapter,[45] but interestingly abbreviate the meta-textual remarks in the equivalent of Chapter CLVII: in each case 'io, Marco Polo' declares tersely that he will now speak of India, but there is no mention of 'the Master'.[46] Without this second reference to Rustichello, the ambiguity generated in the Franco-Italian redaction about the narrating 'I' (or 'we') is a lot less marked. Although both redactions occasionally refer to Marco Polo in the third person, both also have sporadic occurrences of 'io, Marco Polo'.[47] The narrator in these two redactions seems much more clearly identifiable throughout with Marco, and because both, as we have already seen for the Tuscan version, make far sparer use of formulae such as 'si vi dico', 'ora vi dico' or 'Ora vi diremo de' (in Tuscan), 've dirò de', 'ancora ve digo', and

---

[43] I should stress here that I am not assuming BNF f.fr. 1116 is a direct source for any other surviving version, merely that it is the only witness that maintains something approximating to the original's form and language, and also that it is more complete than any other version.

[44] One of the few scholars to have remarked upon this is Bertolucci Pizzorusso ('Enunciazione e produzione', p. 8): 'già gli antichi traduttori si sono affannati ad eliminare le tracce [of pronominal ambiguity]'. She does not, however, go into any detail.

[45] The Venetian text's wording here offers interesting evidence as to how the division of labour between Marco and Rustichello was envisioned by at least one medieval reader, putting Marco firmly in charge: 'E siando in charzere a Zenova, alora se fè' scriver questo libro a misier Ristazo da Pixa, lo qual era prixion chon esso lui: lui lo redusse in scritura, e questo fo ano domini MCCXCVIII' (I, 8: 'And while in prison in Genoa, he had Mr Rustichello da Pisa, who was a prisoner with him, write this book for him; he put it into writing, and this was in the year 1298').

[46] See the Tuscan redaction 153, 14–15, and the Venetian redaction CXX, 12. Although the force of the two versions is the same here, the wording is actually quite different.

[47] See the Tuscan redaction 122, 1; 148, 6; 149, 6; 153, 15; 158, 5; 163, 2. Cf. also 143, 6; 157, 14; 165, 3; 166, 5; 166, 6; and 186, 13–17, for first-person forms used to designate either Marco or Marco and his travelling companions. In the Venetian redaction, which tends always to specify 'io Marco', see CI, 13; CXI, 13; CXVII, 54; CXXI, 13; CXXIII, 6; CXXX, 1; CXXXII, 3; and CXXXIII, 4.

'sì chonteremo innanzi di' (in Venetian), the presence of the narrator is in any case less insistent than when he actually names himself.

The response of the French redactor is quite different, but even more interesting. In every instance where the Franco-Italian redaction reads 'je meser Marc' or some such formulation, this is transformed into the third person. Thus the equivalent passages to the three examples of 'je meser Marc' (or some such) that I quoted above read as follows:

> Or vous conterons de son afaire selonc ce meïsmes que mesire Marc Pol oÿ conter a pluseurs hommes de ces contrees. (40, 3–6; cf. XLI, 2)

> (Now we will tell you all about him according to the very account Mr Marco Polo heard from many men of those lands.)

> [Bangala] est unne prouvince vers midi qui, a .M.C[C].IIII^{xx}. et .X. de Crist, quand ledit messire Marc Pol estoit a la court du Grant Caan, il ne l'avoit pas encore conquestee. (125, 1–3; cf. CXXVI, 1)

> (Bengal is a province to the south, which in the year 1290 of our Lord, when the aforementioned Mr Marco Polo was at the Great Khan's court, he had not yet conquered.)

> Et selonc ce que en celle escripture disoit vous deviseray si comme il est verité et que puis le dit messire Marc Pol le vit et le sot, si comme je le vous diray. (151, 13–16; cf. CLII, 6)

> (And I will relate to you, according to what it said in this writing [a letter written by the Queen of Quinsai to Kublai Khan], the truth, and since the aforementioned Mr Marco Polo saw it [the letter] and knew all about it, just as I will tell you.)

In the last of these examples the distinction between Marco Polo himself and a narrating *je* (by implication, therefore, Rustichello) is particularly clear. This transposition from first to third person is thorough-going. Thus all instances of 'je Marc' in the Franco-Italian redaction are transposed to something along the lines of 'le dit messire Marc'. Equally tellingly, instances of first-person pronouns and verb forms, singular and plural, which seem to relate either to Marco's experience as a traveller or to those of Marco and his travelling companions, but where no specific identity for the 'I' or 'we' is given, are translated to third-person-singular forms and then also given a specific referent, which is to say Marco himself:[48]

---

[48] For two examples of the disambiguation of first-person plural forms designating 'we travellers', compare CLXX, 6, and French redaction 165, 169–72: 'Et vous di encore que le dit mesire Marc Pol, qui tout ce vit, conta comment pluseurs fois il orent de ceste ferine et fu pestrie, et fu li pains moult bons a mengier'. Also CLXX, 7: 'et des autres roiames de l'autre partie ne voç conteron noç rien, por ce que noç ne i fumes mie'; and

Or avoit mesire Marc Pol un compaignon qui avoit a non Susitar et estoit moult sages, et conta le dit Turc a mesire Marc Pol comment il avoit demouré en ceste contree .III. anz pour le Grant Caan, pour faire traire de ces salemandres pour le Seignour. (59, 16–21; cf. LX, 7 quoted above)

(Now Mr Marco Polo had a companion, whose name was Susitar and he was a very wise man, and the aforementioned Turk told Mr Marco Polo how he had stayed in this country for three years on behalf of the Great Khan to extract this salamander for the lord.)

Et selonc ce que le dit messire Marc Pol raconta, il oÿ de ceulz qui tiennent la seccrete pour leur seigneur en ceste cité, qui li conterent par verité, que plus de [.CC^m.] nez y passent [chascun an], lesquelles si vont toutes ensus, sauf les autres qui retournent. Et si y vit le dit messires Marc en unne toute seule fois plus de .X^m. nefz ensemble et en un lieu de ce flun, qui est si larges que il ne semble pas flun mais mer, tant est larges, sique il se puet bien penser[r] que ce est grant fait.
(146, 18–27; cf. CXLVII, 5–6, quoted above)

(And according to what the aforementioned Mr Marco Polo recounted, he heard from those who hold the lord's secret in this city, and who told him truthfully, that more than 200,000 ships pass by there each year, all of which go up river, apart from those that are coming back down. And the aforementioned Mr Mark saw at one time more than 10,000 ships together in one place on this river, which is so wide that it doesn't seem like a river, but rather a sea, so wide is it, so that it really can be thought to be a great thing.)

Et sachiez que le dit mesire Marc Pol aporta de celle dite semence du bresil que cil semment jusques en Venise, et fist la semer et riens n'en crut, et bien croi que ce fu por ce que le lieu est trop froit.
(165, 143–7, cf. CLXIX, 4, quoted above)

(And know that the aforementioned Mr Marco Polo brought some of the said brazil seeds that these people sow back to Venice, and had it sown, but nothing grew from them, and I believe this was because the place is too cold.)

Furthermore, because the French redactor retains the reference to 'the master' in the equivalent of CLVII (156, 77–9: 'Et le maistre le mettra tout ainsi apertement comme le dit messire Marc Pol le conte'), the effect is increasingly clear: Rustichello is the narrating first person, Marco Polo the third-person subject of the experiences he recounts. Marco Polo is therefore represented as a protagonist of the French redaction of the *Devisement*; he is thus possibly represented as one of its authors (thanks to the prologue), but not as its nar-

---

165, 175–8, '[Des] .II. royaumes de l'autre partie de celle ylle ne vous conterons riens pour ce que le dit [messire] Marc Pol n'i fu pas.'

rator. I would suggest, therefore, that the French redactor is doing more than effecting 'une toilette linguistique' ('a linguistic make-over'), as Philippe Ménard puts it, in order to eliminate the 'serious errors' and 'verbal confusion' that 'spoil' the Franco-Italian redaction:[49] he or she is also eliminating some of its more challenging narratological procedures and thereby transforming it fairly radically, making it in some respects similar stylistically and narratologically to earlier historical writing such as Robert de Clari and Villehardouin's respective *Conquêtes de Constantinople*, in which the experiences of an eye-witness are narrated exclusively in the third person by a first-person narrative voice. Ménard has argued passionately that the French redaction is not a *remaniement* since 'C'est le même récit qui nous est présenté avec de temps en temps quelques menues variantes, quelques petites additions ou suppressions' ('It is the same narrative that is presented to us with from time to time tiny variants, a few small additions or suppressions'),[50] but in this instance the cumulative effect of systematic 'tiny variants' is far-reaching: the whole text is disambiguated and thereby simplified.

The situation as far as first-person forms and references to Marco Polo by name are concerned in the *Z* redaction is a little less straightforward. Some of the passages in which 'I, Marco Polo' speaks in the Franco-Italian text are missing in *Z*, but at the point corresponding to CXXVI, 1 ('je Marc'), *Z* reads 'ego Marcus Paulo' (60, 1), which occurs again at the point corresponding to CLII, 6 (85, 6), and on one other occasion where there is no direct equivalent in the Franco-Italian redaction (72, 19, and 85, 6, corresponding to chapter CXXXVIII). However, in six other instances where the Franco-Italian redaction uses a first-person in conjunction with Marco's name, the *Z* redactor transposes this to 'dominus Marcus Paulo' followed by a third-person verb form,[51] and generally the formula 'dominus Marcus Paulo' appears with relative frequency in *Z*.[52] It is as if the *Z* redactor had taken a conscious decision, like the French redactor, to eliminate Marco Polo's first-person narrative voice in his translation (and thereby to eliminate much of the ambiguity concerning narrative voice from his source) but occasionally (and tellingly) nonetheless allowed an 'ego, Marcus Paulo' to slip through, particularly at the beginning of the text. But in any case, since *Z* makes no reference to

---

[49] See 'Intérêt et importance de la version française du *Devisement du Monde* de Marco Polo', in Federico Masini, Franco Salvatori and Sandro Schipani (eds), *Marco Polo 750 anni. Il viaggio. Il libro. Il diritto. Congresso internazionale* (Rome: Tiellemedia, 2006), pp. 183–97 (p. 197), and *Marco Polo: à la découverte du monde* (Paris: Glénat. 2007), p. 10, both quoted at more length in the Introduction above (pp. 24–6).

[50] 'Intérêt et importance', p. 191.

[51] See 86, 11, cf. CLIII, 9, in the Franco-Italian text; 95, 22, cf. CLXII, 15; 100, 1, cf. CLXVII, 1; 102, 5, cf. CLXIX, 4; 103, 13, cf. CLXX, 6; 103, 20, cf. CLXI, 18. Pipino also favours the third person but alternates this throughout with the first person.

[52] It is used once or more in the following chapters: 1, 14, 21, 86, 89, 90, 95, 100, 103, 107, 109, 124.

Rustichello da Pisa, either in the first chapter or in the equivalent of CLVII (90),[53] the effect is to render the narrative voice of the whole text much more straightforward.

Narrative time, narrative space

We have seen in the previous section how the Franco-Italian redaction generates ambiguity at some points in the text concerning first-person pronouns, verb forms and possessives, and how other redactors respond to this by disambiguating to some extent, or entirely. While the ambiguity of first-person-singular forms may call into question the basis of the *Devisement*'s authority as purely an eye-witness account, creating confusion as to the position from which it speaks, the ambiguity of first-person-plural forms may in some instances have the effect of incorporating Rustichello da Pisa into the experiences that are recounted and in others of also inviting readers to identify with the experience of travel in Asia:

> Lor costumes e les couses que hi naisent vos diron tout apertmant; e voç les porés entendre plus cleremant por ce que nos venons aprochant a plus domesces leus. (CLXXXII, 3)
>
> (We will tell you about their customs and about the things that grow there most openly; and you will be to understand about these much more easily as we are approaching more familiar places.)

---

[53] 90, 36–9: 'Sed tamen, quia liber noster non est expletus de hiis que in eo scribere volumus, quoniam adhuc omnia facta Indorum desunt, que bene notifancda sunt hiis qui ea nesciunt et ignorant, quia ibi sunt multa diversa et extranea que in alio mundo alicubi non aparrent, et ideo ben dicendum est utile in nostro libro per ordinem declarare; et aperte dicetur, prout dominus Marcus Paulo videt et dixit per ordinem. Et noveritis quod dominus Marcus Paulo fuit in partibus Yndie tanto tempore conversatus, quod tam ex auditu quam ex visu, satis potuit de Indorum moribus et esse ad plenum cognoscere et videre. Verumtamen ibi sunt tam mirabilia quod multum mirabuntur auditores. Tamen ipsa ponemus in scriptis per ordinem, secundum quod sepedictus dominus Marcus Paulo ea retulit esse vera, incipientes secundum quod per vos poterit comprehendi.' ('Yet our book is not complete with all the things we wish to write in it, since it lacks all the facts about India, which are well worth relating to those who do not know about them, for there are many diverse and strange things that are not found in other parts of the world, and so relating them in our book in good order is useful; and they will be related clearly, in the order that Mr Marco Polo saw and related them. And you should know that Mr Marco Polo stayed in India for such a long time that he was able to see and learn – whether by hearsay or direct experience – a great deal of the customs of the Indians. There are so many marvels there that those who hear about them will be amazed. We will write them down in the right order, according to how the aforesaid Marco Polo truthfully related them, beginning just as you will soon hear.')

Thus, as other commentators have suggested, the movement of the text consciously mimics or recreates a journey through the world, implicitly taking us as readers metaphorically on the same journey as Marco Polo had experienced.[54]

In addition to sustained pronominal ambiguity throughout the text, a further contributing factor to this mimetic strategy is the use of tenses. With the exception of the narrative interludes that make up a relatively small portion of the text,[55] after the 'prologue', where the main tense of narration is the preterit, the dominant tenses of the *Devisement* during the extended sequences of chapters that comprise principally descriptions of numerous cities and provinces, foreign customs and peoples are the present and the future.[56] The effects of this, particularly when combined with pronominal ambiguity, can be striking:

> Or vois laison de ceste cité et ne voç contaron de Endie a cestui point, car voç bien le conterai en notre livre avant, quant tens et leu sera; mes mo retornerai por tramontaine por conter de celle provences e retorneron por un autre voie a la cité de C[h]erman que je voç ai contés, por ce que en les contrés, dont je voç voil conter, ne se puet aler se no da ceste cité de Creman. (XXXVII, 23–4)

> (Now let's leave (talking) to you of this city and we will not tell you about India at this point, for we will tell you about it further on in our book, when the time and the moment are right; but I will return northwards to tell of these provinces and we will return by another route to the city of Kerman that I have already told you about because in these countries I want to tell you about you cannot get anywhere other than from this city of Kerman.)

> Or noç lason de ceste provences et de cest parties e ne iron avant, por ce que se nos alaisomes avant nos entreronmes en Yndie et je ne i voil entrer ore a cestui point, por ce que au retorner de nostre voie vos conteron toutes les couses d'Ynde por ordr<e>, et por ce retorneron a nostres provence ver Baldasciam, porce que d'autre partie ne poron aler. (XLIX, 12)

> (Now let's leave this province and these parts and we will go no further, for if we were to go forward we would enter India and I do not want to enter it now, at this point, for on our way back we will tell you all the things about India, in order, and for this reason we will go back to our province of Badakhshan, because it will not be possible for us to go any other way.)

---

[54] For example, see Segre, 'Chi ha scritto?', pp. 14–15.

[55] For a study of the typology and sources of the narrative interludes in the *Devisement*, see Alvaro Barbieri, 'Il "narrativo" nel *Devisement dou Monde*: tipologia, fonti, funzioni', in Conte (ed.), *I viaggi del 'Milione'*, pp. 49–75; see particularly the tables on pp. 54–6.

[56] On this point, see Bertolucci Pizzorusso, 'Enunciazione e produzione', pp. 22–4.

> Mes plus ne voç en conteron por ce que noç vos en contames en nostre livre en arieres, e de cest et de Quis et de C<h>[er]main, mes por ce que nos alanmes por autres voies, il noç convient encore retorner ci. Mes ensi com je voç ai dit, por ce que noç voç avon contés tout l'afere de cest contree, nos en partiron et voç conteron de la grant Torquie, ensi com vos porés auir apertemant. (CXCVIII, 4–5)
>
> (But we will not tell you any more about this because we told you all about it earlier in our book, about this place, and Kais and Creman, and because we went by another route, we have no need to return here. Rather, as I have said, because we have told you about this country, we will leave and will tell you about greater Turkey, just as you will now hear openly.)

The use of the historical or narrative present is common in Old French texts, as is the use of the present tense to denote the act of narration, particularly in prose romance, but the *Devisement* uses the specific framework of the journey that gives shape to its description of the world to create effects that are nonetheless quite distinct. In the first example, a shared narrative entreprise in the present ('or vos laison') is controlled by a first-person-singular narrator who dictates not only the future of the text but also the route it will follow in terms of both narrative and physical geography ('car voç bien le conterai' and 'mo retornerai por tramontaine').[57] In the second example a first-person narrator is represented as taking a decision in the present that determines the future of the narrative as well as the direction that the journey that is being recounted will take ('je ne i voil entrer ore a cestui point'). Furthermore, alternatives are considered using tenses that indicate a hypothesis considered from the point of view of the present ('se nos alaisomes avant nos entreronmes en Yndie'),[58] and it is suggested that the sequence of places to be recounted in the future needs to observe an order ('por ordre').[59] In the final example, we have a couple of preterits and again a complex sequence of tenses, but interestingly the preterits do not, I suggest, necessarily refer to the same time-line. Whereas the first ('contames') clearly refers only to the earlier narration, the second ('alanmes') could refer to the route of the journey being followed, as well as to the earlier narration, in which case the

---

[57] This is characteristically disambiguated somewhat in the French redaction, see 36, 75–84: 'Or laisserons de ceste gent; nous ne vous conterons ore pas du fait d'Ynde, mais quant temps et lieus en sera, ainz tournerons par tramontane por conter de cele province et retornerons par une autre voie a la [devant dite cité de Creman], por ce qu'en ces contrees dont je vous veul conter, ne s'en puet aler se non [par] la dite cité de Creman.' The only first-person singular here refers to the narration.

[58] The Franco-Italian text's verb morphology is both hybrid and fluid; see Maria Grazia Capusso, *La lingua del* Divisament dou monde *di Marco Polo: 1 morfologia verbale* (Pisa: Pacini, 1980), and p. 31 on imperfect subjunctive forms, which I take these to be.

[59] The order of the journey presumably, see XIV, 2, quoted above p. 17.

two *nos* would implicitly have distinct referents: it would refer in the first instance to Marco and Rustichello, in the second instance either to Marco and his travelling companions (with Rustichello jumping aboard for the ride?), or to Marco, Rustichello and their readers, in which case the text once again becomes a metaphorical journey.

In all these instances, verbs of motion and direction, as well as spatial markers may be applied equally to the text itself and to the journey it describes:[60] *laisser* can mean to stop speaking about something or to leave a place; *retorner* can mean to return to a subject or to return to a place; *aller avant* can mean to go forward in the narrative or to advance physically; *entrer* can be to embark upon a topic or to enter a place; *partir* can mean to leave a subject behind or to leave a place; *a cestui point* can mean at this point (here) in the narration or at this point (here) where we are in our journey. Sometimes verbs of motion seem to refer primarily to the narrative:

> Or ensint avint ceste estoire et ceste matiere com je vos ai divisé, ceste estoire de la desconfiture de les jens dou grant kaan; si en lairon atant, et retorneron a nostre matiere por aler avant de nostre livre. (CLX, 19)
>
> (This is how this story happened, and how this matter was, just as I have related it to you, this story of the misfortune of the Great Khan's men; so we will leave this now and we will return to our subject in order to go forward with our book.)

In others instances, although clearly referring to the narrative as well, verbs of motion seem primarily to evoke the journey itself, particularly when they are combined with spatial markers:

> Autres couses que face a mentovoir en nostre livre ne i ha; e por ce noç partiron de ci e aleron avant e vos conteron d'une grant ysle que est apellé Java. (CLXII, 18)
>
> (There is nothing else here to include in our book: and for this reason we will leave this place and go forward and we will tell you about a great island that is called Java.)

However, because of this ambiguity, words such as *ci* and *avant* may do duty as both temporal and spatial markers, a feature that again recalls the narrative grammar and syntax of prose romance, but which the *Devisement* exploits to different effects. As Susanne Fleischman demonstrated, the alternation of

---

[60] Rieger ('Marco Polo, pp. 309–10) and Segre ('Chi ha scritto?', p. 15) also make this point. Cf. also the suggestive remarks made by Marnette (*Narrateurs et points de vue*, pp. 111–13) on the analogies prose romances suggest between the *chemin* or *parcours* taken by protagonists and the *chemin* or *parcours* taken by the text, but the effects in the *Devisement* are more pervasive.

deictic markers such as *or* (as in 'now the tale tells us') and *ci* (as in 'here the tale tells us') in prose romance suspends the narrative ambiguously between unfurling through the time of (oral) narration or across the space of the physical book.[61] But in the *Devisement* space and time also have the more concrete frame of reference of Marco Polo's journey. Thus, in the last example, are *we* leaving a place or a moment in time behind us? And are *we* moving forward from a point in time or a place in the world? Bearing this in mind and returning to the previous examples, *a cestui point* could designate a point on a route as much as (the more obvious) point *we* have reached in the narrative.

Nowhere does this implicit conflation of time and space, and of the readers' experiences with the narrator's (or the narrators') and the protagonists' experiences, become more obvious than on the two occasions where reference is made to 'the place where we are now':[62]

> Et quant Baian fo venu con toutes seç jens a l'entré dou Mangi, ce est a ceste cité de Coigangiu la ou nos sonmes ore, e de la quel voç conteron tout avant, il dist elz que il se rendesent au grant kaan. (CXXXIX, 8)
>
> (And when Baian came with all his people to the border of Manzi, which is to say to the city of Huai' anzhou, the place where we are now, and about which we will tell you further on, he said that they would submit to the Great Khan.)
>
> Or vos ai devisé les nes es quelz les mercant vont et vienent en Yndie, et adonc partiron de cest mainere de nes e vos conteron de Yndie; mes tout avant vos voil conter de maintes ysles que suunt en cest mer osiane, la ou nos sumes ore. E sunt ceste ysles a levant, et nos comenceron primermant d'une isle que est apellé Çip[a]<n>gu. (CLVIII, 14–15)
>
> (Now I have told you about the ships in which the merchants come and go to India, and now we will leave off about the ships and we will tell you about India; but first I want to tell you about the many islands that are in this ocean, there where we are now. And these islands are to the east, so we will first begin with an island that is called Japan.)

In both instances the precision 'la ou nos sonmes ore' is clearly intended to

---

[61] 'Philology, Linguistics and the Discourse of the Medieval Text', *Speculum*, 65 (1990), 19–37.

[62] The French redaction retains the formulation (see 138, 38, and 157, 66), whereas the Tuscan and Z redactions do so only once (see 154, 13 ('ove noi siamo') and 91, 43 ('ubi sumus ad presens')). Cf. also in the Franco-Italian redaction CVII, 2, 'ceste cité ou nos somes venus' (= French redaction 106, 4–5, 'ceste cité ou nous sommes venu'; Tuscan redaction 106, 2, 'ove noi siamo venuti'; not in Z). The *Devisement* also, of course, conflates time and space by often giving distances in terms of the number of days' travelling required, but this is an unremarkable feature in a medieval text and does not really signify unduly in the context of my argument.

remind the reader of where the text has got to after a digression (on one of the many triumphs of the Great Khan in the first place and on the ships that carry merchandise between China and India). All the same, 'there' (in Asia) is also 'here' (in the book) and vice versa, so that when we as readers are 'here' or 'now' in the book, we are also 'there', in Asia, with Marco Polo.

There with Marco Polo, I would suggest, but not quite then. Despite all the work the text puts into giving us the illusion of being taken on a journey with Marco Polo and his companions, of being, at any particular point in the text, in a specific place with some of the journey behind us and some ahead, the 'prolegue' has made it quite clear that Marco Polo's travels are a *fait accompli* being narrated in retrospect. The references to what will be narrated in the future when the time is right (XXXVII, 23–4, quoted above, p. 63), to the need to follow a particular trajectory, one that distinguishes between the way out and the way home (XLIX, 12, quoted above, p. 63), and to the fact that 'we' take another route from an alternative that is envisaged (CXCVIII, 4–5, quoted above, p. 64), enhance an *effet de réel* whereby the book follows, and will not deviate from, a real journey that is unfolding in the present. However, from time to time we are then reminded that the journey was actually made in the past and by someone else. Such moments draw attention to the fact that the journey on which we as readers are embarked is an illusion – or a fiction – at the same time as it acts as a trope that authenticates what we are reading, for example:[63]

> Or desormés ne voç conterai plus de ceste contree, ne de cestes ysles, por ce que trop <sunt> des<v>oiables et encore que nos ne i somes esté. (CLXI, 18)
>
> (Henceforth, I will not tell you any more about this country, nor about these islands because they are too forbidding and also because we have not been there.)
>
> Or nos avonç contee de cesti roiames que sunt de ceste partie de ceste ysle, e des autres roiames de l'autre partie ne voç conteron noç rien, por ce que noç ne i fumes mie. (CLXX, 7)
>
> (Now we have told you about these kingdoms that are on this side of the island and we will say nothing of the other kingdoms on the other side because we didn't go there.)

---

[63] Some other versions disambiguate in these instances by referring to Marco Polo in the third person; cf. the French redaction 160, 66–7, and 165, 177–8 ('pour ce que le dit mesire Marc Pol n'i fu pas' and 'pour ce que le dit [messire] Marc Pol n'i fu pas'), and Z 103, 20 ('quia dominus Marcus ibi non fuit'). But cf. the Tuscan redaction 157, 14 ('però che non vi sono stato'), and 166, 6 ('però che noi non vi fummo'); also the Venetian redaction CXXXIII, 5 ('io non ge fu' mai').

'We' here cannot plausibly include the readers (who are not in any case in a position to know where 'we' did or did not go in any detail, or whether the text is telling the truth about all the places we have 'been' with it), which suggests a degree of playfulness on the part of the narrator(s). The purpose of this fictional web that is woven around the narrative voice(s) is to authenticate the contents of the *Devisement*: everything it describes is true because 'we' saw it with our own eyes, even though 'we' were not in fact there.

As we have seen, the narrative and stylistic features discussed in the first two sections of this chapter may recall other modes of writing, such as prose romance or chronicles, but they are deployed differently, and together with the narrative frame that launches them (which is to say the 'prologue', its establishment of the dual narration of the text and its narration of the extra-textual journey) they are also what distinguishes the *Devisement* most clearly from the encyclopaedic discourse on which it clearly draws and to which it has also often been compared. While the style of prose encyclopaedias in French is by no means uniform, it is nonetheless clear that the *Devisement*'s use of first-person forms and of tenses makes it quite distinct. Two obvious points of comparison are Gossouin's *L'Image du monde* (c. 1245) and Brunetto Latini's *Tresor* (c.1260–66), both of which contain descriptions of the parts of the world covered by the *Devisement*. Some specific comparison will be instructive as to how the discourse of the *Devisement* differs:[64]

> *Ci commence la seconde partie. Comment la terre est devisée, et quele part ele puet estre habitée.*
> Puis que la terre est si petite comme nous vous avons ci devisé, petit poons prisier ses biens vers ceuls du ciel, ne que l'en fait fiens envers fin or, ne envers gemmes. Car il ne valent riens en la fin. Mais pour ce qu'il nous est avis, ci la ou nous soumes, qu'ele est granz, si la deviserons, si comme nous savrons, briefment. (*L'Image du monde*, p. 102)
>
> (*Here begins the second part. How the world is divided and which part is habitable.*
> Since the world is so small, as we told you, we can value its goods little compared to those of heaven, or excrement compared to pure gold or to gems. For they are worth nothing in the end. But since it seems so big from where we are, we will describe it as best we know how, briefly.)
>
> *Des diversitez d'Ynde.*
> En Ynde si a une moult grant montaingne que l'en apele mont Capien, *et est une grant region. Illec sont gent sanz bien et sanz savoir que Alixandres*

---

[64] Cited from *L'Image du monde de Maître Gossouin: rédaction en prose*, ed. O.H. Prior (Lausanne and Paris: Payot, 1913), and Brunetto Latini, *Tresor*, ed. Pietro Beltrami, Paolo Squillacioti, Plinio Torri and Sergio Vatteroni (Turin: Einaudi, 2007).

encloust la dedenz. Et sont la gent Goz et Magoz qui menjue*n*t char toute crue d'o*mm*es et de bestes comme gent mescreues.

Ceste Ynde dont nous vous parlons si tient .xiiii. regions; et en chascune de ces regions a mo*u*lt de gent.

Si y a si granz bois et si haux qu'il aviennent jusques as nues. [...]

Autres genz y ra q*ue* l'en apele Groi*ng et* Bragman, qui sont plus biaus que ceuls q*ue* nous vous avons no*mm*ez. [...]

Si i ra enquore une autre maniere de gent que, qu*a*nt leur peres et leurs meres *et* leur autres parenz, q*ue*, quant il sont vieill et il sont près de mourir, ile les tuent *et* sacrefient soit a tort ou a droit, et en menjuent la char.
(*L'Image du monde*, p. 111)

(In India there is a very large mountain called Mount Capien, and this is an enormous region. There are people there who are no good and have no wisdom, whom Alexander enclosed there. These are the Gog and Magog people, who eat raw flesh, human and animal, like miscreants.

This India about which we are telling you has fourteen regions and in each one of these there are many people.

There are great trees so high that they reach to the clouds [...]

There is another people there called Groing and Bragman [Brahmin?], who are more beautiful than those whom we have just named for you [...]

And there is yet another people who, when their fathers and mothers or other relatives are old and close to death, they kill them and sacrifice them, rightly or wrongly, and they eat their flesh.)

Ci [comenc]e le devissement du mappemonde, c'est coment la terre est ordenee
Terre est ceinte et environee de mer, selonc ce que li contes a devisé ça arrieres, la ou il parole des elemenz. [...] Et por miauz mostrer le païs et les genz dou monde, traitera li contes briefment de chascune partie por soi, et premierement de Ayse, qui est la premiere et la greignor; et comencera de cel chief qui est vers midi, ou ele se part de Aufrique au fluve dou Nile et au fluve de Tygris, qui est en Egypte. (*Tresor*, 1, 121, 1 and 4)

(*Here begins the description of the map of the world, which is to say how the world is organized.*
The world is girded and surrounded by the sea, according to what the tale has told you before, when it spoke of the elements. [...] And in order better to explain the countries and peoples of the world, the tale will deal briefly with each part separately, first Asia, which is the first and largest part, and it will begin with the part that is most southerly, where it borders Africa on the River Nile and the River Tigris, which is in Egypt.)

Aprés est Bautie, un païs qui fiert contre la terre de Inde. Outre les bau[tr]iens est Pande, une ville de sodia[ni]ens, ou Alexandre fist la tierce Alixandre, por demostrer la fin de ses aleures. C'est li lieus ou premierement [Liber, et puis Ercules, et puis Semiramis, et puis Cire] firent autel, por sign[e] qu'il avoient la terre conquises jusque la, et que plus avant n'avoit point de gent. (*Tresor*, 1, 122, 15)

(After this there is Bactria, a country that borders on India. Beyond Bactria there is Pandia, a town of soldiers, where Alexander built the third Alexandria, to demonstrate the end of his travels. It is the place where first Liber, then Hercules, then Semiramis and then Cyrus made an altar as a sign that the lands they had conquered extended thus far, and that beyond this there were no people.)

Et sachiez que en ceste partie oriental nasqui Jesu Crist, en une province qui est apeles Judee, pres de Jerusalem, en une cité qui est apelee Bethleem. Et por ce comença premierement la crestiene loi en cel païs, selonc ce que li contes devise ça arrieres la ou il parole de lui et ses apostres. En cel païs a mainz patriarches et arcevesques et evesques, selonc les establissemenz de sainte Yglise, qui sont par conte .c. et .xxxiii. Mes la force des sarrazins mescreanz en a une grant partie sorprise, par quoi la sainte loi Jesu Crist ne puet estre co[l]tivé. (*Tresor*, p. 1, 122, 27)

(And know that in this eastern part Jesus Christ was born, in a province that is called Judea, near Jerusalem, in a city that is called Bethlehem. And this is why the Christian religion first began in this land according to the story earlier when it speaks about him and about his apostles. In this country there are many patriarchs and archbishops and bishops, according to the establishment of the Holy Church, which is to say they number 133. But the mighty armies of the miscreant Saracens have overwhelmed a good portion of this land, which is why Jesus Christ's holy law cannot be maintained.)

Gossouin uses both the first-person plural and the present and future tenses in his introduction to his description of the world. However, this 'nous' is strictly academic, and the futures (*diviserons, savrons*) relate only to what comes next in the text, not to any supposed trajectory or journey. The first person is absent from the description itself. A concern to set his geography in the context of a broader Christian understanding of the world is also evident, and although he uses an expression that is almost identical to one used in the *Devisement*, his meaning is entirely different: 'ci la ou nous soumes' means 'on earth' as opposed to 'in heaven'. This preoccupation with Christian geography also governs the structure of Brunetto Latini's chapter on Asia (122), of which I have quoted the beginning, approximate middle and end: Asia begins with Egypt and ends in the Holy Land, which is of almost no interest to Marco Polo. In both Gossouin and Brunetto Latini we see a tendency, as in the *Devisement,* to list places in quick succession ('Autres genz y ra', 'Si ra enquore un autre maniere de gent', 'Après'), but the lack of personal engagement means the sense of order is different. Not only is the first person absent from these lists, but there is also a liberal scattering of impersonal verbs (particularly in Gossouin) and the present tense predominates: this is pure (objective, one might say) description. There is also a strong sense of reliance on written sources, indexed here most clearly in the references to

Alexander. Of course, the *Devisement* also refers to Alexander, as we have seen,[65] but this is often to correct received wisdom rather than to confirm it. We need to bear in mind that the agenda and self-presentation of both these texts are quite different from those of the *Devisement*: both are presented as translations of Latin sources, and both have as their ambition the production of a compendium of knowledge about the world that greatly exceeds geography or ethnography, so in both cases the section on Asia is just a fraction of the whole.[66] But more importantly, the authority which both Gossouin and Brunetto Latini wish by implication to annex comes not from personal experience or an eye-witness, but rather from the objectivity provided by their Latin sources, which they mediate neutrally to their readers. Thus Gossouin's information here derives from Gervase of Tilbury, Solinus and Isidore of Seville: he is confirming what his culture already knows and revealing knowledge only to those who do not know Latin.[67] This is completely different from the *Devisement*, where authority is grounded not only in the person of Marco Polo himself, his experience and trustworthiness as any eye-witness, but also in the text's fictional and rhetorical strategies for implicating the reader experientially in what it describes.

An additional, but rather different, point of comparison emerges with the *Tresor*. Like the *Image du Monde*, the *Tresor* is a tissue of translated quotation, but it nonetheless repeatedly alludes to itself in the section on geography as *li conte* and the conjunction of *li conte* with a future in 121, 4, is quite typical ('traitera li contes briefment'; cf. 121, 27, 'li contes devise ça arieres'). Brunetto's style here is clearly influenced by Old French prose romance, but the future makes his usage distinct: *li conte*, in the *Tresor*, seems to be a relatively neutral term for 'the text' itself rather than the omnipresent but imprecise and possibly fictional source that often haunts Old French prose romance. References to *li conte(s)* are, on the other hand, few and far between in the *Devisement*. For example:

> Mes atant laisse li contes a parlere de Cin[g]hi[s] Can et de sez homes et retorneron au Prestre Johan et as seç homes. (LXVI, 11)
>
> (But on this the tale stops talking about Genghis Khan and about his men and we will return to Prester John and to his men.)

---

[65] See the Introduction, pp. 31–2.
[66] For the *Image du monde* as translation, see p. 57: 'Ce livre de clergie, q*ue* l'en apele l'ymage dou monde, qui est translatez de latin en ro*m*manz' ('this book of learning, which is called the *Image of the World* is translated from Latin into romance'). Cf. the rubric to the first chapter of the *Tresor*: 'Ci comence le livre dou Tresor le quels translata maistre Brunet Latin de Florence en francés et parole de la naissance de toutes choses briefment' ('Here begins the first chapter of the book of Treasure, which master Brunetto Latini of Florence translated into French and which speaks briefly of the beginning of all things').
[67] For precise references, see the notes to Prior's edition, pp. 111–29.

> Or dit li contes que quant le Prestre Johan soit que Cin[g]his Can con toutes sez jens venoient sor lui, il ala con toutes sez jens contre lui. (LXVII, 1)
>
> (Now the tale says that when Prester John knew that Genghis Khan and all his men were advancing towards him, he himself advanced towards him with all his men.)
>
> Or dit le contes que quant Alau soit certainemant comant Berca estoit venus con si grandismes jens, il asenble encore seç parlemant de grant quantités de buens homes. (CCXXIV, 1)
>
> (Now the tale says that once Alau knows for certain how Berca had come with a huge host, he assembles his council with a large number of good men.)

The first two instances here, in fact, make up a single example, in that the formulae 'laisse li conte a parlere de' and 'Or dit li contes que' are used at the beginning and end of chapters to create interlace, in a manner typical of prose romance: the context is the wars between Genghis Khan and Prester John, and the narrative here is moving between the two enemy camps. The second example is similarly used to signal interlace in a narrative context, in this instance the wars between Alau and Berca.[68] As has been noted, scholars often remark that Rustichello da Pisa is responsible for the style of the *Devisement* and particularly for the use of stylistic devices associated with Old French prose romance.[69] If this is the case, then it is striking that there are so few references to *li conte(s)*, particularly when it is considered that Rustichello routinely and frequently handles interlace in his Arthurian prose compilation with references to *li contes*.[70] The style of the *Devisement* is in this respect strikingly distinct from both Brunetto Latini's *Tresor* and from prose romance. Indeed, whereas the context of both references to *li conte(s)* in the *Devisement* is narrative, it is equally true that there are numerous other narrative interludes in the text, including some of the longer anecdotes, in which the perspective of different protagonists is interlaced but from which *li conte(s)* is conspicuously absent.[71] This might suggest that, if the style of the

---

[68] CCXXIII, 19–20, which immediately precede these lines read: 'Mes atant noç lairon de Berca e de sez homes, que bien vos avon devisee une partie de son affere. Et adonc voç conteron de Alau e de sez jens, comant il s'esproitient puis que il soit que Berca e sez homes estoient venus pres <a sa ost>'.

[69] For an example of this specific point, see Larner, *Marco Polo*, p. 111, where he remarks that the 'style of writing' is 'very close to Rustichello's original version, modelled on Arthurian prose epic'; cf. also Burgio's remarks (*Dal viaggio al libro*, p. 135) on the movement in the text between two textual typologies, one deriving from mercantile culture, the other from courtly romance.

[70] See: 2, 1; 16, 1; 16, 20; 17, 1; 53, 1; 56, 25; 57, 1; 60 16; 61, 1; 62, 21; 63, 21 etc.

[71] For example, the story of Kublai Khan's battle with Nayan (see LXXVII–LXXX) or the long account of the wars of the Western Tartars that concludes the text

Devisement is influenced by Rustichello, as many have asserted, he is actually modifying his style (compared with his Arthurian compilation at least) for the rather different discursive context of the *Devisement*, and this even in the narrative interludes.

Since the stylistic features of the *Devisement* I have considered in this chapter (pronominal ambiguity; spatial and temporal ambiguity; both leading to identification between narrator and author, readers and protagonists) all in fact mark the text out as distinct from prose romance, despite any resemblances, it is somewhat surprising that assessments of the *Devisement*'s style have set so much store on Rustichello's being known as an author of romance. This is all the more surprising when it is considered that it is Marco Polo that the text presents as a storyteller, not Rustichello.

Marco Polo, storyteller

The very first mention of Marco Polo in the *Devisement* makes him the subject of the verb *raconter*, which again is the case the next time he is mentioned:

> Et qui trovererés toutes les grandismes mervoilles et les grant diversités de la grande Harminie et de Persie et des Tartars et <de> Indie, et de maintes autres provinces, sicom notre livre voç contera por ordre apertemant, sicome meisser Marc Pol, sajes et noble citaiens de Venece, raconte por ce que a seç iaus meisme il le voit. (I, 2)

> (And here you will find all the greatest marvels and great differences of Great Armenia and of Persia and of the Tartars and of India, and of many other provinces, just as our book will relate in order and openly, as Mr Marco Polo, wise and noble citizen of Venice, relates, for he saw it with his own eyes.)

> Et atant se mestrent a la voie con cest mesajes et alerent un an por tramontane et por grec avant que il fussent la venu; e trovent grant mervoilles et diverses coses les quelç ne voç conteron ci por ce que messier Marc, fil de meser Nicolau, que toutes cestes choses vit ausint, le voç contera en ceste livre avant apertemant. (V, 2)

> (And on this they went on their way with this messenger and travelled for a year north and eastwards before they reached their destination; and they found great marvels and many different things that we will not relate to you now, since Mister Marco, the son of Mister Nicholas, who saw all these things thus, will relate them to you in due course quite openly in this book.)

(CCXXI–CCXXXIII). For a meticulous study of the narrative interludes, see Barbieri, 'Il "narrativo"'. For Barbieri the alternation of description and narrative cannot be mapped closely onto the voices or perspectives of Marco Polo and Rustichello da Pisa.

Marco's role as a purveyor of stories about strange parts of the world is thus marked as central from the outset, but the insistent truth claims indicate that it was expected that some, at least, might not believe his stories. In the first chapter alone we read: 'por ce que notre livre soit droit et vertables sanç nulle ma<n>songe' (3), 'por ce que toutes sunt chouses vertables' (4), 'toutes les granç mervoilles qu'il vit et qu'il oi por verités (5). While, contrary to some scholarly opinion, it is not clear that all medieval readers were overly sceptical about Marco Polo's account of Asia,[72] the greater popularity of Mandeville's fictional (and sometimes fantastic) account, along with the authority Mandeville was clearly afforded in some contexts,[73] does indicate that the contents of the *Devisement* were regarded by some as of questionable authenticity. This is certainly the view that Ramusio, the influential sixteenth-century editor and translator of the text, felt he needed to rebut in his preface. While reporting that he is delighted that recent exploration and recently discovered or translated Arabic texts confirm almost everything that Marco Polo says, he notes that the book was for many years regarded as *favola*:

> Il libro [...] per causa di infinite scorrezioni ed errori è stato molte decine d'anni riputato favola, e che i nomi delle città e provincie fussero meglio sogni. (III, p. 22)
>
> (The book [...] because of its many mistakes and errors has for many decades had the reputation of being fiction and the names of the cities and provinces were thought to have been dreamed up.)

This controversy about whether or not to believe Marco's stories is not, however, confined to the medieval and early modern period if the relatively recent scholarly spat about whether Marco Polo did or not go to China is anything to go by.[74] Although Ramusio's remarks should not be taken as firm evidence of medieval reception, there are two further aspects of his defence of Marco that are interesting in relation to storytelling and fictionality. The first is his comparison with Christopher Columbus, whose journals,

---

[72] See Consuelo W. Dutschke, 'Francesco Pipino and the Manuscripts of Marco Polo's "Travels"', unpublished Ph.D. dissertation, University of California at Los Angeles, 1993, pp. 43–99 ('Contemporary Reaction: Truth or Tale?'), for a full discussion of evidence that, intially at least, the *Devisement* was accorded a good deal of authority. Yet the issue of credibility remains a constant preoccupation; for example, see Larner, *Marco Polo*, pp. 114–15 and 144–6.

[73] For Iain Macleod Higgins, Mandeville's book consciously presents itself as a successor and correction to the *Devisement*. See *Writing East: The 'Travels' of Sir John Mandeville* (Philadelphia: University of Pennsylvania Press, 1997), pp. 51–2.

[74] See p. 6, n. 21. The question is not, however, apparently just of scholarly interest and remains newsworthy; see http://www.telegraph.co.uk/news/worldnews/europe/8691111/Explorer-Marco-Polo-never-actually-went-to-China.html, accessed 23 September 2011.

Ramusio reminds his readers, also contain many an account of incredible and marvellous things. Perhaps, he goes on to suggest, truth can be stranger than fiction?[75] The second is his explanation of Marco's nickname (whence the *Devisement*'s Italian title), for which there are also medieval sources:[76]

> E perché nel continuo raccontare ch'egli faceva piú e piú volte della grandezza del Gran Cane, dicendo l'entrate di quello esser da 10 in 15 millioni d'oro, e cosí di molte alte ricchezze di quelli paesi, riferiva tutte a millioni, lo cognominariono messer Marco Millioni. (III, p. 31)

> (And because in the continual telling of tales he spoke many, many times of the greatness of the Great Khan, saying that his income was between 10 and 15 millions in gold, and so on about the many riches of these countries, always talking in millions, he was given the nickname Mr Marco Millions.)

Marco might have been telling the truth, but his stories of far-flung corners of the world were nonetheless potentially at least perceived as tall stories.

Ramusio's image of Marco telling stories over and over again in which quantities and amounts were always given in millions is, of course, a fictionalization of the process of storytelling, whether or not it has a basis in fact; but we, as readers of the text, nonetheless have to decide how we are going to assess its truthfulness, particularly given the text's insistent and ambiguous use of first-person forms and its use of other techniques that invite identification with the travels of the protagonists. The discourse of the *Devisement*, as we have seen, is neither 'objective', impersonal nor strictly factual. It is frequently fragmented or partial. It thus invites questioning and supplementation from its readers and transmitters, which in turn leads to romanticization, speculation, elaboration.

Furthermore, the reader of the prologue may well realize that in the very act of reading the *Devisement* he or she is being put in the exact same position in relation to Marco as Kublai Khan had been previously. Marco, we are told, was an excellent linguist, and on arrival at the Great Khan's court, he quickly mastered four languages and their scripts, as a result of which Kublai began to use him as an envoy:

> Li jeune baçaler fait sa enbasee bien et sajemant; et por ce qu'el avoit veu et oi plusors fois que le grant kan, quant les mesages k'il mandoit por les diverses partes dou monde, quant il retornoient a lui et li disoient l'anbasee por coi il estoit alés et no li savoient dir autres noveles de les contrees ou il estoient alés, il disoit elz qu'il estoient foux et non saiçhan[ç] et disoi[t] que miaus ameroit oir les noveles et les costumes et les usajes de

---

[75] Ramusio also suggests that Marco Polo was a greater explorer than Columbus, because travelling overland is more onerous than travelling by sea (pp. 22–3).

[76] See Larner, *Marco Polo*, p. 44.

celle estra<n>jes contree qu'il ne fasoit oir celç por coi il li avoit mandé, et Marc, ke bien savoie tout ce, quant il ala en cele mesajarie, toutes les nuvités et tutes les stranges chauses qu'il avoit, met[t]oit son entent por coi il le seust redire au grant kaan. (XVI, 4)

(The young man conducted his embassy well and wisely, and because he had seen and heard several times that the Great Khan, when the envoys he sent out to the diverse parts of the world returned to him and recounted their embassies to him, but couldn't tell him anything else about the countries where they had been, said they were foolish and ignorant and that he would rather hear about new customs and the habits of strange countries than he would hear about the business on which he had sent them, and Marco, who realized this, when he went off on a mission, strived to be in a position to relate to the Great Khan all the novelties and strange things he could.)

In his stories Marco evinces great wisdom for one so young, and it is his consummate skill as a storyteller that lead to his earning the title 'Mr' (XVII, 1–3). Above all, it is Marco's ability to deliver what the Great Khan clearly desires, tales of 'mai<n>tes novités et maintes estranges chouses' (XVII, 6: 'tales of many new things and many strange things'), that leads to his being employed ahead of his rivals at court, much to their annoyance (XVII, 7–8). As others have suggested, we may well be dealing with crude self-aggrandizement here,[77] but how might the model of Marco, storyteller to the Great Khan, inflect our reading of the book as a whole?

What this model suggests is that Marco was a teller of tales not just in the West but also in the East.[78] He is a purveyor of *nuvités* and *estranges chouses* wherever he goes, positioned as a representative of strangeness, foreignness and diversity, both at home and away. This positioning of Marco simultaneously as an insider and as an outsider is as strong in the West as in the East:[79] Ramusio's story of the return of the travellers to Venice in foreign clothes,

---

[77] For example, Larner (*Marco Polo*, p. 42), who tends to have a high opinion of Marco, nonetheless writes: 'the Book's account of Marco's eminent rôle here must be treated with some scepticism.' See also Pierre Racine, *Marco Polo et ses voyages* (Paris: Perrin, 2012), 'Marco Polo au service du grand khan', who laments Marco's 'tendance fâcheuse à manier l'hyperbole'.

[78] For some astute remarks on this point, see Sharon Kinoshita, 'Marco Polo and the Tributary East', in Suzanne Conklin Akbari and Amilcare A. Iannucci (eds), *Marco Polo and the Encounter of East and West* (Toronto: University of Toronto Press, 2008), pp. 60–86 (pp. 71–3).

[79] Cf. Homi Bhabha's remarks on the 'subject that inhabits the rim of an "in-between" reality' in *The Location of Culture* (London and New York: Routledge, 1994), p. 13 (also cited in the Introduction), and also his argument that the post-colonial needs 'to move the location of cultural difference away from the space of demographic *plurality* to the borderline negotiations of cultural translation', a movement that Marco Polo and the *Devisement* would seem to enact perfectly.

unrecognizable and barely able to speak Venetian intelligibly, 'trasfigurati nella faccia' ('their facial features transformed'),[80] is no doubt apocryphal, but it shows the extent to which Marco Polo is perceived in the West as touched by foreignness, and as such he becomes the subject-matter for exotic tales as well as their teller. But the key thing that Marco's storytelling illustrates is in fact that the position of the *estrange* is relative, a point that will be explored further in Chapter 3. For the European reader, what could be newer or stranger than Kublai Khan? But what we see in the prologue is that it is possible to receive strange and new tales about the world from more than one pespective, since Kublai too is a consumer of *nuvités*, in which case the 'new' and the 'strange' might denote quite different things depending on your own position.

The positioning of Marco Polo as someone who addresses listeners in the West and in the East and thus as in both, or perhaps *in between* West and East, is of course a fictional effect of his having told stories to Kublai Khan combined with our knowledge that he is supposed now (at least within the diegetic frame) to be telling stories to us. Again we are drawn into an *effet de réel*, and, like all *effets de réel*, this one is fictional. But if the main point here is that Marco Polo's cultural positioning in the *Devisement* is ultimately ambivalent (he is neither a Westerner nor an Easterner), this ambivalence is then greatly enhanced by the ambiguous narrative voices of the texts. Yet it is not just a question of who speaks in this text. We also have to ask ourselves: from where?

---

[80] III, pp. 28–9; Ramusio reports that he heard the story from a very old man who lived near the Polo family home, who heard it in turn from a very old man when he was a boy. Once they had been recognized, the story goes, the Polos cut the hems of their rags to extract priceless jewels. The account of Marco returning to Venice unrecognized has an obvious literary precedent in Odysseus' return home unrecognized.

2
Language and translation: 'in lingua Galica dicitur'

The question of from where the text speaks is related to another: in which language? The language of the *Devisement* has been problematic in its reception from the outset, though this has been frequently occluded both by early transmitters and by modern scholars. One illustration of uncertainty concerning language comes early in the *Z* redaction. At the beginning of Chapter 4, we read: 'In Iorgia est quidam rex qui David Melic totis temporibus nuncupatur, quod in lingua Galica dicitur Rex David' (4, 1: 'In Georgia their king is always called David Melic, which is to say in French King David'). Here an early Latin translator of a lost version of the Franco-Italian redaction, himself thought to be a Venetian, glosses the Georgian name 'David Melic' (derived from the Arabic *malik*, 'king') by telling us that 'in French' (even though he is writing in Latin) this means 'Rex David'. We are almost certainly dealing here with an instance of the *Z* redactor translating his source unthinkingly, which is characteristic mainly of just the early part of his work: he seems to have quickly become more attentive to such details and to have sought to make his own version increasingly more internally coherent.[1] But the slip is nonetheless symptomatic of the *Devisement*'s early linguistic mobility: it seems to move so easily between languages that, when translated, it invariably retains traces of the language of the source text. Thus, as we will see, the French redaction retains Italianisms from its Franco-Italian source, while the Tuscan redaction retains Gallicisms. Many medieval translations (particularly translations between vernaculars) behave in a similar way, but with the *Devisement* there are nonetheless quite specific issues that are worthy of scrutiny: French was presumably the mother tongue of neither Marco Polo nor Rustichello da Pisa, and if the earliest surviving manuscript of the text,

---

[1] At this point (XXIII,1) the Franco-Italian redaction reads 'en fransois'. Compare *Z* 41, 11, where 'que vaut a dire en françois' (LXXIV, 8) becomes simply 'quod est dicere' ('which is to say'). Whereas the Tuscan redaction frequently introduces glosses on foreign words with 'ciò è a dire en francesco' (see 22, 1; 30, 5; and so on), the Venetian redaction transposes its source, systematically and more coherently, to 'in nostra lengua' (see XIII, 1; XLIX, 4; and so on). On the derivation of 'Melic', see *Z* redaction, p. 13 n. 1; on the likely Venetian origin of the *Z* redactor, see Eugenio Burgio and Giuseppe Mascherpa, '«Milione» latino. Note linguistiche e appunti di storia della tradizione sulle redazioni Z e L', in Renato Oniga and Sergio Vatteroni (eds), *Plurilinguismo letteraro* (Soveria Mannelli: Rubbettino, 2007), pp. 119–58 (pp. 123–8).

the one that is thought to approximate most closely the language of the 'original', is in French, it is nonetheless riddled with Italian forms and syntactic structures that clearly stand out as diverse from the practices found in the more familiar French *scripta* of northern France and England of the period. However fluently and easily its authors spoke French and manipulated the written language, the earliest redactions of the *Devisement* all seem to be marked with forms from, and traces of, their mother tongue. Does this mean that with the *Devisement* the text is always already a translation of sorts, in that in order to produce a written text its authors are translating, sometimes poorly, thoughts (or notes) formulated in another language? If so, are they doing this all the time or only sometimes? And while the language of the *Devisement* in BNF f.fr. 1116 is certainly not Italian, nor is it any form of what one might call Franco-French, which is to say one of the varieties of French spoken and written in France: what exactly then *is* the language of the source text for the French, Tuscan, Venetian or Latin redactions? If 'nostre lengaje' (LXXVI, 1) is implicitly 'fransois' (XXIII, 1; XXXI, 7; XLVII, 3; and so on), it is nonetheless clear that what is meant by 'French' is not necessarily straightforward when dealing with a text like the *Devisement* and that it certainly does not necessarily designate a form of the language spoken and written in France.

Our apprehension of medieval languages has, naturally enough, been refracted through the prism of modern philological traditions, which have tended to privilege forms of languages that were later to evolve into the standard forms of national languages over dialects as well as over so-called regional languages, sometimes assuming these already to be the standard, or at the very least in the process of emerging as the standard, while at the same time also often adopting a comparative approach that seemed to transcend national and nationalistic concerns. This paradoxical relation between Romance philology and nineteenth- and twentieth-century national and nationalistic literary history has been examined extensively over the last few decades.[2] On the one hand, the unabashed aim of Romance philology was to establish the contours of the cultures of some of the pre-eminent modern European nation-states by tracing the histories of their languages and literatures back to the Middle Ages. Thus, as Giulio Bertoni put it in 1941, in the introduction to the first issue of *Cultura Neolatina*, one of the leading journals in the field, 'la storia di un popolo o della sua civiltà o del suo progresso spirituale, è in realtà la storia della sua lingua' ('the history of a people or of its civilization or of its spiritual progress is in reality the history of its

---

[2] An excellent example is 'The Inventions of Philology', in María Rosa Menocal, *Shards of Love: Exile and the Origins of the Lyric* (Durham, NC, and London: Duke University Press, 1994), pp. 91–141.

language').[3] On the other hand, philology has always retained a commitment to internationalism. Thus Gaston Paris, in the first issue of *Romania*, another of the main journals in the field, opined in 1872 that the concept of *Romania* – that is, the culture shared by speakers of different Romance languages – enabled 'la tendance vers une civilisation commune, équitable et éclairée' ('a tendency to create a shared, equitable and enlightened civilization'), a shared civilization which is of course 'sensible dans l'histoire de leurs littératures autant que dans celles de leurs langues' ('discernible in their literary histories as much as in the history of their languages').[4] Both of the impulses articulated here are utopian, grounded in politics that were progressive in their day, however questionable they may seem now: thus, Paris's plea in favour of *Romania* was written in the immediate aftermath of the Franco-Prussian War and explicitly contrasts the civilizing tendencies of the Romance languages with Barbarian/Germanic cultural identities that in his view are grounded rather in racial and blood ties. Some seventy years later Bertoni, writing in the shadow of Italian fascism, vaunts the superiority of philology over other humanistic disciplines because it is grounded in a knowable truth, that of language itself, rather than opinion, the implication being that philology alone remains untainted by prevailing political trends. Philology thus transcends national boundaries to promote civilization, and nowhere is the profoundly internationalist credo of philologists more apparent than in the seminal work of two of Bertoni's German contemporaries, Erich Auerbach and Ernst Curtius, who, as Europe tore itself apart, sought to demonstrate that it had a common culture, expressed in a variety of literary idioms which could all be traced back to a Latinate (or sometimes biblical) common source.[5]

However, exclusionary nationalistic discourses nonetheless always seem to surface at the heart of philology's internationalism. Thus Paris's Romance community is one in which the individuality of nations may flourish, but tellingly he mentions only three: Italy, 'Gaule' and Spain.[6] Meanwhile Bertoni's stress on what he regards as Rome's most significant 'miracle', *la civiltà neolatina* – which is to say, the shared culture of Romance languages – in the first issue of the journal of the Istituto di Filologia Romanza di *Roma* (my emphasis), implicitly underlines Italy's unique position as *Rome*'s cultural heir, particularly since he describes philology as a 'concezione essenzial-

[3] Giulio Bertoni, 'L'istituto di filologia di Roma', *Cultura Neolatina*, 1 (1941), 5–12 (p. 7).
[4] Gaston Paris, 'Romani, Romania, lingua romana, romancium', *Romania*, 1 (1872), 1–22 (p. 21).
[5] Erich Auerbach, *Mimesis: The Representation of Reality in Western Literature*, trans. Willard R. Trask (Princeton: Princeton University Press, 1953), and Ernst Robert Curtius, *European Literature and the Latin Middle Ages*, trans. Willard R. Trask (London: Routledge and Kegan Paul, 1953).
[6] 'Romani, Romania', pp. 21–2.

mente e fontamentalmente italiana' ('a fundamentally and essentially Italian invention'), with no mention of the discipline's largely German origins.[7] So Paris's cultural community turns out to be a community of nation-states opposed to the Hun, thereby occluding some major Romance linguistic communities (e.g. Catalan and Occitan), while Bertoni's intellectual idealism turns out to be grounded implicitly in an imperial nostalgia that elevates Italian culture above that of other Romance languages.[8] This tension between nationalism and internationalism is hardly surprising, given that it is already present in the foundational medieval text for Romance philology, Dante's *De vulgari eloquentia*, which on the one hand shows an awareness of the homogeneity and shared Latinity of Romance languages, while on the other seeking to distinguish between three idioms in order to establish the putative pre-eminence of one.

I have already examined the effects of these philological traditions in some instances of the reception of the *Devisement* in my Introduction: the hybrid language of the Franco-Italian redaction is disparaged by Ménard as 'deformed', 'incorrect' and 'confused'; Varvaro relegates major texts such as the *Devisement* and Brunetto Latini's *Tresor* (major both in terms of dissemination and cultural impact), composed in French by Italians, to the margins of literary history (or at least to the footnotes) because of the awkwardness of placing them in a grand narrative of medieval Italian literature that culminates in Dante (though their placement in mainstream French literary history is, of course, equally problematic). While there have been some notable scholarly contributions in recent years that aim to improve our knowledge and understanding of francophone literature produced and circulating in Italy, the phenomenon remains under-researched both in terms of our empirical knowledge of its extent and in terms of our critical understanding of its causes and effects.[9]

This chapter will seek to assess the cultural freight not only of the *Devisement*'s being composed in French, but also of the form of French in which it was written. This will in turn entail a consideration of the reception of the language of the Franco-Italian redaction, as evinced in almost contemporary translations into other linguistic forms. A comprehensive survey of the material here would be a vast undertaking, given the length of the text, the number of surviving manuscripts, the number of redactions and the complexity of

---

[7] Bertoni, 'L'istituto di filologia', pp. 6 and 13.

[8] For further discussion see Simon Gaunt and Julian Weiss, 'Cultural Traffic in the Medieval Romance World', *Journal of Romance Studies*, 4 (2004), 1–12 (pp. 2–8).

[9] The main scholarly reference point for the production and circulation of French-language manuscripts and texts in Italy remains the indispensable Paul Meyer, 'De l'expansion de la langue française en Italie pendant le moyen âge', in *Atti del Congresso Internazionale di Scienze Storiche IV: Sezione Storia delle letterature* (Rome: Accademia dei Lincei, 1904), pp. 61–104. See also the works cited in notes 57 and 88 of the Introduction for more recent work on the Franco-Italian tradition.

the tradition. My focus in this chapter will be mainly on the language of the Franco-Italian redaction and on how the French redaction adapts its source, but with some consideration also of the Tuscan and *Z* redactions. A number of questions will inform my analysis. How aware were the redactors of early versions of the *Devisement* of effecting a systematic linguistic transposition between clearly and discernibly distinct languages or linguistic forms? Or, to put this slightly differently, to what extent should the early redactions of the *Devisement* be considered translations? Is there any relation between linguistic transposition and other changes made to the text? Finally, what attitude does the text itself have towards language and linguistic difference?

This chapter has three sections. In the first I propose to give a more detailed sense of the language of the Franco-Italian, French and Tuscan redactions and also to look further at the question of translation. In the second I will examine a specific instance of how an episode is treated in the French redaction to consider the ideological ramifications of the redactor's rendering. The third section will discuss the text's own view of linguistic difference and focus in particular on the issue of untranslatability. My conclusion will return to the phenomenon of French in Italy, but also seek to relate the arguments of this chapter to those of Chapter 1.

The languages of the *Devisement*

Let us compare the opening of the text in the Franco-Italian, French and Tuscan redactions.[10]

> Franco-Italian: Seignors enperaor et rois, dux et marquois, cuens, chevaliers et b[o]rgio[i]s, et toutes gens que volés savoir les deverses jenerasions des homes et les deversités des deverses region dou monde, si prennés cestui livre et le feites lire. Et qui troverérés toutes les grandismes mervoilles et les grant diversités de la grande Harminie et de Persie et des Tartars et <de> Indie, et de maintes autres provinces, sicom notre livre voç contera por ordre apertemant, sicome meisser Marc Pol, sajes et noble citaiens de Venece, raconte por ce que a seç iaus meisme il le voit. Mes auques hi n'i a qu'il ne vit pas, mes il l'entendi da homes citables et de verité; et por ce metreron les chouse veue por veue et l'entendue por entandue, por ce que notre livre soit droit et vertables sanç nulle ma<n>songe.
>
> Et chascuns que cest livre liroie ou oiront le doient croire, por ce que toutes sunt chouses vertables; car je voç fais savoir que, puis que nostre sire Dieu pasme de seç mainç Adam nostre primer pere jusque a cestui point, ne fu cristienç, ne paiens, ne tartar, ne yndiens, ne nulç homes de nulle generasion, que tant seust ne cherchast de les deverses partie dou monde

[10] My translation is of the Franco-Italian redaction. Parts of the following analysis draw on my 'Translating the Diversity of the Middle Ages: Marco Polo and John Mandeville as "French" Writers', *Australian Journal of French Studies*, 46 (2009), 235–48.

et de les grant mervoilles come cestui messire Marc en cherche et soi. Et por ce dit il a soi meisme que tropo seroit grant maus se il ne feist metre en escriture toutes les granç mervoilles qu'il vit et qu'il oi por verités, por ce que les autres jens que ne le virent ne <ne> sevent, le sachent por cest livre. Et si voç di qu'il demora a ce savoir en celles deverses parties et provinces bien XXVI anç.

Le quel puis, demourant en le cha[r]tre de Jene, fist retraire toutes cestes chouses a messire Rust[i]ciaus de Pise, que en celle meisme chartre estout, au tens qu'il avoit MCCXCVIII anç que Jesucrit nesqui.

French: Pour savoir la pure verité des diverses regions du monde, si prenez cest livre [et le faites lire]: si trouverez les grandesimes merveilles qui [y] sont escriptes [de] la Grant Herminie et de Persse et des Tartas et d'Ynde et de maintes autres provinces, si comme nostre livres [vous] contera tout par ordre [apertement] des que mesires Marc Pol, sajes et nobles sitoiens de Venice, raconte pour ce que il les vit; mais auques il y a choses qu'il ne vit pas, mais il [l']entendi d'ommes certains par verité. Et pour ce metrons nous les choses veues pour veues et l'entendue pour entendue, a ce que nostre livre soit vrais et veritables, sanz nule mençonge.

Et chascun que ce livre orra ou lira le doi[e] croire, pour ce que toutes sont choses veritables, car je vous fais a savoir que, puis que nostre sire Diex fist Adam, [nostre] premier pere, ne fu onques homme de nul[le] generacion qui tant seust ne cherchast des diverses parties du monde comme cestui mesire Marc Pol en sot. Et pour ce pensa que ce seroit granz maus se ce ne feist metre en escrit ce que il avoit veu ne oÿ par verité, a ce que l'autre gent qui ne l'ont vue ne oÿ le sachent par cest livre. Et si vous di qu'il demoura a ce savoir en ces diverses parties bien .XXVI. ans.

Lequel livre, [puis demourant] en la carsere de Gene, fist retraire par ordre par Mesire Rasta pysan, qui en cele meïsmes prison estoit au temps que il couroit de Crist .MCCXCVIII. anz de l'Incarnation.

Tuscan: Signori imperadori, re e duci e·ttutte altre genti che volete sapere le diverse generazioni delle genti e·lle diversità delle regioni del mondo, leggete questo libro dove le troverrete tutte le grandissime maraviglie e gran diversitadi delle genti d'Erminia, di Persia, et di Tarteria, d'India e di molte altre province. E questo vi conterà il libro ordinatamente siccome messere Marco Polo, savio e·nnobile cittadino di Vinegia, le conta in questo libro e egli medesimo le vide. Ma ancora v'à di quelle cose le quali elli non vide, ma udille da persone degne di fede, e però le cose vedute dirà di veduta e·ll'altre per udita, acciò che'l nostro libro sia veritieri e sanza niuna menzogna.

Ma io voglio che·vvoi sappiate che·ppoi che Iddio fece Adam nostro primo padre insino al dì d'oggi, né cristiano né pagano, saracino o tartero, né niuno huomo di niuna generazione non vide né cercò tante maravigliose cose del mondo come fece messer Marco Polo. E però disse infra·sse medesimo che troppo sarebbe grande male s'egli non mettesse inn-iscritto tutte le meraviglie ch'egli à vedute, perché chi no·lle sa l'apari per questo libro.

E·ssì·vvi dico ched egli dimorò in que' paesi bene trentasei anni; lo quale poi, stando nella prigione di Genova, fece mettere inn-iscritto tutte queste cose a messere Rustico da·pPisa, lo quale era preso in quelle medesime carcere ne gli anni di Cristo 1298.

(My lords, emperors and kings, dukes and marquises, counts, knights and burghers, and all people who wish to know about the various races of men and the diversities of the various parts of the world, take this book and have it read. And here you will find all the great wonders and curiosities of Greater Armenia, of Persia and of the Tartars and of India, and of many other provinces, just as our book will relate to you clearly in due course, just as Mr Marco Polo, a noble and wise citizen of Venice, recounts, since he saw them with his own eyes. But some of this he did not see, rather he heard about it from trustworthy and truthful men; and for this reason we will set down the things he saw as things he saw and hearsay as hearsay, because our book is straight and truthful, with no falsehood.

And all who read or hear this book should believe it, since everything in it is true; for I would have you know that to this day since the time when our lord God formed with his own hands Adam, our first ancestor, there has been no man – Christian, pagan, Tartar, Indian or of any race – who knew so much about nor sought to see so many of the various parts of the world and so many of its wonders as Marco did on his own account. And so he said to himself that it would be a great shame if he did not have all the great marvels he had seen and heard about written down, so that other people who had not seen them and who did not know about them might learn about them from this book. And let me tell you, he stayed in these various places and provinces some twenty-six years in order to acquire this knowledge.

Then, when he was in prison in Genoa, he had all these things related by Mr Rustichello da Pisa, who was in the same prison, in 1298.)

Some aspects of the Franco-Italian redaction deviate immediately from more standard forms of French of the period: the failure to make many adjectives and some nouns agree in the plural (e.g. *deverses region, les chouse veue*), though, as some of these inconsistencies are maintained throughout the text, this suggests less disorder and confusion than an indifference to this particular grammatical norm. Some of the Italianisms could be simply orthographical (e.g. 'ç' for [s] and [tś], as in *voç, seç, cristienç, anç*), but others are more significant, either because they are morphological (e.g. *qui* for 'here', *tropo*, futures and imperfects such as *metreron*), or because they also reflect Italian grammatical or syntactic structures. Note, for instance, the use of the preposition *da* towards the end of the first paragraph and compare this to 'en le chartre de Jene'. The text thus seems to distinguish between Italian *da* and *di*, as if French is by implication being found wanting because it has only one preposition where Italian has two.[11] While it might be pos-

---

[11] Further linguistic research is needed on the Franco-Italian text, but see Valeria Bertolucci Pizzorusso's excellent 'Lingue e stili nel *Milione*', in Renzo Zorzi (ed.),

sible to attribute some of these linguistic features to incompetence on the part of the scribe of BNF f.fr. 1116,[12] this does not explain why some of the peculiar linguistic forms and precise vocabulary found in BNF f.fr. 1116 are also found in other versions, since they are clearly not all taken from the same source, nor why Italianisms that seem authorial should pervade BNF f.fr. 1463, the most authoritative and complete manuscript of Rustichello da Pisa's Arthurian compilation.[13]

The sources of the French and Tuscan redactions, both of which were produced within no more than twelve years of the original, were clearly very close, if not identical, to the surviving Franco-Italian redaction's version of this chapter. The Tuscan redaction abbreviates but in some respects seems to follow its source more closely here than the French, whose redactor works hard to 'correct' the language, eliminating morphologically Italian forms ('qui trovererés' > 'si trouverez'; 'tropo seroit grant maus' > 'ce seroit granz maus') and introducing more systematically a (by now archaicizing) case system for nouns and adjectives (e.g. 'mesire*s* Marc Pol, saje*s* e noble*s* sitoien*s*'). It is striking, however, that neither the French nor the Italian redactions succeeds in eliminating 'foreign' elements entirely: *grandesimes* and *carsere* are Italianisms, 'disse infra·sse medesimo' a Gallicism.[14] It is as if there is always a troubling residue of foreignness in this text, in no matter which language, which suggests, as Valeria Bertolucci Pizzorusso astutely observes on a number of occasions, that some transmitters of this text were well aware of the linguistic hybridity they were producing or reproducing.[15]

L'epopea delle scoperte (Venice: Leo S. Olschki, 1994), pp. 61–73, and Maria Grazia Capusso, 'La mescidanza linguistica del *Milione* franco-italiano', in Silvia Conte (ed.), *I viaggi del 'Milione': itinerari testuali, vettori di trasmissione e metamorfosi del Devisement du monde di Marco Polo e Rustichello da Pisa nella pluralità delle attestazioni. Convegno internazionale Venezia, 6–8 ottobre 2005* (Rome: Tiellemedia, 2008), pp. 263–83. On verb morphology see Maria Grazia Capusso, *La lingua del* Devisament dou Monde *di Marco Polo: 1 Morfologia verbale* (Pisa: Pacini, 1980).

[12] 'Le copiste était ignorant de la langue française et sans doute peu soigneux' (ed. Ménard, I, p. 36).

[13] See Fabrizio Cigni, '"Prima" del *Devisement dou Monde*. Osservazioni (e alcuni ipotesi) sulla lingua della *Compilazione Arturiana* di Rustichello da Pisa', in Conte (ed.), *I viaggi del 'Milione'*, pp. 219–31.

[14] See Ménard's linguistic notes, I, pp. 84–8, and Bertolucci Pizzorusso's n. 5 on p. 4 of her edition.

[15] See particularly Bertolucci Pizzorusso, 'Lingue e stili'; also ' Le versioni storiche del *Milione* in Italia. La versione toscana', in Federico Masini, Franco Salvatori and Sandro Schipani (eds), *Marco Polo 750 anni. Il viaggio. Il libro. Il diritto. Congresso internazionale* (Rome: Tiellemedia, 2006), pp. 199–208 (p. 201), and 'La réception de la littérature courtoise du XIIème et XIIIème siècle en Italie: nouvelles propositions', in Barbara K. Altmann and Carleton W. Carroll (eds), *The Court Reconvenes: Courtly Literature across the Disciplines* (Cambridge: D.S. Brewer, 2003), pp. 3–13 (pp. 6–7). For further comments on the Tuscan text, see her edition, pp. 380–2.

Hybridity is a key concept in post-colonial studies and theory. In his seminal book on the topic Robert Young traces the evolution in meaning of the word 'hybridity' from its origin in seventeenth-century scientific discourse (where it was used in the field of botany), through its simultaneous expansion in the nineteenth century into the spheres of linguistics (hence Bertolucci Pizzorusso's usage) and ethnography (where it was used to discuss miscegenation), then through its twentieth-century usage to describe the mixing of discourses (notably in the work of Bakhtin) and finally into its contemporary usage in post-colonial studies and theory, where, in the wake of Homi Bhabha's work, it enables the exploration of how the cultures, languages and, on occasion, races of the colonizers and colonized intermingle, thereby, potentially at least, subverting the hegemony of the colonizing power.[16] As Young himself argues, one risk in the way the term is sometimes used is that the categories that are supposedly mixed are presupposed, often unquestioned and thereby to some extent reified.[17]

This is indeed a risk. But to return to the *Devisement*: what exactly was the French redactor doing when he gave his source its linguistic make-over? Was he simply adapting it as comprehensibly as possible for his own speech community, a phenomenon that is well attested as texts are copied from dialect to dialect of the same language, or even between different Romance languages, but without any systematic sense of linguistic uniformity or codification, which would indicate an indifference to the remaining hybrid forms and Italianisms?[18] Or was he seeking, rather, to modify his source with a view to eliminating far more deliberately, and in a far more thorough-going way, elements that can be identified as Italian or Italianate (and therefore

---

[16] Robert J.C. Young, *Colonial Desire: Hybridity in Theory, Culture, and Race* (London and New York: Routledge, 1995), pp. 4–26. For Homi K. Bhabha's now classic reorientation of the term see *The Location of Culture* (London and New York: Routledge, 1994), particularly pp. 112–16. The term is not, however, uncontroversial. For some brief discussion, see Bill Ashcroft, Gareth Griffiths and Helen Tiffin, *Post-Colonial Studies: The Key Concepts* (London and New York: Routledge, 2000), pp. 118–21.

[17] *Colonial Desire*, p. 25.

[18] See for example Alison Cornish, *Vernacular Translation in Dante's Italy: Illiterate Literature* (Cambridge: Cambridge University Press, 2011), who comments that 'The alteration of "linguistic dress" is so basic to the behaviour of copyists of vernacular literature that it usually does not register as a scribal intervention, much less as translation' (p. 54). See also Sarah Kay, 'La seconde main et les secondes langues dans la France médiévale', in *Translations médiévales: cinq siècles de traduction en français au Moyen Âge (XIe–XVe siècles). Etude et répertoire*, ed. Claudio Galderisi, 3 vols (Turnhout: Brepols, 2011), I, pp. 461–85. Kay shows how lyrics often do not undergo a thorough-going translation from one Romance language to another, but rather are subjected to a *traduction–translittération* (p. 474) effected 'au moyen de certains traits différentiels plutôt que par le passage d'une langue intégrale dans une autre' (p. 476: 'by means of certain differential traits rather than the integral transposition from one discrete language to another'). Characteristic of the vernacular in certain circumstances, this fluidity would be in stark contrast to the transcription of Latin texts.

perhaps as 'foreign'), motivated by some prior, if not necessarily formalized, notion of standard French, what it ought to look like and how it differed from another Romance idiom that we now call Italian, as well as from the French he found in his source? The answer probably lies somewhere between the two, but the extent of the transformation of the text and its particular linguistic features argues more in favour of the redactor's deliberate revision of his Franco-Italian source with a view to making it into what one might call a 'Franco-French' text. What can be said, then, about the language of the French redaction of the *Devisement*?

With a prose text such as the French redaction of the *Devisement*, which survives in multiple manuscripts, linguistic analysis almost certainly reveals more about the manuscript copy than the text itself, but in the case of the base manuscript used by Ménard and his team for their critical edition (British Library Royal 19 B 1) it is interesting that, although this manuscript is known to have been produced in Paris, the language of the text of the *Devisement* 'est rédigé dans une langue littéraire courante, la scripta franco-picarde. Il s'agit d'une scripta composite: maints picardismes très marqués n'y apparaissent pas. On y décèle de loin en loin quelques italianismes' ('is written in a current literary language, the Franco-Picard scripta. This is a composite scripta: there are not numerous very markedly Picard forms. Some Italianisms are just about perceptible').[19] These Italianisms, described by Ménard as *vestiges*, 'témoignent de la présence d'italianismes dans la version originale du texte. Le français de Rustichello était parsemé d'italianismes. On ne saurait s'en étonner' ('testify to the presence of Italianisms in the original version of the text. Rustichello's French was strewn with Italianisms, which is hardly surprising').[20] For Ménard, what we have then here is a slightly botched attempt at standardization, but just as interesting for my purposes is the presence of Picardisms in a manuscript believed to be from Paris.

As R. Anthony Lodge has demonstrated, if there is no such thing as 'standard' French before the sixteenth century, prestige varieties of French, such as Picard or the French of the royal court, are nonetheless discernible in the literary tradition from the early thirteenth century onwards.[21] And if there is nothing akin in the Middle Ages to the policies that have driven the standardization of modern French,[22] the development of a literary *koine* is a well-attested feature of medieval literary culture in French as it is in

---

[19] See ed. Ménard, I, p. 77, and for detailed analysis pp. 77–89. These findings are confirmed in subsequent volumes: II, pp. XXVII–XXXVIII; III, pp. 26–34; IV, pp. 27–34; V, pp. 43–54; VI, pp. XXXVIII–LXXI.

[20] See ed. Ménard, I, p. 88.

[21] See R. Anthony Lodge, *French: From Dialect to Standard* (London and New York: Routledge, 1993), particularly pp. 87 and 98–101.

[22] On which see Rebecca Posner, *Linguistic Change in French* (Oxford: Clarendon Press, 1997), pp. 33–55.

other Romance languages (for example, Occitan and Italian), with the effect that written language is inherently less variable than we know the spoken language to have been. In the case of French, Occitan and Italian two factors, in particular, seem to have impacted upon the evolution of distinct literary idioms: first, the prosperity of towns and their consequent role in promoting literary culture; secondly, the wealth and prestige of courts. In France, the wealth of the urban north explains the prevalence of Picard forms even in texts known to have come from and/or been copied in other parts of France, while the particular and growing importance of the royal court explains the prevalence of Parisian French.[23] As Lodge puts it, 'whatever the origins of the *koine* [...] the writing systems found in twelfth- and thirteenth-century texts are not fundamentally regional, but attempt to conform, implicitly and with varying degrees of success, to a supraregional written norm.'[24] This 'supraregional written norm' is precisely the French that the French redaction of the *Devisement* most closely reproduces, despite the *vestiges* of Italianisms.

Given the (partial and not always successful) attempt to eliminate traces of the Italian language from the French redaction, differences in the representation of difference are perhaps significant. Thus in the first paragraph 'les deversités des deverses region dou monde' in the Franco-Italian redaction becomes simply the 'diverses regions du monde' in French (the Tuscan stays closer to the Franco-Italian with 'lle diversità delle regioni del mondo'). Similarly there is a reduction in the enumeration of diverse peoples in the next paragraph: 'ne fu cristienç, ne paiens, ne tartar, ne yndiens, ne nulç homes de nulle generasion' in Franco-Italian (which is more or less reproduced in Italian) becomes simply 'homme de nulle generacion' in French. The Franco-Italian redaction thus stresses the plurality of differences to be found in the East, with *les diversités* in the plural. Contrary to what some critics have claimed,[25] the Franco-Italian redaction never simply opposes the East to the West in binary terms, as if the East were a homogenous whole and thereby 'othering' the East in relation to the West, but rather it stresses Asia's great diversity, as we will see in Chapter 4.[26] Thus there is no straightforward opposition here between Christians and Muslims; indeed in the Franco-

---

[23] See Lodge, 'The Selection Norms', in *French*, pp. 85–117. On the importance of court French, see also Serge Lusignan, *La Langue des rois au Moyen Age: le français en France et en Angleterre* (Paris: PUF, 2004). Lusignan's superlative book is also, however, cautionary on the dangers of presuming the hegemony of standard French forms.

[24] Lodge, *French*, pp. 114–15.

[25] See, for example, Syed Manzarul Islam's comment on the *Devisement* in *The Ethics of Travel from Marco Polo to Kafka* (Manchester and New York: Manchester University Press, 1996), p. 151: 'Having inserted a binary frame on the world, the relative difference of the others cannot fail to take on negative values.'

[26] On this point see also Thomas T. Allsen, 'The Cultural Worlds of Marco Polo', *Journal of Interdisciplinary History*, 31 (2001), 375–83 (p. 383), and the nuanced analysis of Steven Shankman, *Other Others: Levinas, Literature, Transcultural Studies* (Albany,

Italian redaction four categories of peoples are distinguished, together with the catch-all 'and all the others', but the French redaction flattens this to 'people of all kinds'.

As we have already seen, Philippe Ménard has argued emphatically that the French redaction should be regarded as neither a *remaniement* nor a translation: 'elle n'est pas une traduction et une adaptation dans une langue étrangère' ('it is not a translation or an adaptation into a foreign language').[27] Ménard's formulation here ('une traduction [...] dans une langue étrangère') is interesting when used of the *Devisement*, even of a version thought to be at least one remove from the original, given that this is a text thought to have been produced by two men who were expressing themselves in a 'foreign' language, or at least not in their mother tongue – a text, therefore, that may have entailed elements of translation not as a secondary process within textual production but rather as primary. According to this logic, one might suggest that the French redaction completes a process of translation begun by Marco Polo and Rustichello da Pisa in the Franco-Italian redaction whereby Marco's account of Asia, of associated parts of the world and of his travels is rendered into increasingly correct French from a linguistically diverse, because overly Italianate, point of departure. But this, of course, is to conceive of the 'diverse' or 'foreign' only from a *French* perspective rather than from the perspective instantiated by the *Devisement* itself in its Franco-Italian redaction, or from the supposed perspective of its authors. It is also to assume that the French language belongs to the French and that its norms may be dictated by their linguistic practices.

In *Le Monolinguisme de l'autre*, Jacques Derrida uses monolinguism as a metaphor to show how no subject may fully inhabit language, given that all language, whether foreign or a mother tongue, is essentially the discourse of the Other, a space that can belong absolutely to none of us, a framework that shapes and determines us far more than we can ever shape or determine it, one we struggle to enter – and then only inadequately. The subject's attempts to establish a place from which he can speak are thus effectively for Derrida a form of translation, what he calls initially 'la traduction absolue' ('absolute translation'), since we are all to some extent speaking a language that does not belong to us, a language that to some extent is therefore foreign.[28] He shortly

---

NY: SUNY Press, 2010), p. 41 (for whom Marco undertakes an ethical quest for the objectively different).

[27] Philippe Ménard, 'Intérêt et importance de la version française du *Devisement du Monde* de Marco Polo', in Masini, Salvatori and Schipani (eds), *Marco Polo 750 anni*, p. 197 and pp. 190–1, for his rebuttal of the idea that the text is a *remaniement*.

[28] *Le Monolinguisme de l'autre ou la prothèse d'origine* (Paris: Galilée, 1996), p. 117: 'une traduction sans pôle de référence, sans langue originaire, sans langue de départ. Il n'y a pas pour lui que des langues d'arrivée, si tu veux, mais des langues qui, singulière aventure, n'arrivent pas à s'arriver, dès lors qu'elles ne savent plus d'où elles partent, *à partir* de quoi elles parlent, et quel est le sens de leur trajet' ('a translation with no reference

reformulates this as 'une traduction interne (franco-française) jouant de la non-identité à soi de toute langue' ('an internal translation (Franco-French) playing on the non-identity of all language to itself').[29] In other words, even in his mother tongue the subject struggles to overcome the alienation the discourse of the Other always induces; he must follow its rules or condemn himself to unintelligibility, but in so doing his point of departure is obscured. This is not necessarily an entirely negative process. As Rey Chow puts it: 'Monolingualism in this instance is less the sign of the imposition by political force or cunning than it is *the promise of the singular*, a promise that remains open ended and thus messianic in character.'[30] The desire to be assimilated to the monolingual discourse of the Other is consequently quite understandable, provided one realizes that one's language will never be identical to it and that the monolingualism of the Other is always going to be open to deconstruction.[31] Ethical error thus, from Derrida's perspective, lies not so much in one's subjection to the Other's discourse (which is inevitable) as in an erroneous belief in its mastery and in one's ability to master it: '*je n'ai qu'une langue, or ce n'est pas la mienne*' ('*I only have one language, and it is not mine*').[32] This subjection to the Other's discourse makes all subjects – even bilingual or multilingual subjects – monolingual on some level, in that the only language in which they may express themselves belongs to another.[33]

The circumstances Derrida takes as the starting point for his discussion – those of a monolingual francophone Jew in multilingual wartime Algeria, stripped of French citizenship and of his Frenchness, but with no other culture or language with which to identify – are, of course, worlds away from those of two Italians composing in French at the end of the thirteenth century. But

point, no original language, no source language. There are for [the monolingual subject] only target languages, if you will, but languages which, with singular happenstance, never quite get where they are going inasmuch as they don't know either where they come from, *from whence* they speak, nor the direction/ meaning of their trajectory').

[29] *Monolinguisme*, p. 123.

[30] 'Reading Derrida on Being Monolingual', *New Literary History*, 39 (2008), 217–31 (p. 225).

[31] See *Monolinguisme*, p. 55: 'Il est impossible de compter les langues, voilà ce que je voulais suggérer. Il n'y a pas de calculabilité, dès lors que l'Un d'une langue, qui échappe à toute comptabilité arithmétique, n'est jamais déterminé. Le Un de la monolangue dont je parle, et celui que je parle, ne sera donc pas une identité arithmétique, ni même une identité tout court. La monolangue demeure donc incalculable' ('It is impossible to count languages, this is what I wanted to suggest. It is incalculable, since the One of a language, which escapes all arithmetic calibration, is never determined. The One of the monolanguage of which I speak, and of the one that I speak, will never have any arithmetical identity, nor any kind of identity at all. Monolanguage remains incalculable'). On these lines, see also Chow, 'Reading Derrida', p. 226.

[32] *Monolinguisme*, p. 15.

[33] Consider the two propositions Derrida explores (p. 21): '1. On ne parle jamais qu'une seule langue. 2. On ne parle jamais une seule langue.'

the analogy I am seeking to make here in terms of a regulatory monolingualism is less with the Franco-Italian redaction of the *Devisement* than with the French redaction. Derrida describes the 'internal translation' of which he speaks as follows: 'Traduction d'une langue qui n'existe pas encore, et qui n'aura jamais existé, dans une langue d'arrivée donnée' ('translation from a language which does not yet exist and which will never have existed into a given target language').[34] Whereas the language of the French redaction is clearly the result of intervention, of the introduction of given linguistic norms over which there seems to have been some degree of consensus, the language of its source is unstable, inconsistent, *ad hoc* and extremely difficult to codify; indeed, it may never have existed, at least not as the idiom of a community of native speakers, and its future certainly turned out to be curtailed, in that subsequent transmitters of all surviving versions of the text (even if we have evidence of other copies having been in circulation) all seem to have sought, though to greater or lesser degrees, to eliminate its idiosyncratic treatment of French. But the language of the Franco-Italian redaction is nonetheless recognizably French, making the French redaction arguably a Franco-French translation.

For Ménard, the changes made by the French redactor to his source simply reflect the normal practices of medieval transcription. He further suggests that this text marked a 'discernible progress' with respect to the Franco-Italian redaction's language, and also that it is linguistically 'more presentable'.[35] But this is again to assume that linguistic correctness according to a single paradigm was both a norm and an expectation, which is of course far from the case with medieval as with modern vernaculars. And despite Ménard's view that the changes the French redactor makes apart from his linguistic make-over amount to no more than 'quelques menues variantes' ('a few tiny variants'),[36] as we saw in Chapter 1, the fact that one at least of these 'tiny variants' pervades systematically the entire text – namely, the elimination of any first-person pronouns and verb forms relating to Marco Polo and their transposition into the third person – represents a fundamental revision of the text. If the French text has been 'improved' according to certain lights, I would suggest nonetheless that the Derridean framework I have outlined allows us to see more clearly the extent to which it has also been domesticated, with some at least of its troubling, ambiguous and foreign elements

---

[34] *Monolinguisme*, p. 123.

[35] See 'Intérêt et importance', p. 191 ('nous restons dans le monde normal de la transcription médiévale') and p. 195 ('Un progrès manifeste apparaît au plan de la morphologie et de la syntaxe'); also 'Le prétendu remaniement du *Devisement du Monde* de Marco Polo', *Medioevo Romanzo*, 11 (1998), 332–51 (p. 351: 'Il s'agit d'une version moins bizarre et moins fâcheuse au plan linguistique, plus présentable, destinée à un large public cultivé').

[36] 'Intérêt et importance', p. 191.

eliminated, or alternatively assimilated to a familiar system for representing foreignness, a familiar and ordered articulation of and in a French *monolangue*. In support of this contention I will examine in the next section a specific instance of translation that also points in this direction, an instance where a 'tiny variant' transforms the text; in the conclusion to this chapter I will return to the idea of French as *monolangue*; and in the next chapter I will discuss how the images found in some manuscripts of the French redaction sometimes also work to occlude some of the text's more troubling elements, thereby reinforcing the impulses of the French redactor whose text they illustrate. But to conclude this section I will consider how the phenomenon of linguistic mobility and hybridity I am describing also resonates strongly with an important question in modern translation studies. To what extent should a translation seek to retain a kernel of foreignness in its linguistic execution, perhaps through deliberately inauthentic syntactic structures, foreign words, neologisms? Or should it aim rather to produce something that sounds completely authentic in the target language?

If traditional approaches to translation have tended to favour the latter approach, modern translation theory has seen the retention of some kernel of foreignness as an ethical imperative, in that the aim of the translator should be to bring a domestic audience into contact with the foreignness of the source text rather than simply to make material available in an obviously accessible, domesticated form.[37] The exemplary translation, according to some modern theorists, needs therefore to disturb and baffle to some extent, to trouble its target language with residues of its source language or with indices of its foreign source, to draw attention to some extent to the fact that it is a translation. While it is clear that the French redaction of the *Devisement* does not succeed in eliminating Italian forms altogether and that the content of the text necessarily means a certain incorporation of the irreducibly foreign, including words that are far more foreign than the occasional Italianisms (as we will see in the third section of this chapter), it nonetheless presents the reader with a text that is a lot less troubling to read (or more agreeable, to use Ménard's formulation) than either the Franco-Italian or the Tuscan redactions.[38] The Tuscan redaction retains the pronominal ambiguity

---

[37] See Lawrence Venuti, *The Scandals of Translation: Towards an Ethics of Difference* (London and New York: Routledge, 1998), particularly pp. 111–12 and pp. 181–2. Venuti is influenced here by Walter Benjamin and Antoine Berman's classic essays on translation which may be consulted for convenience in the same volume: Walter Benjamin, 'The Task of the Translator: An Introduction to the Translations of Baudelaire's *Tableaux Parisiens*', and Antoine Berman, 'Translation and the Trials of the Foreign', in Lawrence Venuti (ed.). *The Translation Studies Reader* (London and New York: Routledge, 2000), pp. 15–25 and pp. 284–97. See also Emily Apter, *The Translation Zone: A New Comparative Literature* (Princeton, NJ, and Oxford: Princeton University Press, 2006), particularly pp. 6–8, where she discusses the vital role of transcoding in Benjamin's model of ethical translation.

[38] Ménard finds twenty Italianisms in the first fifty chapters of the French redaction;

of its source and creates a hybridity of its own through the Gallicisms that occur throughout the text.³⁹ Of course, these Gallicisms would undoubtedly have been quite legible among the Italian merchant classes, where exposure to French in a variety of contexts was not uncommon, not least because French was a *lingua franca* for trade throughout the eastern Mediterranean.⁴⁰ In such multilingual *milieux* – not uncommon in medieval Europe – it is quite possible that the kind of distinctions and boundaries between different languages and dialects that philologists often impose on texts (French vs. Italian, Tuscan vs. Venetian etc.) may simply not pertain in the same way as in the cultivated and literate communities of modern Europe that gave birth to modern philology. Indeed, it is not clear that grammatical 'correctness' and 'incorrectness' were criteria that even occurred to many Italian copyists or authors of texts in French – and possibly Italian too before the language was codified in the wake of Dante. They were simply copying the texts that interested them in a form they could understand, which in turn means that the boundaries between copy/dissemination, translation and reworking are extremely unclear.⁴¹ The risk of recourse to the notion of hybridity I outlined

---

see 'Le problème de la version originale du «Devisement du Monde» de Marco Polo', in François Livi (ed.), *De Marco Polo à Savinio: écrivains italiens en langue française* (Paris: Presses de l'Université de Paris-Sorbonne, 2003), pp. 7–19 (pp. 18–19). On residual Italian forms see also ed. Ménard, I, pp. 84–9, II, pp. XXXVI–VIII, III, pp. 33–4; IV, pp. 33–4; V, pp. 52–4; VI, pp. LXIV–LXX. Cf. Ménard, 'Le prétendu remaniement', p. 350: 'la version française est rédigée en un français plus agréable que le texte hybride du ms. fr. 1116'.

³⁹ To give but three examples from different parts of the text, the ubiquitous use of *uomo* as the equivalent of French *on*, which although common in early Tuscan texts, is undoubtedly calqued on French, see ed. Bertolucci, p. 46 n., glossing the example 'Quando l'uomo si parte di questa terra' (33, 4); *difalta* (98, 1, and n.); *asembiare* (196, 4, and n.).

⁴⁰ See Bertolucci Pizzorusso, 'Lingue e stili' pp. 62–3, and 'Le versioni storiche', pp. 206–7, for comments on Marco Polo's likely exposure to French in the Venetian mercantile *milieu*. On the use of hybrid forms of French as *lingua franca* throughout the eastern Mediterranean (including Italy) see Gianfranco Folena, *Culture e lingue nel Veneto medievale* (Padua: Editoriale Programma, 1990), pp. 227–61 and pp. 269–86, and Laura Minervini, 'La lingua franca mediterranea: plurilinguismo, multilinguismo, pidginizzazione sulle coste del Mediterraneo tra tardo medioevo e prima età moderna', *Medioevo Romanzo*, 20 (1996), 231–301 (particularly pp. 247–8). As both Folena and Minervini demonstrate, Franco-Italian French bears a strong resemblance to the written French of the Levant (Cyprus, *Outremer*, Morea), on which see Cyril Aslanov, *Le Français au Levant, jadis et naguère: à la recherche d'une langue perdue* (Paris: Honoré Champion, 2006).

⁴¹ On this point see Cornish, *Vernacular Translation*, p. 54: on the one hand, 'the alteration of "linguistic dress" is so basic to the behavior of copyists of vernacular literature that it usually does not register as scribal intervention, much less as translation'; on the other, 'The instability of linguistic form suggests that scribes were constantly engaged in subtle, perhaps even unconscious, acts of translation even when they thought they were simply transcribing.' For comments on the Tuscan redaction of the *Devisement*

earlier, that of reifying the very categories one seeks to trouble, is therefore all too apparent here. But in retaining the linguistic fluidity of its Franco-Italian source I would suggest that the Tuscan redaction stays closer to it stylistically and in some respects linguistically than does the French redaction to its source, even though the former is written in a different language and the latter in the same language. I would therefore – perhaps provocatively – suggest that the French redaction *is* a translation of the Franco-Italian *Devisement* whereas the Tuscan redaction is not. After all, the French redactor seems consciously to have aimed to produce a text that was linguistically distinct from its source, which he also sought to revise according to certain stylistic norms, whereas the Tuscan redactor's notion of linguistic distinctness seems a lot less clear, and therefore a lot more in tune with that of the text he was transmitting. And in the French redaction some, though by no means all, of the text's foreignness and hybridity seems to have been intentionally eliminated – lost in translation, as it were.

Translating the Life of the Buddha

What else can get lost in translation when the text is transposed from the hybrid language of its earliest redaction into a more standard form of French? In many respects, and as far as much of the contents is concerned, I am inclined to agree with Ménard's view that the French redaction 'donne un texte assez fidèle (proche de la rédaction franco-italienne) sous son habillage français' ('gives a rather faithful text (close to the Franco-Italian redaction) underneath its French clothing'):[42] thus, the French redaction of the *Devisement* is by far the most complete after the Franco-Italian in terms of the volume of material it transmits, and it also follows the chapter divisions and ordering of the Franco-Italian redaction more closely than any other version. Sometimes, indeed, it seems to follow its source word for word, albeit giving it more or less systematically what Ménard calls 'French clothing'. Nonetheless, some specific instances of translation (or mistranslation) serve to intensify the effects of the systematic revisions I have outlined, as we have already seen with the reduction in the range of diversity evoked in

---

in this regard, see ed. Bertolucci Pizzorusso, pp. 380–1: 'Più che di traduzione vera e propria, si dovrebbe parlare di diffusione; più che di errori di traduzione, di incidenti di tale diffusione.' For a stimulating recent account of the role of multilingualism and linguistic hybridity in literary production, see Catherine E. Léglu, *Multilingualism and Mother Tongue in Medieval French, Occitan and Catalan Narratives* (University Park: Penn State University Press, 2010).

[42] 'Intérêt et importance', p. 195. The question of 'fidelity' is, however, a vexed one in translation studies and theory.

the first chapter. Another example is the French redaction's rendition of the Life of the Buddha.

Marco Polo's Life of the Buddha, which forms the main substance of Chapter CLXXVIII in the Franco-Italian redaction, the second of two chapters devoted to the island of Ceylon (the first being CLXXIII), is one of Western Europe's earliest detailed accounts of the Buddha; it is also highly eccentric in tracing the origins of idolatry back to the origins of Buddhism, while at the same time offering a very positive portrait of the Buddha himself.[43] Having left Ceylon behind them to explore various southern Indian provinces, with a focus largely on religion (St Thomas in Chapter CLXXVI, Brahmins, who like the Buddha seem to provoke a good deal of admiration, in Chapter CLXXVII), the narrators announce 'voç conteron d'une bielle novelles que noç avon dementiqué en l'isle de Sei<l>an' (CLXXVII, 42: 'we will tell you a beautiful story that we forgot that took place in the island of Ceylon'). On the one hand, this makes the Life of the Buddha seem like an afterthought; on the other, it suggests that its inclusion has been provoked by the series of accounts of religious excellence, and it is clearly framed from the outset as a self-contained narrative, a *novelles*.[44] Whereas the Tuscan and Z redactions follow the Franco-Italian closely in their narration of the story,[45] the episode

---

[43] Notable scholarship includes: Ananda Abeydeera, 'Le voyage de Marco Polo dans le pays du bouddhisme', *Corps Ecrit*, 34 (1990),19–28; Eugenio Burgio, 'Marco Polo e gli idolatri', in Nicoló Pasero and Sonia Barillari (eds), *Le voci del medioevo: testi, immagini, tradizioni* (Alessandria: Edizioni dell' Orso), pp. 31–62 = *L'immagine riflessa*, 8 (2005), 31–62; Michael Calabrese, 'Between Despair and Ecstasy: Marco Polo's Life of the Buddha', *Exemplaria*, 9 (1997), 189–229; Leonardo Olschki, *L'Asia di Marco Polo: introduzione alla lettura e allo studio del 'Milione'* (Venice: Fondazione Cini, 1957); Ruggero Ruggieri, *Marco Polo e l'Oriente Francescano* (Rome: Edizioni Porziuncola, 1984). Of these, Burgio and Olschki are by far the most informative. As Olschki notes, the account of the origins of idolatry is 'un' interpretazione esclusivamente poliana' (p. 250). Abeydeera stresses Marco Polo's fascination with Buddhism but also suggests that he probably visited Ceylon twice, once as Kublai Khan's envoy in 1284 and then in 1293 on his journey back to Europe. Calabrese sees in Marco Polo's account of the Buddha's asceticism a counterpoint to Kublai Khan's excessive (and exotic) eroticism, which for Calabrese fascinates Marco far more and was an important precursor of some aspects of modern Orientalism; however, in my view this is to take both Kublai's prodigious sexuality and the Buddha's asceticism out of context (as Calabrese himself concedes, p. 208). Ruggieri attributes Marco Polo's fascination with the Buddha to his Franciscan and missionary leanings (see particularly p. 114); however, this is not really consistent with the fact that the story of the Buddha is not included in Pipino's translation, which is the version with the most marked Christian and/ or missionary orientation.

[44] On the *Devisement*'s use of the Italianism *novelle* here and in CVII, 4, see Bertolucci Pizzorusso, 'Lingue e stili', p. 67, and Alvaro Barbieri, 'Il "narrativo" nel *Devisement dou Monde*: tipologia, fonti, funzioni', in Conte (ed.), *I viaggi del 'Milione'*, pp. 49–75 (pp. 58–9).

[45] See Chapters 174 and 111 respectively. Both also have two chapters on Ceylon, with the Tuscan redaction retaining the remark about having forgotten the story first time round (173, 29).

undergoes a degree of rationalization in the French redaction[46] and is dropped altogether from the Venetian redaction (which is abridged towards the end of the text), which means it is unsurprising that it is also absent from Pipino's translation, though, no doubt, had Pipino found the story in his source, it might not have met with his approval because of its sympathetic portrayal of a non-Christian religious figure and his practices.

Other than in Pipino's version of the text, which frequently seeks to underline the heinous nature of other religions and to oppose their followers, sometimes in an undifferentiated mass, to Christianity, all versions of the *Devisement* frequently go into some detail about others' religions, and their practices, by making analogies with Christianity. I will look at the phenomenon of analogies between other religions and Christianity more generally and in more detail in the third section of Chapter 3. However, one of the principal examples of this is the account of the Life of the Buddha, which vaunts the Buddha's chastity, abstinence and renunciation of the world in order to proclaim that, had he been a Christian, 'il seroit estés un grant sant avec nostre seignor Jesucrist' (CLXXVIII, 22: 'he would have been a great saint with our Lord Jesus Christ'). Dominique Boutet, Thierry Delcourt and Danièle James-Raoul compare this proposition to the familiar formula used of worthy Saracens in the *chanson de geste*, whereby it is remarked that 'had he been a Christian, he would have been a great knight'.[47] But despite the syntactic echo, the two propositions are of a different order because they relate to different frames of reference: the former quite explicitly to Christ's kingdom beyond this world, the latter to the secular sphere of chivalry. Thus the formulation 'had he been a Christian', when used of a non-Christian holy figure in the *Devisement,* underlines parallels between the non-Christian and Christian saint, whereas in the *chanson de geste* it arguably does the opposite, suggesting that, no matter what the Saracen knight does to prove his worth, he is never going to be like a Christian (unless he converts, of course). Furthermore, we are also told that the place where the Buddha is said to have died (in Ceylon) is a site of pilgrimage 'ausi come les cristiens vont a meser Saint Jaque en pelegrinajes' (CLXXVIII, 28: 'just as Christians go on pilgrimage to St James'). Thus another religion is implicitly represented here as capable of offering spiritual enlightenment and as others have remarked

---

[46] Apart from the key difference that I will highlight shortly, the two chapters on Ceylon in the Franco-Italian redaction are amalgamated into one in the French redaction (168), which seems to have triggered some local reordering of the chapters.

[47] See their introduction to the sixth volume of Ménard's edition (ed. Ménard, VI, p. LXXXIX). Their specific point of comparison is *La Chanson de Roland*, ed. Ian Short (Paris: Le Livre de Poche, 1990), line 3164: 'Deus! Quel baron, s'oüst crestïentet'. Cf. also line 899, 'Fust chrestïens, asez oüst barnet'.

the *novelle* of the Buddha's life in the *Devisement* follows the structure of a *vita*, or hagiographical life.[48]

These comparisons are retained in the French redaction, but it differs from other versions in its ascription of the origin of idolatry not to the Buddha's father, as in the Franco-Italian and other redactions, but to the Buddha himself. Here is how the story begins in the Franco-Italian and then in the French redactions:

> Or voç di que il dient que sus cel mont est le menument de Adan nostre primer pere: le sarain dient que celui sepou[c]re est de Adan et les idres dient qu'il est le mo\<n\>ument de Sergamoni Borcam.
>
> E cestui Sergamuni fui le primer homes a cui non fui fait primermant ydres, car selonc lor uxance cestui fui le meior homes que unques fust entr' aus; e ce fu le premer qu'il aussent por saint et a cui nome il faissent ydres. Et ce fu un filz a u\<n\> grant roi e riches e poisant; et cestui son filz fo de si bone vie, qu'il ne vost entend[r]e a nulle chouse mondaine, ne ne vost estre rois. (Franco-Italian redaction, CLXXVIII, 3–5)

(Now I say to you that they say that on this mountain is the tomb of Adam, our first father: the Saracens say that this sepulchre is Adam's and the idolaters say that it is a monument to Sergamoni Borcam [the Buddha].

And this Sergamoni was the first man in whose name idols were made, for according to their custom he was the greatest man who ever lived among them; and he was the first whom they considered a saint and in whose name they made idols. And he was the son of a great king who was rich and powerful; and his son led such a good life that he was not interested in anything worldly, nor did he want to be king.)

> Et vous di que il dient que sus celle montaigne est le monument d'Adam, nostre premier pere. Et ce dient les sarrazins que il est le monument d'Adam.
>
> Et li ydolastre si dient que ce fu le premier ydolastre du monde qu'il nommoient Sargamonyn Boucam. Et le tienent que il fu le meilleur homme du monde et que il fu saint selonc leur usance. Et fu filz, si comme il dient, d'un leur roy, et riche, et fu de si bonne vie que il ne voult onques entendre a nule chose mondaine, ne ne voult estre roy.
>
> (French redaction, 168, 53–63)

(And I say to you that they say that on this mountain is the tomb of Adam, our first father. And the Saracens say this is Adam's monument.

And the idolaters say that it is rather for the first idolater in the world, whom they call Sargamonyn Boucam. And they hold that he was the best man in the world and that he was a saint according to their custom. And he was a son, so they say, of their king, who was rich, and he led such a

---

[48] See Barbieri, 'Il "narrativo"', pp. 54–6 and 65–6; Burgio, 'Marco Polo e gli idolatri', p. 50.

good life that he was not interested in anything worldly, nor did he want to be king.)

Since most of the sentences and details here in the French redaction are so close to the Franco-Italian redaction as preserved in BNF f.fr. 1116 as to be almost identical, it is obvious that the French redactor is working from a source that is very close to it. This makes the few differences all the more striking. Some may result from a process of rationalization or linguistic make-over. But it is hard to tell whether the key difference – concerning whether the Buddha made the first idol or whether it was made in his name by his father – results from a faulty source, from a misunderstanding or from a mistranslation, and, if the latter, how conscious this was.[49] Ménard *et al.*'s edition's base manuscript seems to have reparsed the sentences so that 'et les idres dient qu'il est le mo<n>ument de Sergamoni Borcam' in the Franco-Italian redaction (which makes it clear that Muslims and 'idolaters' have different claims on, and interpretations of, the monument or tomb) becomes instead the separate sentence 'Et li ydolastre si dient que ce fu le premier ydolastre du monde qu'il nommoient Sargamonyn Boucam', which renders the logic a little opaque unless one assumes that 'ce fu le premier ydolastre du monde' has a genitive function in relation to the tomb (giving the meaning 'it [the tomb] belonged to the first idolater in the world').[50] Perhaps the most likely explanation for this stumbling translation in fact comes a little later in the Franco-Italian redaction with the repeated formulation 'a cui non'/'a cui nome', which the Tuscan redaction renders 'a cui nome' (174, 4) and Z 'ad cuius nomen' (111, 6), thus both confirming the reading and making the sense clear. The French redactor seems either to have been puzzled by the now somewhat archaic (in French) though still acceptable form *cui* as a dative relative pronoun used with possessive function because it is preceded here by a preposition, or alternatively to have misunderstood the Italian genitive relative pronoun *cui* ('whose') and therefore the clause 'in whose name', a difficulty that may then have been exacerbated if his source also had the graphy *nome*, as in BNF f.fr. 1116.[51] He did, however, see that the text was

---

[49] For Olschki (*L'Asia di Marco Polo*, p. 258), the idea that the Buddha's father made the first idol is 'une favola che Marco sembra aver aggiunta di suo alla biografia del Buddha', but it actually makes more sense than portraying the Buddha himself as the first idolater.

[50] Or that Adam was the first idolater, which seems less likely? But cf. ed. Badel, p. 408, which uses a different base manuscript for the French redaction and gives the more logical: 'Et ce dient les sarrazins que c'est le monument d'Adam, et les ydolastres si dient que ce fut le premier monument du premier ydo[la]stre du monde que il nommoient Sargamonyn Borcam'; see also ed. Ménard, VI, pp. 240–1 (variants).

[51] The French redaction very occasionally retains the form *cui* (see, for example, 92, 35 and 40; 136, 6), but only as an alternative for *qui*, which is not uncommon in later Old French and Middle French. But this is clearly not consistent across all the manuscripts:

claiming to have identified the first idolater, and so assumed or understood that this was the Buddha himself.

This understanding of the text is again made explicit later in the story:

> E quant cestui filz au roi se morut, il fo porté au roi son pere: e quant il le vit mort, celui que il amoit plus que soi meesme, se il a ire et corus ce ne fa pas a demander. Il fist grand duel; puis fist faire une ymaine a sa semelitudine tout d'or et de pieres precioses, et fai onoré por tuit celz dou pais et aore[r] come dieu [...] Et cestui ont les ydres por le meior dieu e por les plu grant qu'il aient; et sachiés que ceste fu la primer ydres que les ydres ont, e de cestui sunt desendue tutes les ydres.
> (Franco-Italian redaction, CLXXVIII, 23–4, 26)

(And when the king's son died, he was carried to the king, his father: and when he saw that the one he loved more than he loved himself was dead, there is no need to ask of his ire and rage. His pain was extreme; then he had an image of his likeness made all from gold and precious stones, and he has it honoured by all those of the land, and adored as a god [...] And the idolaters consider him to be the best god and the greatest that they have; and know that this was the first idol that the idolaters have and from this one are descended all idols.)

> Et quant il fu mort, si fu dit a son pere. Et quant son pere le vit mort, comme celui qu'il amoit miex de lui meïsmes, a pou qu'il n'issi hors de son sens et fist faire a sa samblance une ymage d'or et de pierres precieuses, et la faisoit aourer a touz ceuz du paÿs [...] et le tiennent pour le plus grant dieu qu'il aient. Et, si comme il dient, par cestui fut faite la premiere ydre que les ydolastres orent onques, si que de cestui dient que toutes les autres ydres en sont descendues. (French redaction, 168, 88–93 and 100–4)

(And when he died, the news was brought to his father. And when his father saw that he whom he loved more than he loved himself was dead, he almost went out of his mind and he had an image of his likeness made in gold and precious stones and had it worshipped by all those of the land [...] and they consider him to be the greatest god that they have. And they say that it was by this man that the first idol that the idolaters had was made, and they also say that all the idols are descended from this one.)

'Et cestui ont les ydres por le meior dieu e por les plu grant qu'il aient; et sachiés que cest fu la primer ydres que les ydres ont' (CLXXVIII, 26) in the Franco-Italian redaction becomes 'et le tiennent pour le [plus] grant dieu qu'il aient. Et, si comme il dient, par cestui fut faite la premiere ydre que les

---

although no variants are picked up in Ménard's edition, Badel's edition (which follows a different base MS) reads *qui* in each of these instances. When preceded by a preposition, *cui* is a perfectly acceptable graphy in Old and Middle French for the regular subject relative pronoun *qui*, but this would make no sense here.

ydolastres orent onques' (168, 100–1). In the first instance, the referent of *ceste* is implicitly the statue made by the father (*ydres* can mean both 'idol' and 'idolater' in the Franco-Italian redaction, which may also have led to some confusion for the French redactor); in the second instance, 'par cestui fut fait' could conceivably refer to the Buddha's father (particularly since he has had a statue of his son made earlier in the paragraph), but syntactically the most proximate referent is the Buddha himself, who is held in the previous sentence to be the greatest god the people have had. This ambiguity again seems to indicate a degree of confusion on the part of the French redactor in his reading of his source.[52]

What difference does this make? Despite the fact that the Buddha is still likened to a Christian saint in the French redaction,[53] he is assimilated nonetheless somewhat unthinkingly to a mass of idolatrous religious others. We might remember here that nowhere does the *Devisement* erroneously represent Muslims as idolaters, as in some vernacular literary traditions,[54] and that the text gives quite a nuanced view of the distinctions between Hindus, Taoists, Buddhists, the Mongols' religion and so on, even if this is not always realized on the level of vocabulary.[55] If some elements of Marco Polo's account of the life of the Buddha and Buddhism are unique (particularly his comments on the origins of idolatry), others have parallels in other sources, and various factors indicate (not least the name he gives the Buddha, which is derived from the Mongol) that his apprehension of Buddhism was filtered through Mongol perceptions.[56] But whether his account derives primarily from written sources, from what he learned about Buddhism at the Mongol court or from what he was told and observed in Ceylon, his fascination with, and admi-

---

[52] Boutet, Delcourt and James-Raoul (ed. Ménard, VI, p. LXXXVIII) also understand the French redaction in this way, but without commenting on the differences between the Franco-Italian and French redactions, even though these are noted in their variants (pp. 240–1). Cf. also later in the chapter, where the somewhat confusing 'Or avés entandu comant les ydres dient qu'il est le filz au roi que fu lor primer ydres e lor primiere dieu' (CLXXXVIII, 30) in the Franco-Italian redaction has as its equivalent in the French redaction simply 'et si dient que il fu le filz le roy si comme je vous ai dit et conté' (168, 111–12), as if in this instance the French redactor were shying away from resolving the genuine syntactic muddle of his source.

[53] Of course, the Buddha *was* a Christian saint to the extent that his life was commemorated in the Josaphat tradition, as noted in an interpolation preserved in two late manuscripts of the *Devisement*; see Marco Polo, *The Description of the World*, ed. A.C. Moule and Paul Pelliot, 2 vols (London: Routledge, 1938), I, p. 410. But this is not acknowledged in earlier versions of the *Devisement*.

[54] Most famously, of course, the *Chanson de Roland*, but other writers about Asia are well aware of the difference between Islam and other non-Christian faiths.

[55] For example, see the juxtaposition of Chapters CLXXVII and CLXXVIII on Hindu Brahmins and Buddhists.

[56] See Burgio, 'Marco Polo e gli idolatri', pp. 53–5, and Olschki, *L'Asia di Marco Polo*, pp. 250–1.

ration for, the Buddha are quite apparent in the Franco-Italian redaction:[57] thus the accounts of the Buddha's absolute eschewal of any luxuriousness, even when offered three thousand virgins to tempt him, and of his horror the first time he confronts mortality in the form of a dead body, strike a tone of great reverence and wonder (CLXXVIII, 9–22). Furthermore, the description of the Buddha's asceticism and beliefs (for instance in reincarnation, CLXXVIII, 25) are in many respects accurate. The precision and subtlety of the Franco-Italian redaction – which may even be read as a parable of how idolatry derives from a misunderstanding of the Buddha's teachings in that he himself never sanctioned idolatry but merely taught asceticism – is either lost on or deliberately suppressed by the French redactor, giving the text over to cruder religious stereotyping.

A burning curiosity underscores the *Devisement*'s mediation of diversity here, as it does in many other parts of the text. This produces a real and unusually open-minded sense of comparative religion as a pagan becomes the incarnation of virtues that are enshrined in Christian teaching. The implications of this openness to knowledge of the other and the concomitant unwillingness to subject the other to a thorough-going Christianizing framework as well as the frequent blurring of boundaries between Christians and others, often through analogy, will be explored further in Chapters 3 and 4, where I will also consider Kublai Khan's role as a promoter of religious syncretism. This role also surfaces in the *Devisement*'s Life of the Buddha as Kublai is so intrigued by the tales surrounding 'le menument de Adan' that he acquires for himself the 'erliques' (CLXXVIII, 41) that are preserved there.[58] For now, I would simply like to conclude this section by noting how this syncretism is further reinforced in the *Devisement*'s Life of the Buddha by the framing of the story as explication of the importance of a site – Adam's Peak in Sri Lanka, as it still known today – that is represented as an important destination for pilgrims of two religions (Muslims and Buddhists), while also concerning Christians, since Adam was '*nostre* primer pere' (CLXXVIII, 3 and 30, my emphasis). The Franco-Italian redaction notes that only God knows who is actually buried there, 'car nos ne [cre]on pas que en celui leu <soit> Adan, car nostre Escriture de Sainte Eglise dit qu'el est en autre partie dou monde' (CLXVIII, 30: 'for we do not believe that Adam rests in this place, for our Holy Scripture says it is in another part of the world'). Benedetto, followed

---

[57] On this point, see particularly Ruggieri, *Marco Polo*, p. 114; also Calabrese, 'Between Ecstasy and Despair', pp. 205–7 and 220.

[58] The term 'relic' suggests a further analogy with Christianity. Kublai believes the relics to be those of Adam: a tooth, some hair and the dish from which he ate (CLXXVIII, 31). These relics are attested in other sources, Christian and Muslim, but although the *Devisement* describes some aspects of Adam's Peak accurately (e.g. the metal rungs that enabled ascent of some parts of the mountain (CLXXVIII, 2)), no mention is made of the object of Buddhist veneration, which is the Buddha's footprint. See ed. Ménard, VI, p. LXXXVI, for some discussion.

by Ronchi, emended BNF f.fr. 1116's 'oron' to '[cre]on' here, presumably on the basis of Z's 'nos non credimus quod in illo loco sit Adam' (111, 49), though 'oron' might also possibly make sense as a hybrid form of the verb 'to hear'. In any event, it is interesting that the French redaction reads simply 'car selonc l'Escripture Sainte de nostre Eglyse, le [monument] d'Adam n'est pas en celle partie du monde' (168, 116–17), thereby eliminating belief (or hearsay) from the equation and making the location of Adam's tomb simply a matter of indisputable fact.[59] Once again we see that the 'tiny variant' may make all the difference in translation.

Foreign languages, foreign words and untranslatability

Quite apart from Marco Polo's ability to move between Romance languages (or, alternatively, his proclivity for confusing them), he is represented in the *Devisement* as a formidable linguist, which presumably also meant that translation was an everyday process for him:

> Or avint que Marc, le filz messer Nicolao, enprant si bien le costume de Tartars et lor langajes et lor leteres <que c'estoit mervoille>; car je voç di tout voiremant que, avant grament de tens puis qu'il vint en la cort dou grant segnor, il soit de <quatre> langaies et de quatre letres et scriture.
> (XVI, 1)

> (Now it happened that Marco, the son of Mr Nicholas, learns the customs, languages and letters of the Tartars so well that it is a marvel; for I say to you truly that before much time had passed after his arrival at the court of the great lord, he knows four languages, and how to read and write them too.)

Similarly, Rustichello da Pisa represents himself elsewhere as a translator:

> Et sachiez tot voiremant que cestui romainz fu treslaitiés dou livre monseigneur Odoard, li roi d'Engleterre, a celui tenz qu'il passé houtre la mer en servise nostre Sire Damedeu pour conquister le saint Sepoucre. Et maistre Rusticiaus de Pise, li quelz est imaginés desovre, conpilé ceste romainz, car il en treslaité toutes les tresmervillieuse novelles qu'il treuvé en celui livre et totes les greigneur aventures. (*Il romanzo arturiano*, 1, 2)

> (And know truly that this romance was translated from the book of my lord Edward, the king of England, at the time when he went to the Holy Land in the service of our Lord God to conquer the Holy Sepulchre. And Master Rustichello da Pisa, who is portrayed above, compiled this romance, for

---

[59] Z's reading and its partial agreement with the Franco-Italian redaction make it unlikely that the first clause was entirely absent from the French redactor's source.

he translated all the marvellous stories that he found in that book, and all the greatest adventures.)

Neither of these assertions is verifiable, nor necessarily entirely truthful. While scholars are agreed that the forms of place-names and words from Oriental languages used in the *Devisement* suggest that Marco Polo knew Persian and Mongol, it is not clear which other Oriental languages he knew; and while many are convinced he knew no Chinese, this need not necessarily pose a problem (as some have asserted) for his having been some kind of administrator for the Mongol empire in China, as the *Devisement* states.[60] For Rustichello's part, he clearly did not translate all the *novelles* and *aventures* in his book, because some are lifted from other vernacular sources, such as the *Tristan en prose*, as the verb *conpiler* here suggests; and although he does not mention a source language, by implication this must be Latin (see 236, 5, though this passage is copied from another source). In both instances the reference to different languages plays a role within the diegetic frame. Thus Marco Polo's knowledge of languages contributes towards his (self)-image as a high-ranking functionary and confidant of Kublai Khan: in the next sentence he is described as 'sajes et proveanç outre mesure' (XVI, 2: 'wise and worthy beyond measure), as a result of which Kublai employs him as an envoy (XVI, 3–4), thereby linking Marco's linguistic abilities to his general value as a gatherer and teller of exotic tales. Rustichello, on the other hand, deploys the standard 'I found this in a Latin book' conceit in order to authenticate and authorize his own text. We are also dealing with different forms of multilingualism: whereas Rustichello's knowledge of Latin is not surprising for a man of his supposed background, Marco Polo's ostensible knowledge of Oriental languages is far more unusual. Nonetheless, quite apart from the text's own hybrid language, the two forms of multilingualism combine in the *Devisement* (Rustichello is a *mestre*: CLVII, 18) to position the text within a multilingual framework in which movement between languages is the norm.

This positioning of the text within a multilingual framework and in some respects *in between* languages again resonates with some modern theoretical approaches to translation. Homi Bhabha, for example, insists that 'it is the "inter" – the cutting edge of translation and negotiation, the *in between* space – that carries the burden of the meaning of culture' and that 'exploring this Third Space' may liberate the subject from what he calls 'the politics of

---

[60] See Giorgio Cardona's 'Indice ragionato', in *Milione*, ed. Bertolucci Pizzorusso, pp. 491–761, for detailed information on the Oriental languages from which words used in the *Devisement* may derive. These include Arabic, Chinese, Mongol, Persian, Sanskrit and Turkish. For some discussion of Marco's knowledge of Oriental languages, and the debates surrounding the question, see John Larner, *Marco Polo and the Discovery of the World* (New Haven, CT, and London: Yale University Press, 1999), pp. 64–5.

priority'.[61] Similarly, Emily Apter's notion of the 'translation zone' suggests a space belonging directly to no one, ascribing to no one language, in which hegemonic structures may be rethought, challenged, disputed.[62] The historical frames of reference that inform Bhabha and Apter's work are vastly different from mine: Bhabha's main focus is on the process of decolonization and its implications in the second half of the twentieth century; Apter's is broadly on global conflicts post-9/11. But there are nonetheless obvious structural parallels with the *Devisement*, in that the occupation of a culturally and linguistically 'in-between' space enables ideological work that could not otherwise be envisaged.

Subsequent to the prologue, the *Devisement*'s comments on linguistic difference are confined to two types: first, provinces and cities are frequently described as 'having a language of their own'; secondly, a range of words from Oriental languages are used in the text and then either translated or glossed (as we saw in the opening paragraph of this chapter). I will explore the implications of places 'having a language of their own' in Chapter 4, but would just note here that the text never identifies the languages in question or makes any reference to the practicalities of learning languages, using interpreters and so on. This would seem to suggest that it is linguistic difference *per se* to which our attention is being drawn rather than the specific details of differences between different languages. With this in mind, I would like now to focus on the use of words from unidentified (in the text at least) Oriental languages in a text in French (or Italian or Latin, for that matter).

The use of words from a language that does not belong to the same 'family' of languages (i.e. non-Romance languages for French and Italian) and their subsequent glossing serves, on the one hand, simply to add exotic flavour to the *Devisement*; on the other, it also suggests that these words are basically untranslatable. And, as suggested earlier, preserving their foreignness may be seen as responding to an ethical imperative not to over-assimilate the foreign but to offer, rather, some tangible and irreducible residue of its difference and otherness.

For Derrida, proper names, which of course abound in the *Devisement*, represent the degree zero of untranslatability. Consider the opening of his seminal essay 'Des Tours de Babel':[63]

---

[61] *The Location of Culture*, pp. 38–9.
[62] *The Translation Zone*, pp. 5–6.
[63] Jacques Derrida, 'Des Tours de Babel', in *Psyché: Inventions de l'autre* (Paris: Galilée, 1998), pp. 203–35 (p. 203), cited here from http://www.jacquesderrida.com.ar/frances/tours_babel.htm, accessed 8 August 2011. Some parts of what follows are drawn from my 'Untranslatable', in Emma Campbell and Robert Mills (eds), *Rethinking Medieval Translation: Ethics, Politics, Theory* (Cambridge: D.S. Brewer, 2012), pp. 243–55.

Babel: un nom propre d'abord, soit. Mais quand nous disons Babel aujourd'hui, savons-nous ce que nous nommons? Savons-nous qui? Considérons la survie d'un texte légué, le récit ou le mythe de la tour de Babel: il ne forme pas une *figure* parmi d'autres: Disant au moins l'inadéquation d'une langue à l'autre, d'un lieu d'encyclopédie à l'autre, du langage à lui-même et au sens, il dit aussi la nécessité de la figuration, du mythe, des tropes, des tours, de la traduction inadéquate pour suppléer à ce que la multiplicité nous interdit. En ce sens il serait le mythe de l'origine du mythe, la métaphore de la métaphore, le récit du récit, la traduction de la traduction. Il ne serait pas la seule structure à se creuser ainsi mais il le ferait à sa manière (elle-même *à peu près* intraduisible, comme un nom propre) et il faudrait en sauver l'idiome.

(Babel: a proper noun in the first instance, perhaps. But when we say Babel today, do we know what it is we are naming? Do we know of whom we speak? Let us consider the survival of a text bequeathed, the narrative or the myth of the tower of Babel: it is not just one figure among others: speaking as it does of the inadequacy of one language to another, of one place in the encyclopaedia to another, of language to itself and to meaning, it also speaks of the necessity of figuration, of myth, of tropes, of towers [or turns], of inadequate translations to supplement that which plurality forbids us. It would in this sense be the myth of the origin of myth, the metaphor of metaphor, the narrative of narrative, the translation of translation. It would perhaps not be the only structure to demarcate itself thus, but it would do so in its own way (itself more or less untranslatable, like a proper noun) and we need to rescue [or save, or preserve] its idiom.)

But why should proper names be untranslatable?

Babel, Derrida asserts here, is not just a figure among others: Babel retains its status as foundational myth precisely because it figures not just the failure of different languages to correspond to each other but rather the inadequacy of all language to man's aspirational drive for wholeness (figured by 'one tongue' and 'the same speech' in Genesis 11:1: 'labii unius et sermonum eorundem') and mastery (figured by the impossible proposed heights of the offending tower in 11:4: 'faciamus nobis civitatem et turrem cuius culmen pertingat ad caelum').[64] And for Derrida, embedded as he is in the 'linguistic turn', the impossibility of linguistic wholeness and mastery implicitly stands for, but also outweighs, the impossibility of other forms of wholeness and mastery. Thanks to Babel, Genesis, tells us, mankind's language(s) will be both confounded (11:7: *confundamus*, says the one and indivisible Hebrew God, intriguingly, but perhaps prophetically, using the first-person plural) and confused (11:9: *confusum*). God thereby instantiates linguistic difference as both a punishment and an injunction to translate: people are condemned not to understand their neighbour's speech (11:7: 'non audiat unusquisque

---

[64] Cited here from http://www.latinvulgate.com/, accessed 8 August 2011.

vocem proximi sui'), yet the implication is surely that they should try to do so. Thus if universal understanding is prohibited by God, translation is divinely ordained.

Of course, the parable or fable of Babel in Genesis 11 layers irony upon irony. Thus although God recognizes mankind's original wholeness (11:6: 'ecce unus est populus et unum labium omnibus'), mankind itself needs to be dispersed and thereby fragmented (11:9: 'inde dispersit eos Dominus super faciem cunctarum regionum') to realize its prior unity, let alone the value of this: from a human perspective 'one people' and 'one language' are retroactive constructs that were heuristically always already lost, by which I mean they would seem to be destroyed by their very conception or articulation. And this inherent fracturing of linguistic unity is nicely figured in the translation history of the Vulgate Genesis 11 itself, where a single Latin verb (*confundere*, of which *confusum* is the past participle) gives rise to two verbs (in English at least): to confound and to confuse. Implicit, then, in the Babel myth, as Derrida saw, is not just destruction but the process he called *différance*, whereby meaning moves relentlessly along the signifying chain, never to come to rest, and which deprives man of unmediated access to stable meaning. Indeed, meaning is always displaced and at one remove; hence Babel is not just a myth, metaphor, narrative or translation but rather 'le mythe de l'origine du mythe, la métaphore de la métaphore, le récit du récit, la traduction de la traduction'. Babel thus offers another way of understanding the 'absolute translation' to which mankind is condemned. But maybe the final irony of Genesis 11 is that in some ways the people of Babel got what they wanted. They built their tower so that their name might be 'celebrated' (11.4: 'celebremus nomen nostrum'), and while most translations give this phrase perhaps audacious overtones of creation (for example, see the King James Bible: 'Let us make us a name'),[65] *celebrare* suggests rather a desire for renown, perhaps commemoration.[66] And in this respect the Babelonians certainly got what they wished for.

I do not aspire to say anything new about Genesis 11 or indeed about Derrida, but I would like to unpack a little the intriguing last sentence of his introduction to 'Des Tours de Babel', as it seems to me to pose some pertinent questions for both the *Devisement*'s treatment of proper names and for its use of foreign words: 'Il ne serait pas la seule structure à se creuser ainsi mais il le ferait à sa manière (elle-même *à peu près* intraduisible, comme un nom propre) et il faudrait en sauver l'idiome.' First, what is the subject of this sentence? A number of referents for the pronoun 'il' are possible: Babel

---

[65] Cited from http://www.kingjamesbibleonline.org/book.php?book=Genesis&chapter=11&verse=, accessed 8 August 2011.

[66] A point marked only relatively infrequently in translations. For example, see the Douay–Rheims Catholic Bible: 'let us make our name famous', cited from http://www.drbo.org/chapter/01011.htm, accessed 8 August 2011.

itself, the proper noun, the text, the narrative and the myth. Characteristically, Derrida's pronominal indeterminacy here mimes what he is talking about (structural parallels), as it does again in the parenthesis: does *elle* refer to *structure* or to *sa manière*? And equally characteristically, Derrida then introduces what will prove to be one of the main themes of his essay in a parenthesis, which is to say that proper names are untranslatable. Yet even that isn't quite it. Something here (the unspecified *il*) is *more or less* untranslatable, *like* a proper name. But why is a proper name untranslatable, and how can something be *more or less* untranslatable? Surely translations of proper nouns abound, and something either is or is not translatable? And why explain the idea here – whatever it is – through an analogy?

This raises, I suggest, not simply the question of when translation founders but also the problem of the untranslatable. Yet, as I have already suggested, perhaps the untranslatable should be regarded not only as a problem but also as an opportunity, an invitation for further thought (particularly within the 'translation zone') and as an ethical necessity.

While some place-names in the Middle East and even India may have been familiar to medieval readers from texts in the Alexander tradition or encyclopaedias, texts about the Far East often accumulate in quick succession series of similar but deeply foreign-sounding place-names that readers are almost certainly never going to have encountered before, and which they are unlikely therefore to be able to situate. The *Devisement* is no exception: consider chapters CXXX–CXXXVIII, which relate to Caingiu (Changzhou), Cacianfu (Hezhonfu), Cianglu (Changlu) Ciangli (Jiangling), Candinfu (Dongpingfu), Singiu (Zhenzhou), Ligin (Liucheng), Pingiu (Pizhou) and Cingiu (Tongzhou). When such sequences of place-names occur, what exactly is the effect? As Michèle Guéret-Laferté suggests, one effect is undoubtedly to enhance the text's *effet de réel*.[67] This reality effect is produced partly by the way the cities are positioned spatially and even temporally in relation to each other. (Cacianfu is *ver midi* in relation to Caingiu (CXXXI, 1); Candinfu is six days south of Ciangli (CXXXIV, 1) and so on.) The singular situation of all these places in space and time is then echoed in the way their names are individuated. Empirical research on the *Devisement* identifies nearly all the numerous places mentioned with real places, so it is generally believed that Marco Polo was attempting to recall, as best he could, and to convey to his francophone readers, foreign place-names.[68] In order to do so he does not Gallicize them, and thus one might say he respects their specificity rather than assimilating them to a francophone symbolic. Yet the specificity of these

---

[67] Michèle Guéret-Laferté, 'Le vocabulaire exotique du *Devisement du Monde*', in Conte (ed.), *I viaggi del 'Milione'*, pp. 287–305 (p. 291).
[68] Stephen G. Haw suggests it is possible positively to identify 90 per cent of the place-names in the *Devisement*; see *Marco Polo's China: A Venetian in the Realm of Khubilai Khan* (London and New York: Routledge, 2006).

places for the text's francophone readers, who have no experience of the various places' geographic and temporal situation, is primarily a product of linguistic differentiation. Indeed, given how similar the descriptions of a lot of these places make them sound, one might say that the real difference between, as it were, Cingiu, Pingiu and Singiu is just one letter, as if the core of untranslatability comes down to what Lacan famously termed 'the insistence of the letter' in the structuring of the Real.[69]

The words from Oriental languages other than proper nouns that appear in the *Devisement* do not, however, function in quite the same way. In her recent study of these words Michèle Guéret-Laferté suggests that while 'tout récit de voyage fait une vaste opération de traduction, une transposition qu'opère celui qui décrit la réalité étrangère de façon à ce qu'elle soit assimilée' ('any travel narrative undertakes a vast task of translation, a transposition operated by the person who described the foreign reality so that it might be assimilated'),[70] the traveller will nonetheless encounter 'l'intraduisible' (the untranslatable):

> C'est cette altérité qui ne trouve pas d'équivalent dans le monde et la langue du narrateur qui est mise en évidence par l'insertion de termes étrangers. Ce signe autre, signe de l'Autre, constitue bien une preuve qui vient renforcer la valeur du témoignage et il produit sur le lecteur un incontestable «effet de réel», tout en dégageant, par son incompréhensibilité même, une aura d'étrangeté.
>
> (It is this alterity that finds no equivalent in the narrator's world and language which is highlighted by the insertion of foreign terms. This other sign, or sign of the Other, plainly constitutes a further proof of the value of eye-witness, and produces for the reader an undeniable 'reality effect', while all the while giving off, by virtue of its very incomprehensibility, an aura of foreignness').[71]

Guéret-Laferté identifies and discusses thirty-seven words from Oriental languages that the Franco-Italian redaction records, some of which are glossed and some of which are not. Where a word is glossed, she suggests that the *volonté traductrice* ('will to translate') is Rustichello da Pisa's rather than Marco Polo's.[72] This part of her argument is perhaps less persuasive than the remarks I have just quoted about the effect of foreign words and their 'aura of foreignness'. Furthermore, the different ways in which the Oriental words are

---

[69] Jacques Lacan, 'L'instance de la lettre dans l'inconscient ou la raison depuis Freud', in *Ecrits* (Paris: Seuil, 1966), pp. 493–528. The English phrase 'insistence of the letter' stems from the influential early translation of this essay; see Jacques Lacan, 'The Insistence of the Letter in the Unconscious', *Yale French Studies*, 36/7 (1966), 112–47.

[70] 'Le vocabulaire exotique', p. 290.
[71] 'Le vocabulaire exotique', p. 291.
[72] 'Le vocabulaire exotique', p. 301.

glossed warrant further scrutiny. Sometimes a direct equivalent or translation is given: for example, 'toscaor, que vient a dire en nostre lengue home que demorent a garde' (XCIV, 3: '*toscaor*, which means in our language men who mount guard') – though, as we can see, 'translation' is already tipping over into paraphrase here, and more often than not this is the case. But in many instances attempts at 'translation' work quite explicitly through analogy, as with the 'mainere d'osiaus que sunt apelés bargherlac des queles le fauconz se passent. Il sunt grant come perdis, il ont fait les pies come papagaus, la coe come rondiaus' (LXXI, 6–7). If this bird surpasses a falcon, is bigger than a partridge, has feet like a parrot and a tail like a sea swallow, it is in fact none of these things; it is quite specifically a *bargherlac* (probably a Turkish word).[73] The trouble Marco Polo (or Rustichello da Pisa) has taken here to render the bird easier to picture for the francophone reader, even if the resulting image resembles a legendary hybrid beast, may, as Guéret-Laferté suggests, confirm 'la rigueur de l'information' ('the accuracy of the data') and illustrate 'l'objectif encyclopédique de l'oeuvre polienne' ('the encyclopaedic intention of Polo's work'),[74] but in also underlining, as Guéret-Laferté likewise notes, its specificity, the text effectively confronts its readers with the untranslatable, a foreign reality which in practice cannot be assimilated. And as the *Devisement* seems to realize, if alterity is to be ultimately respected, the translator must surely in the end abandon equivalence, paraphrase and analogy, leaving us just with the untranslated and untranslatable foreign word. Perhaps translation can only become really interesting precisely at the point where the process of translation reaches its limits and is effectively abandoned. Perhaps, as Derrida suggests in his elliptical parenthesis in the opening paragraph of 'Des Tours de Babel', everything is more or less untranslatable, like a proper noun, and to acknowledge this we must 'save' or 'rescue' its idiom. And can we perhaps do this by not even attempting to translate it? This points to one of the fundamental paradoxes of the success of any text in translation, but one particularly pertinent to the *Devisement*. To translate a text is to lose something, but without a translation fewer people (in some cases dramatically fewer) will have the opportunity to read it.

Conclusion

Earlier in this Chapter I suggested that in some contexts French might be regarded as a *monolangue* in the Derridean sense of the term. As Alison Cornish has put it, 'Because there was a literature in French [in Italy] a

---

[73] Guéret-Laferté relies, for her understanding and etymologies of Oriental words, on the 'Indice Ragionato' prepared by Giorgio R. Cardona to Marco Polo: *Milione*, ed. Bertolucci Pizzorusso; see the entry under *bugherlac* (p. 570).

[74] 'Le vocabulaire exotique', p. 291.

good hundred and fifty years before there was one in Italian, for a long time, French literature *was* vernacular literature',[75] and as we saw in the introduction, it is traditional to attribute the popularity and ubiquity of French as a literary language in western Europe and around the Mediterranean to the nobility and refinement of French courtly culture. Is this why Marco Polo and Rustichello da Pisa produced the *Devisement* in French? It is also often taken to be the implication of the much-quoted remarks of two other thirteenth-century Italians writing in French, Brunetto Latini and Martin da Canale: the 'patois de France' is 'la parleure [...] plus delitable et plus comune a touz languages' ('the *patois* of France is the most delightful and popular speech of all languages') and 'por ce que lengue franceise cort parmi le monde, et est la plus delictables a lire et a oir que nule autre, me suis je entremis de translater l'ancienne estoire des Veneciens de latin en franceis' ('because the French language is found throughout the world and is more delightful to read and hear than any other, I have undertaken to translate the ancient history of the Venetians into French').[76] However, it is striking that both Brunetto Latini and Martin da Canale stress the international currency and mobility of French ('commune', 'cort parmi le monde') and do not specifically mention its cultural prestige. While there is no doubt that the use of French by non-native speakers of French in written texts in the Middle Ages was to some extent determined by literary tradition, the situation may also be analogous to that of two tourists today in Thailand (or India, or Peru or Botswana) – say a Greek and a Sri Lankan (or a Pole and an Argentinian) – speaking to each other in English. They do not use English because of Shakespeare (though Shakespeare may form part of their education and may influence some of their idioms), and their use of English is obviously not innocent of political freight since the ubiquity of English cannot be disassociated from several centuries of European wars and British imperial expansion. But their use of English is nonetheless largely pragmatic. In the same way Marco Polo, Rustichello da Pisa, Brunetto Latini and Martin da Canale may well have admired the French literary tradition, but they may also have adopted French simply because they wished to have a broad and international readership. This ties the use of French less to high French culture than to the trade routes across and around the Mediterranean, up over the Alps not just into France but also into Germany, the Low Countries, the British Isles and Scandinavia. French, I venture to suggest, is not just the language of high vernacular culture in the thirteenth and fourteenth centuries but also the vernacular language of the translation zone, the contact zone, the language that inhabits the space in between, a space that by its very nature is mobile and in flux. To quote Cornish again: 'French was a literary

---

[75] '*Translatio Galliae*', p. 310.

[76] Cited from Brunetto Latini, *Tresor*, ed. Pietro Beltrami, Paolo Squillacioti, Plinio Torri and Sergio Vatteroni (Turin: Einaudi, 2007), 1, 1, 7 and Martin da Canale, *Les Estoires de Venise*, ed. Alberto Limentani (Florence: Olschki, 1972), p. 1.

(and performative) instrument, not a birthright.'[77] Thus French may function as a *monolangue* in some circumstances: for example, I have argued, in the French redaction of the *Devisement*, where an albeit unsuccessful attempt is made to foreclose other idioms and exclude differences of a variety of kinds, not just linguistic or cultural but also, as we saw in Chapter 1, ambivalent narrative techniques. In the Franco-Italian redaction, however, the use of a hybrid form of French, marked by internal diversity, may have a destabilizing effect, troubling the position from which the text speaks, an effect that works in conjunction with the ambivalent narrative voice of the Franco-Italian redaction I discussed in Chapter 1.

In one intriguing instance, which is not found in any other version of the *Devisement*, the narrator of the Z redaction seems to show an awareness that in any language, or family of languages, there are degrees of familiarity and foreignness:

> Sed scire debetis quod per totam provinciam Manci una servatur loquela et una maneries litterarum. Tamen in lingua est diversitas per contratas, veluti apud laycos inter Lonbardo<s>, Provinciales, Francigenas, etcetera; ita tamen quod, in provincia Mançi, gens cuiuslibet contrate potest gentis alterius intelligere ydioma. (90, 33–4)
>
> (But you must know that in all the provinces of Manzi, one mode of speech is used and one script. Yet the language is different according to the region, as it is among the lay people of Lombardy, Provence, France etc.; in the same way, in the province of Manzi, people from one region can understand the idiom of the people of another.)

The text here affirms what any Romance philologist knows: that Romance languages may on occasion be mutually intelligible without translation ('gens cuiuslibet contrate potest gentis alterius intelligere ydioma'); indeed, in an echo (or perhaps in anticipation) of Dante in *De vulgari eloquentia*,[78] different Romance idioms are represented here as a single linguistic system with internal diversity according to the region ('in lingua est diversitas per contratas'). But even more interesting than this observation is the *structural* parallel made between different Romance languages and different forms of Chinese. Difference is thus once again rendered intelligible through analogy, but without it being assimilated. Or, as Derrida would say, 'Il ne serait pas la seule structure à se creuser ainsi mais il le ferait à sa manière' ('It would perhaps not be the only structure to demarcate itself thus but it would do so in its own way').

---

[77] '*Translatio Galliae*', p. 310; see also *Vernacular Translation*, p. 71.

[78] *De vulgari eloquentia* is traditionally dated 1302–5; a precise date for the Z redaction is not possible, though it must of course post-date the *Devisement*'s initial composition in 1298.

The first two chapters of this book have been an attempt to show how two structures in the *Devisement* – narrative voice and language – work in parallel to problematize the position from which the text speaks. The next two chapters will turn more explicitly to the text's subject-matter, but bearing in mind always that its treatment cannot be divorced from the structures that are the vehicle for its transmission.

3

Knowledge, marvels and other religions: 'oculis propriis videt'

The main interest of the *Devisement du monde* has always been its subject-matter. Though several thirteenth-century Latin texts based on eye-witness accounts of the Far East preceded it,[1] the wealth of detail and also possibly the fact that it circulated in the vernacular as well as in a variety of redactions seem to have ensured the *Devisement* its immediate success and its impressively long shelf life. European readers were apparently avid for information about the strange lands that lay to the East, and although these had always been represented as extraordinary, Marco Polo's account suggested they were extraordinary in new and unexpected ways, since his differed so substantially from previous accounts deriving from ancient textual traditions (encyclopaedic material deriving from Pliny, Solinus and so on; the Alexander tradition), with their barbaric hordes in need of enclosure, monstrous races and exotic, sometimes quasi-supernatural, creatures. Readers seem to have been spellbound by Marco's tales of the untold wealth of Kublai Khan's empire, of its astonishing economic and material infrastructure, of the amazing variety of human societies – many of them clearly far from barbaric – to be found in Asia, of the range of religions as compared to the Christian/pagan dichotomy found in some popular vernacular texts, and of exotic but nonetheless naturalistic animals and plants.

The most frequent word used to qualify this wondrous diversity is 'marvel', used twice already in the very first chapter of the text and 120 times altogether in the Franco-Italian redaction:[2] 'Et qui trovererés toutes les grandismes mervoilles et les grant diversités' and 'tropo seroit grant maus se il ne feist metre en escriture toutes les granç mervoilles qu'il vit' (I, 2 and 5). Indeed, marvels seem to have been recognized as an essential ingredient

---

[1] See Christopher Dawson, *Mission to Asia* (Toronto: Toronto University Press, 1980), for English translations of the accounts by John of Plano Carpini and William of Rubruck.

[2] See Sergio Marroni, 'La meraviglia di Marco Polo. L'espressione della meraviglia nel lessico e nella sintassi del *Milione*', in Silvia Conte (ed.), *I viaggi del 'Milione': itinerari testuali, vettori di trasmissione e metamorfosi del Devisement du monde di Marco Polo e Rustichello da Pisa nella pluralità delle attestazioni. Convegno internazionale Venezia, 6–8 ottobre 2005* (Rome: Tiellemedia, 2008), pp. 233–62.

of the *Devisement* in some branches of the tradition: thus the famous BNF f. fr. 2810, itself entitled 'Des Merveilles du Monde', has running headers that read variously for the *Devisement* 'Cest le livre de Marc Paul | Et des merveilles', 'Le livre de | Marc Paul', 'Le livre de Marc Paul | Marc Paul et les merveilles'; similarly, British Library Royal 19 D 1 introduces the *Devisement* with the rubric 'Ci commence li liures du grant Caam, qui parole de la grant Erminie de Persse et des Tartars et dynde, et des granz merueilles qui par le monde sont' (fol. 58: 'here begins the book of the Great Khan, which speaks of greater Armenia, of Persia and of the Tartars and of India and of the great marvels to be found throughout the world').[3] This apparently aligns the text with traditional accounts of the marvels and wonders to be found outside Europe, such as those found in the *Roman d'Alexandre*, here cited in Thomas de Kent's twelfth-century version, the *Roman de Toute Chevalerie*:[4]

> Veu ad les merveilles des terres indien[e]s
> E les foreins realmes e les mers aufrikienes,
> E le mont Caricason e les genz prasienes,
> Olimpum e Taurum e les pleines libien[e]s,
> Le Nil e Eufraten e les mers gaudienes
> Et totes les merveilles ethiopienes
> Qe mult sunt poy seues entre les cristien[e]s.
> Dirray vous merveilles solum gestes paienes. (6,600–6,607)
>
> (He [Alexander] saw all the marvels of the Indian lands and the foreign realms and the African seas, and Mount Caricason, and Prasian peoples, Olympus, Taurus and the plains of Libya, the Nile, the Euphrates and the seas of the Gaudiens, and the Ethiopian marvels, which are very little known among Christians. I will relate marvels to you according to pagan sources.)

These lines preface a section in which Alexander encounters (among other marvels) a people that crowns a dog as their king (6,717–22), archers with four eyes (6,725), a monstrous race of people with no noses (6,751–4) and so on. Such parades of outlandish beings, introduced by Thomas of Kent as marvels, draw upon and partake of a lengthy tradition of texts – in Latin and the vernacular – devoted to the wonders or marvels of the East, texts

---

[3] Pipino, however, begins his book 'Incipit prologus in librum domini Marchi Pauli de Veneciis de consuetudinibus et condicionibus orientalium Regionum' (p. 1: 'Here begins the prologue of the book of Master Marco Polo of Venice about the customs and condition of the regions of the Orient'), reserving the word *mirabilia* in the prologue for the wonders of God's creation in the animal world.

[4] Thomas de Kent, *Le Roman d'Alexandre ou Le Roman de toute chevalerie*, ed. Brian Foster and Ian Short, trans. Catherine Gaullier-Bougassas and Laurence Harf-Lancner (Paris: Champion, 2003).

that derive directly or indirectly from Pliny.⁵ But these traditional monstrous races are conspicuously absent from the *Devisement*, which suggests that it uses insistently a familiar term only to reorient its meaning, while appealing with equal insistence to the authority and truthfulness of Marco's own eye-witness account: 'fu verité selonc ce que je Marc Pol vit puis apertemant a mes iaux' (CLII, 6: 'and this was true according to what I, Marco Polo, saw clearly with my own eyes').⁶

However, despite the fact that, as we will see, the *Devisement*'s marvels are often highly naturalistic, a number of factors have combined over the last seven centuries to cause some readers to doubt its truthfulness. At first, the fact that Marco's account of the marvels of Asia was so at odds with almost all others led to doubts in some quarters, particularly when more traditional accounts, such as Mandeville's, continued to be produced; the inaccessibility of Asia and particularly China for almost two hundred years after Marco's extended stay there no doubt exacerbated incredulity.⁷ More recently, the text's formal and stylistic properties, together with the claims it makes about

---

⁵ On this tradition see: Mary C. Campbell, *The Witness and the Other World: Exotic European Travel Writing, 400–1600* (Ithaca, NY, and London: Cornell University Press, 1988), pp. 47–86; Lorraine Daston and Katherine Park, *Wonders and the Order of Nature, 1150–1700* (New York: Zone Books, 1998), pp. 21–66; John Block Friedman, *The Monstrous Races in Medieval Art and Thought* (Cambridge, MA, and London: Harvard University Press, 1981); Jacques Le Goff, *L'Imaginaire médiéval* (Paris: Gallimard, 1985), pp. 17–39 and 189–200; Debra Higgs Strickland, *Saracens, Demons and Jews: Making Monsters in Medieval Art* (Princeton and Oxford: Princeton University Press, 2003), pp. 29–61; Caroline Walker Bynum, 'Wonder', *American Historical Review*, 103 (1997), 1–26. Despite the similar terminology, what is generally referred to as the *merveilleux* in medieval romance (giants, fairies, magic spells etc.) is a rather different phenomenon, even though the two traditions do not remain discrete.

⁶ On the importance of the *Devisement* for value placed on the idea of eye-witness accounts, see Andrea Frisch, *The Invention of the Eyewitness: Witnessing and Testimony in Early Modern France* (Chapel Hill: University of North Carolina Press, 2004), pp. 41–60. As Frisch contends, however, the value of such accounts may be undermined where what is being reported is at odds with hegemonic discourse.

⁷ The Black Death, which precipitated the disintegration of the Mongol empire, also seems to have put an end to European travel to the Far East. For example, the last date for which there is evidence of Genoese merchants using the land route to Cathay is 1344. See Janet Abu-Lughod, *Before European Hegemony: The World System, AD 1250–1350* (New York and Oxford: Oxford University Press, 1989), p. 169. Another factor that may have exacerbated the scepticism that some modern scholars have expressed with regards to Marco Polo's account of China may be that he visited China in the immediate aftermath of the Mongol conquest, when it was in the grip of major social, political and economic change. As Stephen Haw suggests, this period in China differed greatly from what preceded it and what followed, with subsequent Chinese sources seeking to play down the impact of Mongol government, which makes the *Devisement* a unique source, with information that by definition is not going to be confirmed in other sources. See Stephen G. Haw, *Marco Polo's China: A Venetian in the Realm of Khubilai Khan* (London and New York: Routledge, 2006), Chapter 12.

the involvement of a writer of romance in its composition, have encouraged some readers to align the text with fiction, often pointing to things that Marco does not say about China, rather than what he does say, as signs of his account's inauthenticity.[8] For my part, I am persuaded by Stephen Haw's arguments that almost everything the *Devisement* tells us about the Far East and China is true enough in the sense that it was almost certainly grounded in Marco Polo's direct experience of the regions described, whatever the inaccuracies or tendency to hyperbole.[9] But to my mind the question of whether or not the *Devisement* tells the truth is not necessarily the most important or interesting issue when assessing how the text was and is read as an account of far-off lands that most readers of the text, in the Middle Ages at least, were never likely to visit. The more telling problem is the investigation of how knowledge of distant and unknown lands is relayed by a mobile, unfixed observer and of the effects this has on how this knowledge might be apprehended, both by medieval readers (almost none of whom would have had any direct experience of the lands the *Devisement* describes) and by readers now.

This chapter has three sections. First, I will discuss the phenomenon of the marvel in the *Devisement* and consider, in particular, how it seeks to correct received knowledge about the Far East. I shall argue that 'marvel' is an epistemological rather than an ontological category in the *Devisement*. This point is hardly new, but I wish to explore how it relates to the question of where the narrator(s), the protagonists and the readers are situated: that which is a marvel for us might be quite banal for the Mongols, for example, and vice versa. The second section will be devoted to Kublai Khan, since his person, court and government take up a larger proportion of the book than any other topic and constitute the main marvel of the text. Here my focus will be on how Kublai on the one hand figures the utterly, magnificently strange, but on the other offers a utopian model of government, and particularly with regard to his attitude to the various religions of the peoples he governs. I will suggest that this makes him a figure of what Freud called the uncanny. Finally, I will examine further the *Devisement*'s treatment of different religions to show that the *Devisement* – unusually for a medieval text – does not erect distinct and insuperable boundaries around Christianity, but on the

---

[8] In fact, some of the text's most significant lacunae are easily explained. For instance, the Great Wall of China as we know it post-dates Marco Polo's time in China, and existing fortifications would have been unremarkable. Foot-binding was not as widespread in the late thirteenth century as it was to become; and Mongols did not drink tea, so since Marco seems to have frequented primarily the Mongol ruling elite, is not surprising that he fails to mention it. Furthermore, the lacunae in other contemporary accounts of China are far greater than any in the *Devisement*, though the wealth of accurate information it offers far outweighs that of any other account. See Haw, *Marco Polo's China*, Chapter 4.

[9] Haw, *Marco Polo's China*. See also Pierre Racine, *Marco Polo et ses voyages* (Paris: Perrin, 2012), '*Le Devisement du monde*: un grand reportage', on the *Devisement* as reportage.

contrary represents diverse religions leaking into each other, even morphing into each other, conjuring up a troubling elsewhere where the most important categories of medieval Christendom do not seem to pertain.

Marvels: 'la greignor mervoille dou monde'

As already noted, the *Devisement* not infrequently seeks quite explicitly to correct received knowledge about the world outside Europe:

> Et <est> cest la provence ke Alexandre ne poit paser quant il vost aler au ponent por ce que la vie est estroit et dotose: car de l'un les est la mer et de l'autre est gran montagne que ne se poent cavaucher. La vie est mout estroit entre la montagne et la mer; et dure cest estroit vie plus de quatre liegues, si ke pou homes tendront le pas a tout le monde. Et ce fo la caxon por coi Alexandre ne poet passere. Et voç di ke Alexandre hi fist fermer una tore et hi fist une forteçe por coi celle jens ne poesent pasere por venir sor lui et fu apellé la port dou fer et ce est le leu que le livre Alexandre conte comant il enclouse les Tartarç dedenç deus montagnes. Et ce ne fu pas voir qu'il fuissent Tartar, mes furent une jens qui estoient apellés Comain et autres jenerasion asseç: car Tartarç n'estoient a celui tens. (XXIII, 6–10)

> (And this is the province where Alexander could go no further when he wanted to travel west because the road was so narrow and difficult: for it is hemmed in by the sea and high mountains over which it is not possible to ride. The road is so narrow between the mountain and sea, and this narrow road lasts for more than 4 leagues, so that a few men can hold the pass against many. This is why Alexander could not pass. And I tell you that Alexander had a tower built and a fortress so that the people could not attack him, and it was called the Iron Gate. And this is the place where the book of Alexander relates how he enclosed Tartars between two mountains. And it is not true that they were Tartars; rather, they were a people called Comanians, and other races besides, for there were no Tartars in those days.)

> Et en ceste montagnes meisme se trouve une voine de la quel se fait la salamandre; et sachiés que salamandre ne est pas beste come ue<n> dit, mes est tes choses come je vous dirai desout. Il est verités que voç savés bien que por la nature nulle bestes ne nulz animaus ne pout vivre en feu, por ce que chascu<n> animaus est fait des quatre alimens. Et por ce que les jens ne savoient la certance de la salamandre le disoient en la mainere qu'il di<en> encore que salamandre soit beste, mes il ne est pas verité. (LX, 4–6)

> (And in these very mountains is found a seam from which salamander is made; and you should know that salamander is not an animal, as is said, but rather it is as I will tell you. It is true, as you well know, that it is not in the nature of any beast or animal to live in fire, since every animal is made up of the four elements. And since people did not understand the truth about salamander they said as they still do that it is a beast, but this is not true.)

Il ont leofans sauvajes et ont unicornes aseç que ne sunt mie gueres moin que un leofans: il sunt dou po[i]l dou bufal, les pies a fait come leofant, il a un cor enmi la front mout gros e noir. Et voç di que il ne fait maus <du cor, mes> con sa langue: car il a sus sa langue le spine mout longues, si que le maus que il fait <il le fait> con <la> langue; il a le chief fait come sengler sauvajes; et toutes foies porte sa teste enchine ver terre; e demore mout voluntieres entre le bue et entre le fang; elle est mout laide beste a veoir. Il ne sunt pas ensi come nos de ca dion e deviçon: que dient qu'ele se lai<se> prendre a la poucelle, mes vos di qu'il est tout le contraire de celz que nos qui dion que il fust. (CLXVI, 14–16)

(They have wild elephants and many unicorns, which are hardly smaller than elephants: they have hide like buffalo, feet like elephants and a very large black horn in the middle of their forehead. And I tell you that it does not inflict harm with its horn, but with its tongue; for on its tongue it has long spines, so that the harm it inflicts is done with its tongue; it has a head like a wild boar; and yet it carries its head bent towards the ground; and it prefers to wallow in the mud and bog; it is a very ugly beast to see. They are not as we say here and describe: for it is said they will let themselves be captured by a virgin, but I tell you that they are quite the contrary to what we here say they are.)

Whether appealing to historical accuracy (as in XXIII), verisimilitude (as in LX) or the authority of eye-witness accounts (as in CLXVI), the *Devisement* seems concerned to set the record straight, and the insistence with which it is asserted that others – and other texts – have lied is as central to the text's impact as its repeated claim to be telling the truth.[10] After debunking the myth of the unicorn with a naturalistic description of what is obviously (for the informed modern reader) a Javan rhinoceros (which is single-horned), the text goes on to accuse of 'grande mensoigne et grant deceverie' (CLXVI, 18: 'great lies and great deception') those who bring back embalmed monkeys from India and pass them off as 'peitit homes' ('little men'). For men this small simply do not exist (CLXVI, 20).

Despite its frequency in the text as a whole, the word *mervoille* is conspicuously absent from these passages. Sergio Marroni's exhaustive study of the word *mervoille*, its cognates and associated syntactic structures in the Franco-Italian and Tuscan redactions of the *Devisement* reveals that overwhelmingly, when *mervoille* is not being used generically simply to reinforce a statement either positively or negatively ('que c'estoit mervoille'), it qualifies human customs or products, with only a minority of occurrences relating to nature or (more significantly) to the supernatural; furthermore, when *mervoille* does

---

[10] See in particular Marroni, 'La meraviglia', p. 255, who compares the frequency with which reflexes of *vero* occur in the Tuscan redaction to their relative infrequency in contemporary texts in Italian.

qualify what might be thought of as supernatural, the referent is frequently Christian, though even here it is worth noting that the Franco-Italian redaction has a marked preference for the word *miracle* while the Tuscan redaction seems to prefer *meraviglia* for Christian miracles.[11]

A typical example of a marvel in the *Devisement* is Kublai Khan's relay messenger service, which enables rapid communication throughout his empire:

> Et en ceste mainere que voç avés oi, vunt por toutes pars les mesajes dou grant sire; et ont herbergies et chevaus aparoilés a ogne jornee. Et ce est bien la greignor autesse et la graignor grandese que aie ne aust onques nul enperaorç, ne nulç rois, ne nulz autre homes teroine; car sachiés tout voiremant que plus de CC^M chevaus demorent a cestes postes propemant por les seç mesajes. Et <en>core voç di que les paleis sunt plus de X^M, que sunt ensi forni de riches arnois come je voç ai contés, et ce est chouse si merveilose et de si grant vailance que a poine se poroit bie<n> conter ne scrivre. (XCVIII, 9–11)

> (And in the manner that you have heard, the messengers of the great lord go everywhere; and they have lodgings and horses ready all the time. And this is the greatest achievement and the greatest accomplishment of any emperor or king, or any other early man; for you should know truly that more than 200,000 horses are kept in these staging posts exclusively for his messengers. And I tell you furthermore that there are more than 10,000 of these posts thus supplied with ample equipment as I have related to you, and this is such a marvellous and worthy thing that it can hardly be related or written.)

Although it is these kinds of figure that seem to have given Marco Polo the nickname 'Marco Millions', Stephen Haw has argued that, while not completely accurate, such figures are nonetheless not necessarily overly exaggerated; thus Pierre Racine estimates that in reality there were probably around 3,000 staging posts in the Mongol communications network, using between 125,000 and 150,000 horses.[12] The scale of the infrastructure, the cultural achievements and the buildings, the sheer size and wealth of the Mongol empire (particularly once it had absorbed China) and the considerably more advanced technology meant that many of the things Marco encountered in

---

[11] 'La meraviglia', pp. 241–2. The usage in the Franco-Italian redaction is as follows (with the figures for the Tuscan redaction in brackets): customs 30 (16); first encounter with a foreign population 3 (2); generic 18 (9); nature 12 (8); commercial exploitation of nature 9 (6); cultural artefacts 24 (12); the supernatural 24 (19). The disparity between the two redactions here is not accounted for simply by the abbreviated nature of the Tuscan redaction, which indicates the Tuscan redactor is making lexical choices that diminish the importance of marvels.

[12] Haw, *Marco Polo's China*; Racine, *Marco Polo*, 'En route pour Khanbaliq'.

1 Monstrous Races illustrating *Le Devisement du Monde*. MS Bodley 264, fol 218 r.

the East were indeed marvels, verging on the unimaginable for Westerners who had not seen them with their own eyes. This concords with Pierre-Yves Badel's contention, for which he draws on Gervase of Tilbury's *Otia imperialia* (c. 1211), that in the *Devisement* the marvellous is that which, although natural as opposed to supernatural, we do not understand or, perhaps more accurately, do not yet understand.[13] The marvellous is primarily therefore an epistemological challenge, something to be computed and understood, rather than an absolute category of beings or objects *per* se. Furthermore, the *Devisement*'s avoidance of traditional Eastern marvels alongside the focus on cultural achievements seems to suggest a deliberate attempt to reorient the semantic field of the marvel.

[13] 'Lire la merveille selon Marco Polo', *Revue des Sciences Humaines*, 55 (1981), 7–16 (pp. 12–13). See also John Larner, *Marco Polo and the Discovery of the World* (New Haven, CT, and London: Yale University Press, 1999), pp. 80–1.

The presentation of the text in some manuscripts indicates that some readers, at least, may have been perplexed by this. Thus, in the exquisitely illustrated Oxford Bodleian 264, a copy of the French redaction which, as we saw in the introduction, is bound together with a version of the *Roman d'Alexandre*, the rubric to the first chapter of what is announced as the 'liure dynde' declares that it 'deuisera toutes les m*er*ueilles qui y sont et les manieres des gens' ('will recount all the marvels that are there and the customs of the people', Chapter CLVIII in the Franco-Italian redaction, 157 in the French). This is followed by an illustration of some of the monstrous races (see opposite).

From left to right we see a Blemmyae, a one-eyed wild man, a sciapod and a cynocephalus – in other words, some of the *merveilles* traditionally thought to be found in India but none of which is mentioned in the *Devisement*. Of course, discrepancies between images and the texts they illustrate are not uncommon in medieval manuscripts, and often they may result from an artist (or his studio director) making only a cursory reading of the text, or sometimes not even of the text itself but of a rubric. Alternatively, an artist may have been following an iconographic programme. Here one of the best-known high medieval illustrations of the monstrous races bears no relation to the text it illustrates but seems simply to have been triggered by the word *merveilles* in the rubric (or in an instruction to an artist). A similar phenomenon occurs in the famous *Livres des merveilles*, Bibliothèque Nationale f.fr. 2180 (fol. 29r). As has been frequently remarked, the gap in these instances (and two others in these manuscripts) between what the text tells us may be found in India and what the images suggest may be found there draws attention to the extent to which the *Devisement* confounds contemporary readers' expectations of the marvels of India.[14] Whereas the disparity between text and

---

[14] Laurence Harf-Lancner, 'From Alexander to Marco Polo, from Text to Image: The Marvels of India', in Donald Maddox and Sara Sturm-Maddox (eds), *The Medieval French Alexander* (Albany: State University of New York Press, 2002), pp. 235–57, and 'Divergences du texte et de l'image: l'illustration du *Divisement du monde* de Marco Polo', *Ateliers*, 30 (2003), 39–52; Philippe Ménard, 'L'illustration du *Devisement du Monde* de Marco Polo: étude d'iconographie comparée', in François Moureau (ed.), *Métamorphose du récit de voyage* (Paris: Champion/Slatkine, 1986), pp. 17–31 (pp. 28–9), and 'Réflexions sur l'illustration du texte de Marco Polo dans le manuscrit fr. 2810 de la bibliothèque nationale de Paris', in *Mélanges in memoriam Takeshi Shimmura* (Tokyo: France Tosho, 1998), pp. 81–92 (p. 90); Debra Higgs Strickland, 'Artists, Audience, and Ambivalence in Marco Polo's *Divisament dou Monde*', *Viator*, 36 (2005), 493–529 (pp. 502–6), and 'Text, Image, and Contradiction in the *Devisement dou monde*', in Suzanne Conklin Akbari and Amilcare A. Iannucci (eds), *Marco Polo and the Encounter of East and West* (Toronto: University of Toronto Press, 2008), pp. 23–59 (pp. 44–8); Rudolf Wittkower, *Allegory and the Migration of Symbols* (London: Thames and Hudson, 1977), pp. 76–92 ('Marco Polo and the Pictorial Tradition of the Marvels of the East') (p. 86). Bodley 264 has a further image of monstrous races on fol. 262r, and BNF f.fr. 2180 on fol. 76v. The latter illustrates Chapter CLXXII (167 in the French redaction) on the Andaman

image may be attributed to inadvertence or incompetence,[15] the programme of illustrations in both manuscripts is sophisticated and generally attentive to textual detail.[16] Rudolf Wittkower and Debra Higgs Strickland have consequently argued that these artists deliberately 'interpret and even "correct" the text so as to harmonize it with traditional conceptions', producing 'verbal-visual disjunctions' that are 'carefully planned glosses on the text and not simply examples of "artistic error"'.[17] If this is the case, then the visual presentation of the French redaction in these two manuscripts further enhances the simplification of the text in this version that I outlined in Chapters 1 and 2 through the disambiguation of narrative voice and through its linguistic make-over. Not only does the reader get what s/he is expecting here, but in the case of Bodley 264 the iconographic programme of the manuscript as a whole, as well as the disposition of the texts, subordinates the *Devisement*'s account of Asia to that of the Alexander tradition, while in BNF f.fr. 2810 the illustrations show the influence of iconographic programmes associated with the Alexander tradition.[18] In other words, the images confirm what the reader already knows about India from other sources, regardless of what the text says.

If marvels in the *Devisement* are not quite what contemporary readers were expecting, it is striking that after the opening chapter the first marvel the reader encounters is not a marvel of the East but, on the contrary, one of the West, which is to say the Polo brothers Niccolò and Maffeo, who, when they are unable to return home from Bukhara during their first journey to Asia because of local wars, become marvels for a Mongol messenger on his way to Kublai Khan:

> Et endementier qu'il hi demoroient, adonc hi vint un messajes d'Alau, le sire dou levant, qui aloit au grant sire de tous les Tartars qui avoit a nom C[h]oblai. Et quant ces mesajes voit messier Nicolao et meser Mafeo,

---

Islands with cynocephali. The text tells us here that the men 'ont chief come chienz et dens et iaux come chiens' (2: 'have heads like dogs and teeth and eyes like dogs'). For some commentators (e.g. Ménard, 'L'illustration', p. 29) this is a textual reference to cynocephali, but other scholars agree that the text is offering a straightforward analogy here that the artist of BNF f.fr. 2810 embellishes with gusto; see Strickland, 'Artists, Audience', pp. 505–6, and Wittkower, *Allegory*, p. 81.

[15] For Ménard they are are 'de graves infidélités au texte'; see 'Réflexions', p. 90.

[16] On the former see particularly Consuelo W. Dutschke, 'The Truth in the Book: The Marco Polo Texts in Royal 19 D 1 and Bodley 264', *Scriptorium*, 52 (1998), 278–300, and on the latter see particularly Maria Luisa Meneghetti, 'Quando l'immagine dice di più: riflessioni sull'apparato decororativo del *Livre des Merveilles du monde*', in Pietro G. Beltrami, Maria Grazia Capusso, Fabrizio Cigni and Sergio Vatteroni (eds), *Studi di Filologia Romanza offerti a Valeria Bertolucci Pizzorusso*, 2 vols (Pisa: Pacini, 2006), II, pp. 1023–49.

[17] Wittkower, *Allegory*, p. 76, and Strickland, 'Text, Image, and Contradiction', p. 24.

[18] Wittkower, *Allegory*, pp. 91–2.

il n'a grant mervoille, por ce ke jamés ne avoient veu nul latin en celle contree. (IV, 5-6)

(And while they were staying there, a messenger from Hülegü, lord of the Levant, who was going to the great lord of all the Tartars, who was called Kublai. And when this messenger sees Mr Niccolò and Mr Maffeo, he considers this a great marvel, for he had never seen a Latin (Westerner) in that land).

When he invites the Polo brothers to accompany him, his explicit reason is that Kublai has never seen a 'Latin' at all (IV, 9). While this is unlikely to be true, it clearly establishes a paradigm according to which Westerners such as the Polos, who return from Asia with marvellous tales, are themselves first perceived, while in the East, as objects of curiosity – marvels – a paradigm that is reinforced later in the 'prologue' as Marco amazes Kublai Khan with his knowledge of languages and his tales of 'maintes novités et maintes estranges chouses' (XVII, 6: 'many novelties and many strange things'; cf. also XVI, 4).

The most striking instance of the Polos as a source of marvels or of the Polos as marvels (the distinction between the two is not absolute) comes in Chapter CXLVI, which narrates the siege of Sanyanfu (Xiangyangfu) by the Mongols, its eventual fall and absorption into Kublai Khan's empire.[19] The Franco-Italian redaction relates how, after three years of siege, the Polos build trebuchets that hurl rocks into the city, allowing the siege to be raised 'por les trebuche que fist faire meser Nicolau e meser Mafeu e meser Marc' (CXLVI, 21: 'by the trebuchets that Mr Nicholas, Mr Maffeo and Mr Marco had had made'). The Polos' trebuchet, we are told, 'as Tartarç senbloie la greignor mervoille dou monde' (CXLVI, 14: 'seemed to the Tartars the greatest marvel in the world'). Given the insistent use of *mervoille* and its cognates throughout the *Devisement*, this epithet of 'the greatest marvel in the world' is noteworthy, particularly since a trebuchet is a rather banal piece of medieval European engineering, hardly a marvel at all from a European perspective. The fact that the trebuchet *seemed* like a marvel is also significant. What is a marvel from one perspective might in fact seem perfectly ordinary from another.

Interestingly, this account of the siege of Sanyanfu is one of the few instances in the *Devisement* where the text demonstrably does not tell the truth. It is rightly maintained that the conquest of the city was vital to the Mongol conquest of southern China: it was indeed one of the wealthiest and most strategically important cities of the region; it did indeed hold out against a lengthy siege (though for six years rather than three, as the *Devisement*

---

[19] Some parts of what follows draw from my '*La greigneur merveille du monde*: Marco Polo and French as a Marker of Cultural Relativity', *French Studies Bulletin*, 100 (2006), 63-6.

claims); and it did indeed open the door to the conquest of the rest of China (CXLVI, 4 and 20). However, the Polos cannot have had any hand in raising the siege, since the town (Xiangyang) fell in 1273, when they were still on their way to China (where they are thought to have arrived only in 1275), while the Mongols had had sophisticated and effective siege engines at their disposition for some time (built by Muslim engineers from Persia).[20] The idea that the Polos bestowed this technology upon them for the first time is simply not credible. It is also interesting that this is one of the few episodes transmitted in a wide range of versions for which different redactions diverge sharply:

> French redaction: is longer than the Franco-Italian redaction, but with a longer (ed. Ménard, 145) and a shorter (ed. Badel, CXLV) version. Both embroider the Polos' role in the siege, in comparison with the Franco-Italian redaction. The occurrence of the phrase 'la greigneur merveille du monde' and various other details, such as the Polos' having in their retinue a Nestorian Christian and a German, suggest derivation from a source similar to BNF f.fr. 1116.

> Tuscan redaction: seems to paraphrase the episode compared to the Franco-Italian redaction but adds the detail that 'quel fue il primo mangano che mai fosse veduto per neuno Tartaro' (142, 12: 'this was the first trebuchet ever seen by any Tartar'). The details concerning the Polos' helpers suggest a source similar to BNF f.fr. 1116.

> Venetian redaction: again seems to paraphrase, but also has the details concerning the Polos' helpers and remarks that 'lli Tartari che erano in l'oste se ne fèno grande meraveglia' (CXII, 7: 'the Tartars in the host thought this a great marvel'), again suggesting a source similar to BNF f.fr. 1116.[21]

> Z redaction: greatly abbreviated. The siege is mentioned: 'Et noveritis quod civitas ista multo tempore se defendit ex quo se diderat provincia tota Manci' (79, 7: 'And you should know that this city resisted for a long time after the rest of the province of Manzi surrendered'). But the Polos are given no role in raising the siege.

While it is possible that Z derives from a more sober source that is prior to the version found in BNF f.fr. 1116, whose redactor would then have embellished a story about the Polos making trebuchets that led to the other versions, the truncated nature of the reference to the siege in Z, which offers no explanation of the context of the remark made in 79, 7, makes a faulty

---

[20] See ed. Ménard, V, pp. 142–3.
[21] Pipino curiously offers an abbreviated version of this episode, but narrated in the first-person plural, specifically identified as 'dominum Nicolaum patrem meum et dominum Matheum fratrem eius et me marchum'. While it is explicitly stated that siege engines were unknown in the region, they are not called marvels. See pp. 136–7.

source more plausible (or even a deliberate decision to cut), and this is by no means the only place where *Z* seems to abbreviate radically. Similarly, the Tuscan and Venetian redactions may have had sources that had shorter versions of the tale of the siege, but on the other hand both redactions abbreviate throughout, and so their sources could equally well have been very similar to the surviving Franco-Italian redaction here. Be that as is it may, and whatever the 'original' reading may have been, what constitutes 'the greatest marvel in the world' in the Franco-Italian and French redactions depends entirely on your point of view.

Kublai Khan and the uncanny

If the greatest marvel of the world, for the Tartars at least, was the siege engine at Sanyanfu, the *Devisement* nonetheless makes it clear that one person embodies so many great marvels as to surpass all others:

> Or vos vueil comencier a contier en nostre livre tous les grandismes fait e toutes les grandismes mervoies dou grant kaan que aorendroit regne que Cublai Kaan est apeléç: que vaut a dire en nostre lengaje le grant seignors des seignors. Et certes il ha bien ceste nom a droit, por ce que cascun sache voiremant que ceste grant kan est le pius poisant homes de jens et de teres et de treçor que unques fust au monde, ne que orendroit soit, da Adam notre primer pere jusque a cestui point. Et ce voç mostrerai je tout apertamant en nostre livre que ce est veritables chouse: si que chascaun sera content que il est le greignor sire que unques fust au monde, ne que orendroit soie, e voç most<re>rai raison comant. (LXXVI, 1–3)

> (Now I want to begin to relate in our book all the very great deeds and all the very great marvels of the Great Khan that reigns now, who is called Kublai Khan, which means in our language the great lord of lords. And indeed he deserves this name, because let everyone know truly that this Great Khan is the most powerful man, in terms of people, land and wealth, that there is or has ever been in the world, from the days of Adam, our first father, up to this point. And I will demonstrate clearly in our book that this is true, so that everyone will happily agree that he is the greatest lord there is or ever was and I will explain why.)

The twenty-seven chapters (LXXVI–CIV) that the Franco-Italian redaction devotes to describing Kublai Khan's person, his court, his palaces, lifestyle, concubines, family and government represent a substantial portion of the book as a whole.[22] They pile superlative upon superlative, hyperbole upon

---

[22] Of the main redactions only *Z* does not have these chapters.

hyperbole, not infrequently qualifying what is described explicitly as a marvel (see LXXXIV, 15; XC, 6 and 7; XCIV, 24; XCV, 1; XCVIII, 11), although since the whole section is about 'toutes les grandismes mervoies dou grant kaan', everything about him may be considered marvellous.

Marco Polo's admiration for Kublai Khan seems to have known no bounds. Indeed, without the slightest hint of righteous Christian censure, the *Devisement* offers a striking image of his being worshipped by a vast assembly of subjects 'as if he were a god':

> Et encore voç di que le maintin de celle feste, avant que les tables soient mises, tuit les rois et tous les dux et marchois et cuenz, baronç, chevaliers, astronomique, mires, fauconer, et maintes autres ofitiaus et reg[e]or de jens et de teres et de ost, vienent en la grant sale devant le seignor; et celz que ne hi chevent demorent dehors le palais en tel leu que le grant sires les puet bien veoir [...] Et quant il sunt tuit asetés, chascun en son leu, adonc se leve un grant prolés et dit a haut vos: « Enclinés et adorés». Et tant tost que celui a ensi dit, il s'enclinent maintinant et metent lor front en tere; et font lor orassion ver le seignor et l'aorent ausi com se il fust dieu.
> (LXXXIX, 10, 12–13)

> (And what is more, I tell you that the morning of this great feast, before all the tables are laid, all the kings and dukes and marquises, counts, barons, knights, astronomers, doctors, falconers and many other officers and leaders of men and lands and armies, come into the great hall before the lord; and those who can't fit in stay outside the palace in such a place as where the great lord can see them [...] And when they are all settled, each one in his place, then a powerful prelate stands up and says loudly: 'Bow down and worship.' And as soon as he has said this they all bow down, their foreheads to the ground; and they offer greetings to the lord and worship him as if he were god.)

Furthermore, although the *Devisement*'s representation of Kublai's dominion verges on the utopian with its extraordinary economic and administrative structures (XCVI–XCVII), sophisticated transport infrastructure (XCVIII), elaborate social support mechanisms (XCIX) and so on, it is quite possible that many of the expansive figures and details given for the scale and extent of his palaces (LXXXIV–LXXXV), the number of his wives and concubines (LXXXII), courtiers (XC) or members of his escort (LXXXVI), or the details he gives about the scale of his hunting parties (XCI–XCIV), his feasts (LXXXVII–XC) and so on, may not be far short of the mark. The very magnificence of Kublai and everything associated with him makes him exceptional, marvellous and therefore quintessentially strange.

This makes it all the more striking that Kublai's substantive introduction to readers of the *Devisement* comes in a narrative interlude that on the one hand underlines quite explicitly his association with Christian values (even though he is not a Christian, of course), but on the other tells of his defeat of a rebellious Christian subject, his kinsman Nayan.[23] While it might be argued that Kublai's association with Christian values is simply part of an attempt to render him and his empire more acceptable for a Christian readership, with a view to justifying the text's palpable positive bias in favour of a man who is a pagan emperor and of his pagan realm,[24] the fact that he defeats a Christian prince in this episode blurs the boundaries between the familiar and the foreign, troubling the line that is usually drawn between 'us' and 'them' when other cultures and non-Christian religions are represented in medieval texts. This paradoxically, I suggest, accentuates Kublai's strangeness more than if he had been represented as a caricature pagan emperor implacably opposed to and incapable of understanding everything Christian: he does not fit any neat categories that distinguish the familiar from the strange. As such, Kublai is an example of what Freud called the uncanny, which is to say that which can seem at one and the same time familiar and strange, creating a troubling cognitive dissonance.[25]

My own use of the notion of the uncanny when reading the episode of Nayan's rebellion that introduces Kublai is also informed by two influential reactions to Freud's famous essay on the uncanny. First, whereas I take from Julia Kristeva the idea that Freud neglected to elaborate on how central (Western) representations of the strange and the stranger might be to the uncanny, concentrating as he did on his reading of Hoffmann's *The Sandman*, I question her historical narrative, in which the Enlightenment marks a crucial rupture in the history of the representation of the stranger, before which the world is 'closed in on itself' and the stranger regarded as radically separate, and after which the stranger is increasingly perceived closer to home.[26] Thus, rather than seeing a text such as the *Devisement* as a 'clin d'oeil avant la

---

[23] The *Devisement* says Nayan is Kublai's uncle (LXXVII, 6). In fact, he was a descendant of one of Genghis Khan's half-brothers: see Morris Rossabi, *Khubilai Khan: His Life and Times* (Berkeley and Los Angeles: University of California Press, 1988), p. 222. Some parts of what follows draw on my 'L'inquiétante étrangeté de la littérature de voyage en français au moyen âge', *Medioevo Romanzo*, 36 (2010), 57–81.

[24] For example, see Syed Manzarul Islam, *The Ethics of Travel from Marco Polo to Kafka* (Manchester: Manchester University Press, 1996), p. 195: 'the defeat of a Christian protagonist by a heathen power is, paradoxically, turned by Marco Polo into a victory for Christianity.'

[25] Sigmund Freud, *The Uncanny*, trans. David McClintock, with an introduction by Hugh Haughton (London: Penguin, 2003). My account here is commensurate with Frisch's view that Marco's ethos is out of step with his readers' ideological horizons; see *Invention of the Eyewitness*, pp. 56–60.

[26] Julia Kristeva, *Etrangers à nous-mêmes*, 2nd edn (Paris: Gallimard, 1991). She concludes: 'A reconnaître *notre* inquiétante étrangeté, nous n'en souffrirons ni ne jouirons de dehors. L'étrange est en moi, donc nous sommes tous des étrangers' (p. 248: 'in recognizing *our* uncanny foreignness, we will neither suffer nor enjoy from outside. The foreign is in me, we are thus all foreigners').

lettre à l'Unheimlich de Freud' ('a prescient wink to the uncanny of Freud'),[27] as Kristeva does, I would prefer to see it as integral to a longer history of European engagement with the foreign. Secondly, as Freud's *tour de force* in playful philology in the first part of his essay on the uncanny demonstrates, the meaning of *das Unheimlich* ('the unhomely') in German has an unnerving capacity to collapse into its opposite, *das Heimlich* ('homely'). Freud attributes the capacity of the uncanny to provoke anxiety (it is not for nothing that the French term is *l'inquiétante étrangeté*) largely to the relation he posits between the uncanny and the return of the repressed. Lacan does not take issue with this, but he does usefully point up how the uncanny works to trouble and blur the boundaries between categories that might otherwise have been thought distinct and discrete, and he suggests that *this* is *also* a primary cause of anxiety.[28] Not only do we find that the Other resides in us (just as we reside in it), as Kristeva argues, but 'l'homme trouve sa maison en un point situé dans l'Autre au-delà de l'image dont nous sommes faits' ('Man finds his home at a point situated in the Other beyond the image from which we are made').[29]

The story of Nayan's rebellion, which immediately follows the general introductory chapter about Kublai quoted above (LXXVI) and precedes the lengthy description of his person, court and so on (LXXXII–CIV), is exceptional among the narrative interludes of the *Devisement* in that it is clearly intended to underscore the reader's perception of a person, rather than a place. Its positioning suggests its purpose is to offer the reader a matrix with which to read the character of Kublai and his dominion.

One of the most significant factors in the story of Nayan is that he is a Christian. But it is equally significant that this apparently has nothing to do with his motivation for rebelling against the young Kublai: the text tells us simply that he no longer wishes to recognize the Great Khan's authority, the implication being that he has no desire to kowtow to a 'jeune enfanz' (LXXVII, 6: literally 'young child'). The subsequent account of the rebellion and its decisive battle, into which Kublai himself leads his troops, follows literary convention in a number of key respects. Thus, in this story we have something akin to the rite-of-passage *enfance* episode common in contemporary Old French romances and *chansons de geste*, enabling us to see how a boy becomes a man but also giving us the assurance that at any moment the venerable elder statesman may step down from his throne to become a military superhero once again. One effect of the story of Nayan's rebellion is therefore to align Kublai with European literary paradigms such as King Arthur or Charlemagne, though of course the ensuing description of his many and vast palaces, of his numerous wives and prodigious sexual appetite, of

---

[27] Kristeva, *Etrangers*, p. 165.
[28] Jacques Lacan, *Le Séminaire livre X: l'angoisse* (Paris: Seuil, 2004).
[29] Kristeva, *Etrangers*, p. 60.

his astonishingly opulent recreational activities, of the sophistication of the economy, transport system and military machine over which he presides, and of his global and extremely varied empire, can leave the reader in no doubt that the power and magnificence of his European counterparts pale in comparison.

As the description of the decisive battle between Nayan and Kublai's men densely accumulates stylistic devices and conventions that recall Old French *chansons de geste* and prose romance, there is no doubt that if, on the one hand, our apprehension of Kublai's prodigious youthful exploits is being familiarized by being mediated in a familiar form, on the other this familiar form is being deployed also to intimate the extent to which Kublai surpasses the models that are evoked:

> Et que voç en diroie? Il comancent la meslee mout cruele et felones[c]: or poit l'en veoir voler sagites, car toit l'air n'estoit plien, come [s]e il fuist pluie; or poit bien veoir chevaliers et chevaus mort caoir a la tere; il hi estoit si grant la grié et <la> remoute que l'en ne o[is]t le dieu tonant. Et sachiés que Naian estoit cristienz bateiçiéç et a ceste bataile avoit il la crois de Crist sor la enseigne.
>
> Et porcoi voç firoie je lonc conte? Sachiés tout voirement que cele fu la plus perilieuse bataille et la plus dotouse que jamés fust veue; ne a nostre tens ne furent tantes jens en un canp a bataille et propemant homes a chevaus. Il hi morurent tant homes et d'une part et d'autre que ce estoit mervoille a veoir. Elle dure ceste meslee dou maintin jusque a midi, mes au dereain venqui la bataille le grant kaan. (LXXIX, 10–14)

(So what can I tell you? They begin the cruel and desperate battle. So you can see arrows flying, for the air is full of them, as if it were raining arrows. Now you can see knights and horses falling dead on the ground. So great was the din and the turmoil that it is as if God were thundering. And let me tell you that Nayan was a baptized Christian and that in this battle he had the cross of Christ on his banner.

So why should I make this into a long story for you? You should know that this was the most perilous and fearful of battles ever seen. Never in our time have so many men been seen on a battlefield, nor indeed so many knights. So many men died on both sides that it was a marvel to behold. The battle lasted from daybreak until midday, but in the end the Great Khan won the battle.)

But if the intention here is to establish Kublai's worthiness, why repeatedly stress Nayan's Christianity?

The reason becomes clear as his grisly end and its aftermath are narrated. Nayan is rolled in a carpet, then dragged around by horses until he dies. This unusual (for Westerners) form of execution is chosen because 'il ne vuelen que le sanc dou leignajes de l'enperer soit espandu sor la terre (LXXX, 3: 'they do not want blood from the royal line of the emperor spread on the ground'). But the full extent of Kublai's magnanimity only emerges as he pacifies his subjects after the execution:

> Et aprés que le grant kaan ot ce fait et vencu cest bataille, les generasionz des jens qui hi estoient, saracinç, ydres et juif, et maintes autres jens que ne creoent en Dieu, fasoient gas de la cruis que Naian avoit aportés sor sun gonfanç; et disoient contre les cristienz que i estoient: « Veés comant la crois dou vostre dieu a aidiés Naian qui estoit cristienç! » Il en fasoient si grant gas e si grant escherne qu'ele vindrent devant le grant can. Et quant le grant can oi ce, il dist maus <paroules> a celz que gas en fasoient devant elz; puis apelles mant cristienz que illuec estoient et [li] comance a conforter et dit: « Se la crois dou vostre dieu ne a aidiés Naian, elle a fait grant raisonz; por ce que elle est bone ne devoit faire se bien non et droit. Naian estoite desliaus et traitres que venoit contre son seignors et por ce est grant droit de ce que li est avenu, et la crois dou vostre dieu fist bien, se elle ne l'aide contre droit; pour ce qu'ele est bone couse ne devoit faire autre que bien». Les cristiens responderent au grant kan: « Grandisme sire – font il – vos dites bien verités: car la crois ne vost faire maus ne desliautés come fasoit Naian que estoit traites et desloiaus contre son seignors, et il a bien eu ce de que elle estoit doigne». (LXXX, 6–10)

> (And when the Great Khan had done this and won the battle, the different types of people who were there – Muslims, idolaters, Jews and many other people who do not believe in God – mocked the cross that Nayan had on his banner; and they said to the Christians present: 'Just see how your god's cross helped Nayan, who was a Christian.' And they so mocked and derided it that the Great Khan got wind of this. And when the Great Khan heard this, he chastised those who were behaving thus in his presence. Then he summoned the many Christians who were there and begins to comfort them, saying: 'If your god's cross did not help Nayan, then it was quite right in this, because it is good and so must do nothing but what is good and right. Nayan was disloyal and a traitor, since he rebelled against his lord and for this reason what befell him was quite right, and your god's cross was quite right not to help him when he was in the wrong, for it is a good thing and should do nothing but good.' The Christians replied to the Great Khan: 'Oh greatest of lords,' they said, 'you speak the truth: for the cross should never do anything wrong or disloyal, as Nayan did, for he was a traitor and disloyal to his lord, and he got what he deserved.')

Kublai has an uncanny and better understanding of Christian values than many Christians. The foreign Other offers the Christian reader a truth here about Christianity that in some respects is contingent on the circumstances, but which in others is clearly a universal truth. However, perhaps more importantly, without himself being a Christian, Kublai validates the power of the cross, even though he has just had a Christian executed. The nuanced ethical complexity of his judgement that 'the cross is good and so should do nothing but good' contrasts with the crude jingoism of a better-known line such as 'Paiens unt tort e crestïens unt dreit' ('the pagans are wrong and the Christians are right') from the *Chanson de Roland*.[30] The representation of the Mongol court as multi-faith and of Kublai himself as a promoter of religious tolerance is in some respects historically accurate: thirteenth-century Mongol emperors, and Kublai in particular, discouraged religious discrimination (largely, it would seem, in order to encourage trade), had a penchant for employing administrators who belonged to religions of the Book and also frequently seem to have had a genuine curiosity for other religions. Indeed, communities of Muslims, Jews and Nestorian Christians thrived in the Far East during Kublai's reign. One reason given in the *Devisement* for Kublai's relation with the Polo family seems to have been his curiosity about Christianity (VIII), and in the course of the thirteenth and fourteenth centuries several very high-ranking Mongol nobles converted to Christianity or Islam – with far-reaching effects, since the conversion of the Khans of the Golden Horde and Ilkhanate (in Syria, Iraq and Iran) after the disintegration of Kublai's empire to Islam was a major factor in the subsequent dominance of Islam in the Middle East.[31] But the choice to introduce Kublai with this episode, which illustrates his tolerance towards Christians and his wisdom, is not, I suggest, motivated simply by a drive for historical accuracy. Placing Kublai on a higher plane of understanding regarding Christianity than Christians themselves troubles any clear distinctions the Christian reader may bring to the text between 'us' and 'them', seriously disturbing any certainty he or she may bring to the text regarding the automatic superiority of Christianity. Indeed, the text seems to suggest here a point that is hinted at, without ever fully being made, throughout the lengthy description of Kublai, which is that religious tolerance and syncretism are a key ingredient of social order and economic prosperity. And what could be more 'worryingly strange' for many medieval readers than this?

The troubling nature of this episode is further underlined in one of the three manuscripts of the French redaction in which it is illustrated. Two of the surviving illustrations of Nayan's execution are inaccurate, in that one depicts a hanging, the other a beheading: the illustrators probably simply read the rubric, or an instruction based upon the rubric, without reading the text (French redaction 79: 'Ci devise le .LXXXIX. chapitre comment le Grant Caam fist ocirre Naian'). But it is nonetheless striking in London, British Library, Royal 19 D 1 that there is a clearly marked racial difference between Nayan and his executioners:[32]

---

[30] *La Chanson de Roland*, ed. Ian Short (Paris: Le Livre de Poche, 1990), l. 1015.
[31] Larner, *Marco Polo*, p. 119.
[32] On this image and other representations of Nayan's execution, see Strickland, 'Artists, Audience', pp. 499–500, and 'Text, Image, and Contradiction', pp. 53–4.

2 The execution of Nayan. British Library, Royal 19 D 1, fo 85.

Nayan is depicted as a Caucasian noble, but his executioners as stereotypical, dark-skinned Saracens. On the one hand, this may reflect the tendency in this manuscript to Westernize the Great Khan and other high-class Mongols (since Nayan is Kublai's uncle).[33] On the other, not only are lower-class Mongols represented as 'other' in the process of killing a white man in this image, but they are watched by a crowned figure (Kublai) with noticeably darker skin than the man being executed, though lighter than that of the executioners. Even if, as is possible, this results from the illustrator's inattention, what is actually represented in the image is far more stereotypical than what is related in the text. If, on the other hand, the image does not result from the illustrator's inattention but represents rather a conscious choice (which is what the carefully differentiated skin tones might suggest), then this indicates that what the text narrates was deemed problematic.

It is sometimes suggested that Western Europe fantasized about an alliance with the Mongols which would lead to the launching of a new crusade against Muslims in the Middle East, resulting in the reconquest of the Holy Land, and that the *Devisement* should be read in this context.[34] There are some explicit advocates of the idea that the Mongols might come to Christendom's aid against the Islamic world: for example, the virulently Islamophobic Hayton, an Armenian prince turned monk. His *La Flor des estoires de la terre d'Orient*, probably composed in Poitiers in 1307, draws extensively on the *Devisement* to recount a history of the Mongol empire: like the *Devisement*, it was originally composed in French then subsequently translated into Latin, and, again like the *Devisement*, it is suggested that the text was dictated.[35] Hayton concludes by urging the Pope to preach a crusade so that 'la Terre Sainte, que fu arosée du precieus sanc Nostre Seignor Jhesu Crist, soit delivrée du poer des ennemis mescreans' (p. 252: 'the Holy Land,

---

[33] See David J.A. Ross, 'Methods of Book Production in a XIVth Century French Miscellany (London, B.M. Royal 19.D.1)', *Scriptorium*, 6 (1952), 63–75 (pp. 68–9).

[34] For a recent account that reads the *Devisement* in this light, see Antonio García Espada, *Marco Polo y la cruzada: historia de la literatura de viajes a las Indias en el siglo XIV* (Madrid: Marcial Pons Historia, 2009).

[35] See Hayton, *La Flor des estoires*, in *Recueil des historiens des croisades: documents latins et français relatifs à l'Arménie*, II (Paris: L'Académie des Inscriptions et des Belles Lettres, 1906), p. 253 (accessible at: http://gallica.bnf.fr/): 'Lequel livre je Nicole Falcon de Toul, escris premierement en françois, si come le dit freire Hayton me disoit de sa bouche, sanz note ne exemplaire, et de romanz le translatei en latin' ('I, Nicole Falcon de Toul, first wrote this book in French, just as the aforementioned Hayton spoke to me, without notes or draft, and I translated it from Romance into Latin'). *La Flor des estoires* offers evidence that a copy of the *Devisement* had already found its way to France by 1307, which may corroborate the information given in Thibaut de Chepoy's prologue (see p. 19 above), although if Hayton's work went into circulation in 1307, this might suggest that copies of the *Devisement* had been in circulation outside Italy earlier than this. The *Devisement* is associated with Hayton's *La Flor des estoires* in several manuscripts: Bibliothèque Nationale f. fr. 2810 and New York, Pierpont Morgan Library, 723.

which was watered with the precious blood of our Lord Jesus Christ may be delivered from the power of our miscreant enemies'). In the chapters leading up to this, Hayton has expressed some consternation that the Mongols have not yet come to the aid of Christendom (p. 246), but the implication is nonetheless that their enmity for the 'Saracens' and the practical consideration of their nomadic lifestyle were such that they would favour the Christians:

> Et je, qui assés connois la volunté des Tartars, croi fermement que toutes les cités et les terres que les Tartars conquerroient sur les Sarazins que volentiers les dorroient à garder as Crestiens franchement e quitement, car les Tartars ne porroient demorer en celes contrées por la grant chalor que i fait au temps d'esté. (p. 245)
>
> (And I, who know well the Tartars' wishes, believe firmly that they would willingly give all the cities and the lands that they conquer from the Saracens freely and without obligation to the Christians to govern, for Tartars cannot stay in those lands because of the great heat of the summers.)

It is unclear whether this is wishful thinking on Hayton's part or whether he is being deliberately disingenuous with a view to swaying the Pope. Either way, he misunderstands or underestimates the Mongols' capacity to take over the lands they conquer by assimilating themselves to their cultures and religions, whether this be in China or the Middle East, where, as already noted, the Mongol rulers converted to Islam. The hope that help against the Muslim world might come to Christendom from the East was also perhaps encouraged by the ubiquity of one of the most successful literary hoaxes of all time, the *Letter of Prester John*,[36] which from c. 1165 onwards encouraged belief in a powerful Christian kingdom in the Orient that might indeed outflank the Muslims of the Middle East.

Readers of the *Devisement*, however, could hardly regard Prester John as a potential crusading ally, since a narrative interlude tells us that he had died several generations earlier during the course of an unsuccessful war with Genghis Khan (LXVI–LXVIII). This passage again offers readers an account of something they might expect to find in Asia, but again foils expectations by announcing Prester John's death. Furthermore, a Christian is once more represented as subordinate. More generally, if, in the early thirteenth century, there had been aspirations that the Mongols might be potential allies for Christendom against Islam, these had been tempered by the savage onslaughts of Mongol armies on Eastern Europe in 1237 and 1240. After this,

---

[36] For the text of the letter, and an excellent study, see Michael Uebel, *Ecstatic Transformation: On the Uses of Alterity in the Middle Ages* (New York: Palgrave, 2005). For Romance vernacular versions, see *La Lettre du Prêtre Jean: les versions en ancien français et en ancien occitan, textes et commentaires*, ed. Martin Gosman (Groningen: Bouma, 1982).

learned circles in Europe were in any case relatively well informed about the Mongol empire, even before the *Devisement* started to circulate widely in the early thirteenth century, because of the reports written by papal envoys to the Far East such as John of Plano Carpini (who went to Asia in 1245–7) and William of Rubruck (who travelled to the Far East before 1260).[37] Western reactions to the Mongols can perhaps best be summed up by Joinville's *Histoire de Saint Louis*: here we learn that following diplomatic contact in 1248–9 while he is in Cyprus, Louis IX is initially hopeful that the Mongols will help him conquer Jerusalem, only to be quickly disappointed by their overweening pride and arrogance.[38] In any event, there is certainly no trace, in the *Devisement*, of any fantasy about an alliance between Christendom and the Mongols against Islam. This is not to say that there are not shades of anti-Muslim prejudice in *Le Devisement* (as we will see in the next section), but in the Middle and Far East, at least, Christians and Muslims alike are uniformly represented as subject to the Kublai Khan's supreme sovereignty, which is the guarantor of progress and prosperity for all. Kublai, in other words, represents a promise for the future for adherents of both religions.

Religious syncretism

One of the sharpest markers of difference in medieval European culture was religion. Learned writers were naturally aware that Judaism, Christianity and Islam shared sacred texts and prophets, but this did not stop them suggesting an absolute divide between Christianity and other religions. To quote the *Chanson de Roland* again, 'Paiens unt tort e crestïens unt dreit' (1015), and such sentiments certainly pervade Pipino's redaction of the *Devisement*, with its repeated qualification of Muslims and idolaters as 'abominable', 'wicked' and 'evil'.[39] In other redactions, however, analogies between other religions and Christianity are far more typical:

> Car sachiés tout voirement que chascun ydres ont feste en lor <jor> només come ont les nos <saint>. Car il ont grandisme moster et abaie, que je voç di que il hi a si grant mostier come une pitete cité, es quelz a plus de II^M

---

[37] See Dawson, *Mission to Asia*.

[38] See Jean de Joinville, *Histoire de Saint Louis*, in *Historiens et chroniqueurs du moyen âge: Robert de Clari, Villehardouin, Joinville, Froissart, Commynes*, ed. Albert Pauphilet (Paris: Gallimard, 1952), pp. 195–366, Chapters XCIII–XCIV.

[39] Pipino's prologue (pp. 1–2) informs the reader that the purpose of his translation is to reveal the truth about the peoples who live in blindness and darkness. The prologue is reduced to ten chapters that narrate the Polos' journeys, but once the description of the world begins, value judgements come thick and fast, for example in Chapter XII: 'Turchi lingam propriam habent et Machometi abhominalibilis legem' (p. 17: 'the Turks have their own language and Mohammed's abominable law').

nonain selonc lor costumes, que vestrent plus honestemant que ne font les autres homes. Il portent le chief ras e la barbe rase. Il font les greignors festes a lor ydres con greignors cant et con greignors luminarie que [j]amés fose veue; et encore voç di que cesti bacsi en i ont entr'aus de tiaus que, selonc lor ordre, puent prandre mollier, et il ensi font, car il en prennent et ont filz aseç.

Et encore voç di qu'il est un autre mainere de religions, que sunt appelés sensi<n>: qui sunt homes de grant astinence, selonc lor costumes, et moinent si apres vie come jes voç conterai. Sachiés touti voiremant que il ne menuent en toute lor vie for que semule, <ce> est canille, c'est l'escorse que remanent de la farine dou forment; car il prenent celle semule, ce est canille, et la metent en eive chaude et la hi lassent demorer auquant; puis le menuent. Il degiunent maintes foies l'an et ne mengient rien dou monde for que cel canille que voç ai contés. I[l] ont grant ydres et asez et tel foies aorent le feu. Et voç di que les autres regules dient que cesti que <vi>vent en si grant astinence sunt come paterin, por ce que il ne aorent en tel mainere les ydres com il font. (LXXV, 30–38)

(Now you should know truly that every idol has a day's festival named after them, like our saints. For they have such great churches and abbeys that I can tell you there is one church that is as big as a small city, in which there are more than 20,000 nuns,[40] according to their customs, who dress more modestly than the other people. They have shaved heads and faces. They celebrate their idols elaborately with exuberant singing and more light than has ever been seen; and I can also tell you that these *bacsi* have some among them who, according to their order, can marry, and indeed they do, and takes wives, and have many sons.

And I can also tell you that there is another type of religion, whose adherents are called *sensin*: these men are extremely ascetic, according to their customs, and live such a harsh life as I will describe to you. You should know truly that they only ever eat throughout their lives semolina, which is to say *canille*, which is the residue left by the wheat flour; for they take this semolina, this *canille*, and they put it in hot water and leave it there a while, then they eat it. They fast many times in the year and eat under no circumstances anything other than this *canille* I have told you about. They have many great idols and sometimes worship fire. And I can tell you that the other orders say that those who live so abstemiously are like heretics, for they do not worship as other idolaters do.)

This description begins with an explicit analogy (the idolaters' idols have festivals named after them, 'like our saints'), but the sequence of implicit

---

[40] The reading of BNF f.fr. 1116 (*nonain*), retained by Benedetto and Ronchi, may be problematic given that the text goes on to talk of shaved faces as well as shaved heads. The French redaction reads *moinnes* (74, 134), Z *monachi* (42, 4), the Tuscan redaction *monaci* (74, 27) and the Venetian redaction *munexi* (LX, 31). However, the reference to modest dress might seem more appropriate for women than men.

analogies suggested by the vocabulary chosen is even more telling. The idolaters have 'churches' and 'abbeys', they behave according to 'their order' (which is suggestive of a religious order), and different sects are referred to as *regules* ('rules'). But perhaps the most telling choice of vocabulary concerns the non-orthodox *sensi<n>*, (non-orthodox because they are the most abstemious), presumably Taoists,[41] who are said to be like *paterin*. *Paterin* is a somewhat colloquial word for heretic, particularly used for the Cathars, that derives from a popular movement in twelfth-century Milan.[42] Though of Italian origin, it was no doubt widely understood in French by the late thirteenth and early fourteenth century, but the significance of its use here, I suggest, is its implicit yet quite specific local (i.e. Italian-French) frame of reference: everything about the religious practices described, included eventual deviations from the norm, is conveyed by suggesting that these practitioners of exotic other religions are in many respects just like ourselves: their monks and nuns sing and light candles like ours, they have saints' days like us, they even have heretics like us. Although Z eliminates this local colour by translating *paterin* as *hereticos* (42,10), the implicit analogy between Christians and idolaters that runs through this passage is reinforced by the translation of 'un autre mainere de religions' as 'alius ordo religiosorum' (42, 7), which is, of course, strongly suggestive of monastic orders.

These implicit analogies recur whenever another religion is described. The most striking accumulation comes in the long chapter on the 'Brahmins' of India (CLXXVII), a term that appears to designate both Hindu Brahmins and a range of other India religious groups, such as Yogis and Jains. Their abstinence, honesty, peaceful nature and general lack of luxuriousness are repeatedly praised (CLXXVII, 3–4; see also 16–17, 23, 35), with several of their practices being likened rather strikingly to Christian rites or beliefs. For example: 'Encore vos di que il ardent le oisi dou buef et en font poudre, puis s'en ongent en plusors leu dou cors con grant reverence, bien con ausi grant com font le cristiens de l'eive beneete' (CLXXVII, 26: 'And I can tell you further that they burn the bones of cattle and make a powder with which they anoint their bodies in several places with great reverence, easily as much reverence as Christians have for holy water').[43] Anointing oneself with a paste made from ground cattle bones must have been alien and rather difficult to picture for European readers, yet it is nonetheless daringly normalized (and positively marked) by the reference to holy water. This leads into a detailed account of exotic beliefs and customs that consist-

---

[41] See ed. Ménard, II, p. 80, n. to 74, 139.

[42] See ed. Ménard, VI, pp. 139–40, n. to 169, 199, and *Milione*, ed. Bertolucci Pizzorusso, pp. 689–90.

[43] Though the contents of this chapter are for the most part retained in the French redaction (172), they are abbreviated, and this clause is dropped, which may indicate some discomfort with the analogy itself.

ently oscillates between foregrounding qualities that are similarly positively marked in a Christian system of values and practices that must have seemed outlandish if not frankly bizarre. Thus the Yogis eat leaves, but not when they are green, since they believe this indicates they are still alive and therefore have souls (CLXXVII, 27); to eat anything alive would be a sin (*pechiés*), and the Yogis will avoid sin at all costs. They go naked, but when challenged on this they say, first, that they wish for nothing other than that which they entered the world, but add that since they have never sinned with their genitals they have no need to cover them, unlike others (CLXXVII, 29–30). Indeed, so strong is their insistence on chastity that any man who gets an erection when (deliberately) tested by the manual ministration of a comely maiden is instantly expelled from the community as given to luxuriousness (CLXXVII, 36–8). This whole sequence is a mixture of accurate observation of beliefs and customs, together with some garbled, possibly incredulous and certainly somewhat prurient perceptions of the relation between Eastern spirituality and sexual drives.[44] Even here it is striking that what is actually being described is a devotion to chastity (a positively marked Christian practice) so extreme that few Christians manage to attain it. Although it is conceded that all these 'Brahmins' are 'si crueli et si perfidi ydres que je vos di' (CLXXVII, 40),[45] such stock condemnations of non-Christian beliefs and practices are far outweighed by the positive vocabulary used throughout the chapter and the positive spin that is put on the abstinence and asceticism of the 'Brahmins' throughout. Naturally Christians should know that to deny carnal appetites is a good thing, but, perhaps most tellingly of all, one consequence of their healthy lifestyle is that they live exceptionally long lives, and, as the text comments, 'ce est bien gran mervoie' (CLXXVII, 34).

As already noted in the previous chapter, except in the French redaction this sequence immediately precedes the Life of the Buddha, making for an even longer, and possibly therefore more troubling, sequence of proponents of other (pagan) religions embodying Christian virtues. This blurring of boundaries between Christianity and rival religions is particularly marked when the *Devisement* is talking about the Far East and about 'idolaters'. Indeed, although a superficial reading might suggest that the *Devisement* is given to the kind of knee-jerk Islamophobia or 'anti-Islamic paranoia' so

---

[44] Some have argued that Marco Polo was preoccupied with sexual mores, alternatively representing the East as a kind of sexual paradise or betraying his own interests as a sexual tourist. See, for example, Michael Calabrese, 'Between Despair and Ecstasy: Marco Polo's Life of the Bhudda', *Exemplaria*, 9 (1997), 189–229 (pp. 196–222). However, explicit references to sexual practices or to sexual opportunities in the *Devisement* are actually comparatively rare. For one exception, see CXVII, 6–9, which relates how in a particular province hospitality requires that husbands offer guests their wives' sexual favours.

[45] The French redaction strengthens this statement as follows: 'Et il sont si creueulz et si parfais ydolastres que ce est deablie' (172, 87–8: 'they are so cruel and such perfect idolaters that this is diabolic').

often found in medieval texts,[46] in fact, in many parts of the world, three main religions (Christianity, Islam, idolatry) are represented as co-habiting unproblematically:

> La provence s'apelle Tangut. Il sunt tuit ydres, bien est il voir qu'il a auques cristienç nestorin; et encore hi a saracinç. (LVIII, 2–3)
>
> (The province is called Tangout. They are all idolaters, but it is also true that there are some Nestorian Christians and also some Saracens.)

Jews are mentioned, but rarely (LXXX, 6), which perhaps indicates exceptionally low levels of another common medieval 'paranoia', and overtly anti-Islamic statements are confined to parts of the text that describe parts of the world through which the Polos passed either at the beginning or at the end of their travels (XXVI, 3; XXX, 8–9; CXCIII, 41; CXCIII, 46, CXCIV, 3): it is as if, the closer to Europe, the greater the risk of what one might call default Islamophobia, and conversely the farther from home, the more a collective 'we' can be used of Christians and Muslims – as when we see Adam referred to as 'our first father' in the Life of the Buddha (CLXXVIII, 3), a context where 'our' clearly refers to both Christians and Muslims.

Scholars who see the *Devisement*'s main agenda as anti-Islamic or pro-Christian are perhaps reading the text in the light of subsequent writers such as Hayton, who wish to see the Crusades relaunched and whose work is littered with anti-Islamic remarks. Yet this is not just a modern mode of reception of the *Devisement*, since the text has a tendency in transmission to absorb and elaborate on prejudices and expectations that were not so prevalent in its earliest redaction. Pipino's addition of anti-Islamic adjectives throughout his redaction has already been mentioned, but consider also the following passage found only in the French redaction from the end of the narration of the miracle of the moving mountain:

> En tel maniere [ala] ce fait comme vous avez oÿ, [de quoy] ce fut moult grant miracle. Et ne vous merveilliez se li Sarrazin heent les Crestiens, car la maloite loy que Mahoms leur donna, si commande que touz les maus que ils pueent faire a toutes manieres de gens et meïsmes aus Crestiens que il [le] doivent faire, et d'embler le leur et de tous les autres maus, puis que il n'est de sa loy. Et veez con sanglante loy et com mauvais commandemens que il ont. Et tous les Sarrazins du monde se maintiennent en ceste maniere. (28, 44–54; after XXIX, 9, in the Franco-Italian redaction)
>
> (And the event took place as you have heard, so it was a very great miracle. And do not be amazed if Saracens hate Christians, for the cursed law Mohammed gave them commands them to inflict wickedness on all kinds of people, even Christians, and to steal from them and other kinds of wicked-

---

[46] Islam (*Ethics*, p.155) charges Marco Polo with anti-Islamic paranoia.

ness, because they are not of their religion. And just consider what a bloody law and what wicked commandments they have, and all the Saracens in the world behave in this way.)

This episode, near the beginning of the text, narrates how the Christians of Baghdad are rescued from Muslim persecution by the power of prayer, and this enables them to move a mountain at the request of their persecutors. But the episode ends far more neutrally in the earlier Franco-Italian redaction, with 'En cele mainere ala ceste mervoile come il avés oi' (XXIX, 10: 'in this manner the marvel you have heard came about'), instead of the Islamophobic lines I have just cited, which are in fact an expanded and more virulent version of sentences that occur in the Franco-Italian redaction at XXX, 8–9, but which, as reworked in the French redaction, have far greater pro-Christian and anti-Islamic force.

Far from showing 'anti-Islamic paranoia' or representing idolatry as 'the other religion by excellence',[47] the *Devisement*'s sense (like Kublai Khan's) of the relative value of, and similarities between, different religions is striking. I would like to conclude this section with an examination of two episodes that illustrate this most poignantly. Chapter CXCIII comes after we have been told that 'nos venons aprochant a plus domesces leus' (CLXXXII, 3: 'we are approaching more familiar places'). The main body of the chapter is devoted to narrating how the Christian king of Abyssinia takes revenge on the Muslim sultan of Aden and on 'celz chiens saracinz' ('those Saracen dogs') for the forcible circumcision of one of his bishops, since 'il ne est digne couse que les chiens saraçin doient sovrestere les cristiens' (CXCIII, 46: 'it is not fitting that Saracen dogs lord it over Christians'). But the most interesting feature of this chapter, from my current perspective, is not the story itself but an arresting detail concerning the social organization of Abyssinia:

> Les jens cristiene de ceste provence ont trois seigne en mi le vix: ce est le un dou front jusque a dimi le nes, et pois en ont de chascune goe un. E ce sunt fait con fer chaut e ce est lor batesme: car puis que il sunt batiçés en eive, et il se font puis celz seigne que je voç ai dit, e ce est por gentilise e por compliment dou batesmo. Et encore voç di que il hi a juif; et cesti juif ont II seigne: ce est da cascune goe un. E les saracinz ont un seigne tant solamant, ce est dou front a demi les nes. (CXCIII, 3–6)

> (The Christians of this province have three marks on their faces: one on the forehead right in the middle above the nose, and then they have one on each cheek. And they are made with a hot iron at their baptism: for when they are baptized in water they make these marks I have told you about, and this is a kindness and in order to complement baptism. And I tell you further that there are Jews there and these Jews have two marks, one on

---

[47] Islam, *Ethics*, p. 155.

each cheek. And the Saracens have just one mark, which is in the middle of the forehead, over the nose.)

The *Devisement* is not the only text to record the practice of branding adherents of different religions in the region, so it is likely that what is described here has a basis in fact.[48] However, within the overall dynamic of the *Devisement* it is striking that the custom is explicitly located in a region that is said to be split, in terms of sovereignty, between Christians and Muslims (CXCIII, 2), and that the seemingly barbaric practice of branding children is represented as an act of kindness (*gentilise*) towards Christians in particular, who are distinguished by three 'signs', as if marked physically by the Trinity. It would seem that being able to distinguish clearly between Christians, Muslims and Jews here (perhaps as we reach more familiar places?) is important, but the very fact that a visual sign, one that is literally emblazoned on the body, is necessary for this suggests paradoxically that otherwise they would be extremely easy to confuse. Boundaries between different religious groups are rigidly enforced here, but only precisely because they are so fragile, as the reader of the *Devisement* has already learned just a few chapters previously, when told that the Christians of the island of Scotra (Socotra) 'vont tuit nus a la mainere et a la uçance de les autres yndians ydres' (CXC, 6: 'go about entirely naked in the manner and following the customs of other Indians who are idolaters').

The second episode I should like to examine is unique to Z, and although Benedetto was convinced of its authenticity,[49] its status in my view is less certain. While Marco Polo is staying with his uncle Maffeo in Fugiu (Fuzhou, the subject of CLV–CLVI in the Franco-Italian redaction), he is told by a Saracen scholar of a community whose religion is generally thought to be baffling since 'ydolatria non est, quia ydola non retinent; non adorant ignem; non profite<n>tur Macometum; nec etiam habere videtur ordinem christianem' (89, 40: 'they are not idolaters, since they do not have idols; they do not worship fire; they do not recognize Mohammed as prophet; nor do they look like Christians'). Marco Polo is asked to investigate, is instantly intrigued by the sect and sets about getting to know them, rather like a good anthropologist. Though they initially resist his attempts to understand their culture and religion, fearful that Kublai Khan will ban their religion (89, 46–7), Marco and Maffeo are persistent, apparently taking considerable trouble since they learn the language of the community and translate its holy texts (89, 48: 'inceperunt scripturam interpretari et traslatari de verbo ad verbum et de lingua in lingua<m>'), only to discover a Psalter, the Gospels and so on. The story has a happy outcome in that, thanks to the Polos' ministrations, these Christians are given a special charter to practise their religion

---

[48] See ed. Ménard, VI, p. 189, n. to 187, 6–9.
[49] See ed. Benedetto, p. CLXIX.

freely by Kublai Khan, and clearly this might be thought to send a cosy and reassuring message to a European and Christian readership, albeit one that evokes the uncanny: however far you travel from home, you will find something familiar, something that will not trouble your world view, for the 'other religion' will strangely morph into your own. But perhaps this reassuring message can also be turned on its head. In a world in which distinctions between different religions are thought to be absolute, how troubling is it then to encounter people like you and yet fail to recognize them? What can we know for certain under such circumstances? Perhaps the only solution is indeed branding?

Benedetto wrote of this passage:

> Nessuno all' infuori di M. Polo può avere scritto il cap. singolarissimo [...] ove Matteo e Marco ci appaiono finalmente nella loro giusta luce, quali autentici esploratori, curiosi di apprendere i riti e le credenze dei popoli, condotti dalla loro curiosità, grazie al loro tatto pratico e al loro sapere, a scoprire nel cuore del Fu-Kien idolatra un forte nucleo cristiano. Tutto respira la sincerità: il tono piano e ingenuo, i particolari precisi e minuti, tra cui alcuni storicamente preziosissimi circa l'organizzazione religiosa del gran impero.[50]

> (No one other than Marco Polo can have written the very singular chapter in which Matteo and Marco finally appear to us in their true light, as authentic explorers, curious to learn about the rites and beliefs of the populations of peoples, driven by their curiosity and thanks to their practical sense and wisdom able to discover in the heart of idolatrous Fu-Kien a strong Christian community. Everything seems sincere: the simple and ingenuous tone, the precise and minute details, some of which are historically invaluable on the religious organization of the great empire.)

Benedetto's belief in the sincerity of the passage and his evident passion for his object of study are touching, but his commentary begs a number of questions, albeit in an interesting manner. If Marco and Maffeo are *finalmente* seen in their 'true light' here, one might ask why it is that this has taken such a long time and why their 'true light' flickers here, in the margin of the tradition, only to be immediately extinguished? In fact, the only lengthy narrative concerning the Polos in other redactions is the tale of the siege of Sanyanfu, which, as noted previously, is clearly fictional and which Z omits. This is not the only occasion when Z offers an anecdote about Marco that is unique to this redaction, the most notable other example being 68, 19–59. Though this passage is largely about rituals associated with the alluring virginity of Chinese girls, it concludes with an account of how Marco Polo found a ring that he had lost thanks to the services of an old woman who appealed to

---

[50] Ed. Benedetto, p. CLXIX.

idols for help: 'Et ego, Marcus, inveni quemdam meum anulum perditum isto modo; sed non quod eis aliquam fecerim oblationem vel homagium' (68, 59: 'And I, Marco, found in this way a ring I had lost, but without making any offering or paying homage to them'). This curious episode simultaneously implicates Marco in and distances him from idolatrous practices, but again the personal detail is exceptional. Generally speaking, in the entire tradition narrative details pertaining to the Polos and their lives abroad are few and far between, and often oblique, which in itself may suggest that the detail and elaboration of the episodes concerning the unrecognized Christian sect and the lost ring are suspect. Benedetto clearly *wanted* Marco Polo and his uncle to be 'authentic explorers', to be driven by curiosity and by a tactful thirst for knowledge, but, rather than being an early piece of high-quality anthropology, the passage smacks, in my view, of romanticized extemporization, no doubt inspired in part by Marco Polo's account of himself as a linguist and underpinned by a fantasy in which the true way of practising Christianity needs to be revealed to wayward Oriental Christians by their Occidental co-religionists. Benedetto's desire to find 'authenticity' and 'sincerity' – if by these terms one means unmediated autobiographic narration – in a text where these qualities are rather thin on the ground is all too evident, and it is perhaps precisely the sparseness of autobiographical detail that has encouraged modern readers to speculate and hypothesize about Marco's experiences and life. Be that as it may, this passage in Z is also a response to the *Devisement*'s overall tendency to collapse distinctions between religions, which, as I have suggested, may be read as reassuring or challenging, depending on your perspective. One thing is clear, however: for some at least – for instance, the Saracen scholar in the episode I have just examined or the branded Abyssinians – an inability to maintain clear distinctions between adherents of different religions is a problem.

Conclusion

This chapter has been about how the *Devisement*, particularly in the Franco-Italian redaction, challenges the received knowledge of its day, while also blurring the boundaries that have traditionally been erected around the categories on which knowledge rests. It does this (as we have seen in Chapters 1 and 2) without offering the reader a stable position from which to construct an alternative framework for knowledge. The subject and site of knowledge are mobile, and as they move so the nature of knowledge and its content move with them. Another world – textual and real – is presented in which important categories and elements of the knowledge base the European reader takes for granted are called into question, challenged and ultimately (sometimes) dissolved. As the reader is brought back to Europe, some distinctions re-emerge – and perhaps even more starkly, if the need to distinguish different religions through branding is anything to go on – but the question then is: once we know about this other, more fluid, world, can we still hold on securely to the old world view? The evidence of some manuscripts and redactions (the French redaction and particularly the illustrated manuscripts of this redaction; Pipino) suggests that some, perhaps many, medieval readers and transmitters resisted the challenge the *Devisement* represented (even if they could not resist the temptation of reading the text in the first place), recuperating it at least partially into more familiar frameworks and into a more familiar account of otherness. These manuscripts and redactions tend to suggest a more straightforward and clear-cut opposition between 'us' and 'them' than the *Devisement* in fact offers, one that the text itself often resists: indeed, as we saw in Chapters 1 and 2, the *Devisement*'s more troubling features have a remarkable tendency to survive in transmission, sometimes even when transmitters are seeking to eliminate them. Some modern readers, however, have responded far more to the conservative agenda set by some medieval transmitters of the *Devisement* than they have to the more radical potential of the text's earliest incarnations, perhaps because this enables the confirmation of a widely held view of medieval culture as grounded unthinkingly in blind prejudice – prejudice that has to be thrown off to produce modernity. Indeed, the *Devisement* resists any straightforward opposition between 'us' and 'them'. One reason why this is so is the strong investment in the idea of 'diversity': this is the subject of my final chapter.

4

Diversity and alterity: 'diversarum regionum mundanas diversitates'

In the thirteenth and fourteenth centuries Christian Europe confronted two related problems concerning its relation to the rest of the world. First, how was Christendom to turn back the apparently relentless and frequently bellicose expansion of Islam, in particular its reconquest of the Holy Land, to which many believed Christianity had inalienable historic rights? Secondly, was the vast, and in medieval terms global, empire of the Mongols that had made its presence felt sharply from the 1240s onwards, friend or foe, a potential ally against Islam or another, potentially devastating, threat? From the brutal Mongol invasions of Russia, Poland and Hungary in the early 1240s through the fall of Acre in 1291, Europe felt beleaguered. While the onslaught of plague from 1347 focused attention on problems closer to home (and also weakened Europe's ostensible enemies), it failed to lessen anxiety about European Christendom being overwhelmed. One reaction to this fear was a sharp sense of the alterity of the rest of the world and, perhaps almost inevitably, xenophobia.

There are certainly texts that inscribe virulent xenophobia – and in particular Islamophobia – while also exploring the possibility that the Mongols might become allies against Islam. A case in point, as we saw in the last chapter, is Hayton's *Flor des estoires* (1307), which ends with a stirring appeal to the Pope to mount a new crusade against Muslims so that 'la Terre Sainte, que fu arosée du precieus sanc Nostre Seignor Jhesu Crist, soit delivrée du poer des ennemis mescreans' ('the Holy Land, which was watered with the precious blood of our Lord Jesus Christ, may be delivered from the power of our miscreant enemies').[1] Hayton recalls the shedding of Christ's blood in the Holy Land here precisely to anticipate the shedding of far larger quantities of blood on the part of the *ennemis mescreans* of Christendom, which implies a violent and confrontational model of cultural encounter. Literary scholarship inspired by post-colonial theory and many historians of Christian–Muslim relations have tended to pick up on this view, suggesting that

---

[1] See Hayton, *La Flor des estoires*, in *Recueil des historiens des croisades: documents latins et français relatifs à l'Arménie*, II (Paris: L'Académie des Inscriptions et des Belles Lettres, 1906), p. 252 (accessible at: http://gallica.bnf.fr/).

medieval European culture had an essentially binary view of the world. On the one hand there were Christians, taken to be white and either from north-western Europe or at the very least from the Frankish diaspora; on the other hand there was the rest of the world, made up of Muslims (also known as pagans or Saracens) and 'idolaters', who were frequently assimilated to an undifferentiated category of non-Christian others. According to this view, the purpose of the copious tradition of medieval writing about the Orient was to represent 'the exorbitant otherness of an "outlandish" world'.[2] This gathering of all others into a single category of the 'exorbitantly foreign' is not only ideologically pernicious: its refusal to acknowledge the irreducible specificities of others amounts to ethical failure.[3]

As we saw in the last chapter, the *Devisement* does not bear out the claim that the main concern of Europeans writing about Orient is exorbitant otherness. In this chapter I will explore further how the *Devisement* toys with the uncanny and hybridity, presenting a challenging view of the world that assumes neither the pre-eminence of European culture nor a stark, binary contrast between Europe and the rest of the world. As we have seen, the *Devisement* offers a challenging engagement with difference that troubles the European subject's cultural, racial, religious and linguistic identity. This in turn suggests an openness to difference that is more in keeping with the kind of cultural traffic that Sharon Kinoshita sees at work in a range of twelfth- and thirteenth-century French and Occitan literary texts:[4] Kinoshita offers a view of medieval francophone literary culture that is as interested in crossing borders and blurring boundaries as it is in reifying them. But many medievalists are loath to accord the Middle Ages this kind of openness, so strong is the commitment to locating the pernicious ideological roots and preconditions of colonialism in medieval culture.[5] Thus, and perhaps paradoxically, the violent and confrontational world view exemplified by Hayton prevails in modern scholarship, rather than the more open models found in the *Devisement*.

The *Devisement* subverts an oppositional, binary view of the world in a variety of ways. For example, as we saw in Chapter 3, although xenophobic anti-Islamic sentiments surface in the text, particularly when it is describing places close to Europe, these knee-jerk positions are far outweighed by the way different religions – widely regarded as distinct – are represented as co-existing and as having a tendency to leak into each other. But perhaps the

---

[2] Syed Manzarul Islam, *The Ethics of Travel from Marco Polo to Kafka* (Manchester and New York: Manchester University Press, 1996), p. 149, writing of Marco Polo.

[3] See Geraldine Heng, *Empire of Magic: Medieval Romance and the Politics of Cultural Fantasy* (New York: Columbia University Press, 2003), p. 254, for whom Mandeville writes 'in the face of the exorbitantly foreign'.

[4] Sharon Kinoshita, *Medieval Boundaries: Rethinking Difference in Old French Literature* (Philadelphia: University of Pennsylvania Press, 2006).

[5] See further my 'Can the Middle Ages Be Postcolonial?', *Comparative Literature*, 61 (2009), 160–76.

most crucial way in which a different view of the world is offered is through the focus on diversity as an organizing principle of knowledge. The first section of this chapter will consequently be devoted to the category of diversity and how it is used in the *Devisement*: I will argue that the *Devisement*'s mode of representing difference is grounded primarily in what Derrida calls *différance* ('deferral') rather than binary opposition and also show how this is a process that informs its view of the symbolic order more generally.[6] Thus the focus on diversity does not simply have epistemological ramifications; it also inflects the *Devisement* on formal and structural levels. The second section is devoted to a discussion of a feature of Kublai Khan's realm that clearly particularly impressed Marco Polo: paper money. I hope to explain why Marco Polo found paper money so fascinating and the role the *Devisement* suggests it plays in the construction of an alternative symbolic order, one that can transcend difference. The final section will consider what is generally taken to be a radical form of alterity: cannibalism. To what extent do cannibals represent a radical otherness, playing the role of what, following Judith Butler, one might call the 'constitutive outside',[7] which is to say, that which is excluded from the dominant culture in order better to delineate its norms and boundaries, or are they too absorbed into a differential system? If they are so absorbed, this may imply an ethical openness to alterity that some have deemed impossible in medieval culture.

Diversity, division, devising

As we have already seen, the *Devisement* insists in its very first sentence on the world's diversity:

> Seignors enperaor et rois, dux et marquois, cuens, chevaliers et b[o]rgio[i]s, et toutes gens que volés savoir les **deverses** jenerasions des homes et les **deversités** des **deverses** region dou monde, si prennés cestui livre et le feites lire. (I, 1)
>
> (Lords, emperors and kings, dukes, marquises, counts, knight and burghers, and all you people who wish to know about the diverse kinds of men

---

[6] See Jacques Derrida, *De la Grammatologie* (Paris: Les Editions de Minuit, 1967), and *L'Ecriture et la différence* (Paris: Les Editions de Minuit, 1967).

[7] Judith Butler, *Gender Trouble: Feminism and the Subversion of Identity* (London and New York: Routledge, 1990), p 77: 'what remains "unthinkable" and "unsayable" within the terms of an existing cultural form is not necessarily what is excluded from the matrix of intelligibility within that form; on the contrary, it is the marginalised, not the excluded, the cultural possibility that calls for dread of minimally, the loss of sanctions [...] The "unthinkable" is thus fully within culture, but fully excluded from "dominant" culture.'

and all the diversities of the diverse regions of the world, take this book and have it read.)

This indicates from the outset a debt to the encyclopaedic tradition, which associated diversity particularly with India.[8] *Diversité* in this sense indexes the extraordinary variety to be found in the world and may be used to distinguish different kinds of people, animals, birds, plants, languages, products, geographical features, minerals, precious stones, religions and so on. The *Devisement* only very rarely (if ever) plays on the negative sense of *divers* and *diversité* as 'evil' or 'wickedness':[9] overall diversity is clearly something at which Marco Polo, Rustichello da Pisa and their readers might wonder.[10]

Katherine Park has drawn out with a good deal of finesse how the *Devisement*'s positive view of diversity as a primary feature of nature draws on an encyclopaedic tradition that its author(s) most probably knew in the vernacular, but which was of course more widely disseminated in Latin.[11] The *Devisement* is thus shot through, for Park, with categories deriving ultimately from Aristotle and Pliny, but she further suggests that diversity is viewed less as a philosophical category than as a motor for trade, which for Marco Polo is the means by which wealth and prosperity are created: 'Natural variety generates trade [...] and trade generates profit; thus Asia's extraordinary wealth compared to the relative poverty of Europe, can be traced directly to its diversity.'[12] This leads her to conclude: 'Placed in this economic and ethical context, Polo's *Divisament* acquires special meaning. A hymn to the world's diversity, it is also a sermon naturalizing and justifying trade.'[13] Whereas I think Park is quite correct that the *Devisement*'s debt to the encyclopaedic tradition is deliberate, it challenges, as we have already seen, some of the

---

[8] For example, *L'Image du Monde de Maître Gossouin: rédaction en prose*, ed. O.H. Prior (Lausanne and Paris: Payot, 1913), p. 111, where the chapter on India is headed 'Des diversitez d'Ynde'; Brunetto Latini, *Tresor*, ed. Pietro Beltrami, Paolo Squillacioti, Plinio Torri and Sergio Vatteroni (Turin: Einaudi, 2007), 1, 122, 21 ('Et sachiez que en inde et en cel païs la outre a maintes diversitez de genz'); Thomas de Kent, *Le Roman d'Alexandre ou Le Roman de toute chevalerie*, ed. Brian Foster and Ian Short, trans. Catherine Gaullier-Bougassas and Laurence Harf-Lancner (Paris: Champion, 2003), 6702–4 ('En Ethiope ad gent de diverse nature, / De diverse lignee, de diverse parleure, / Car trestoz en sunt de diverse engendrure'). Ethiopia and India are often represented as contiguous to each other in medieval sources.

[9] For a possible example see CLXI, 6, discussed below, p. 170.

[10] For dictionary entries, with numerous examples, see Godefroy, 2, 731, and 9, 398; TL, 2, 1968; FEW, 3, 107.

[11] Katherine Park, 'The Meaning of Natural Diversity: Marco Polo on the "Division" of the World', in Edith Sylla and Michael McVaugh (eds), *Texts and Contexts in Ancient and Medieval Science: Studies on the Occasion of John E. Murdoch's Seventieth Birthday* (Leiden and New York: Brill, 1997), pp. 134–47.

[12] 'The Meanings of Natural Diversity', p. 144.

[13] 'The Meanings of Natural Diversity', p. 146.

premises medieval writers drew from Pliny (whether directly or indirectly) about natural diversity, in that it has no truck with the monstrous races and corrects received wisdom on a number of exotic species and phenomena. I am also not persuaded that trade is the *Devisement*'s principal or main preoccupation. To be sure, attention is often paid to the commodities that are produced or traded in specific places, to the passage of merchants and indeed to currency and exchange. But so many other aspects of the natural world and human civilization are subject to scrutiny that trade needs to be seen as just part of the picture the text is painting and, as already noted in the introduction, as a 'merchants' manual' the *Devisement* is not particularly helpful since it lacks the practical details and guidance that might be expected.[14] Rather than linking diversity to Marco's putative mercantilism, I shall argue that 'diversity' in the *Devisement* functions primarily as a philosophical and epistemological category in that it is first and foremost a means of conceptualizing and organizing the representation of difference.

One index of this is the semantic leakage of *diversité* (< Latin *diversus*) or ontological diversity (i.e. the material or morphological differences between, for instance, different types of animal, different types of precious stone or, indeed, different races of people) into the epistemology of diversity, which is to say the apprehension and conceptual organization of diversity (*diviser* 'to divide', *estre divisé de* 'to differ from', < Latin *dividere, divisum*), and then the act of describing it (*devisement*, 'devising', 'description', also < Latin *dividere*), a leakage that may be enhanced in the Franco-Italian redaction by the exceptional mobility of the idiom's orthography and morphology.

Thus early in the *Devisement* we encounter the expression *estre divisé / estre devisé de* used to indicate the difference between different species of animals, but spelt differently in the space of two sentences:

> Et la pro<v>ense de coi nos comi<n>son ore est apellé Reobar. Les sien fr[u]it sunt datarl et pome de paraise et pistac et autres fruit, les quelz ne sunt en nostre leu froit. Et en ceste plaign a une generation d'osiaus que l'en appelle francolin, que sunt devisé a les autres francolin des autres pais: car il sunt noir et blance mesleemant, et les pies et les beco ont rouges. Les bestes sunt ausi divisee et voç dirai des bue primerament: les buef sunt grandisme et sunt tuit blance come nois, le poil ont peitet et plain, et ce avient por le caut leu; il ont les cornes cortes et groses et non agues, entre les spaules ont un çinb reont haut bien deus paumes. (XXXVI, 3–6)
>
> (And the province with which we begin now is called Rudbar. Its fruits are dates and apples of paradise, pistachios and other fruits not to be found in our cold climates. And on this plain there is a species of bird that is called

---

[14] Stephen G. Haw has recently argued that the field in which the *Devisement* shows most sustained interest is natural history: *Marco Polo's China: A Venetian in the Realm of Khubilai Khan* (London and New York: Routledge, 2006), Chapter 9.

francolin, which is different from the francolins of other countries: for they are piebald and their feet and beaks are red. Animals are also different [or possibly 'There are many different kinds of beast] and first I will tell you about the oxen: they are very large and entirely white as snow, with short and fine hair because of the hot climate of the place; they have short, thick horns, which are not sharp, and between their shoulders they have a round hump that is at least two hands high.)

The alternating spelling *devise / divisee* here is not significant since in Old and Middle French the orthographic distinction between the two Modern French verbs *diviser* and *deviser* has yet to emerge: indeed since both verbs derive from the same Latin etymon, in the medieval language it would seem that a single verb has a number of different senses and alternative spellings. 'To divide' something also means 'to describe' something, in other words 'to apprehend its diversity'; this then gives the sense 'to talk discursively' more generally, and eventually 'to converse'. Whereas some instances of ambiguity could have been resolved on a case-by-case basis, in others ambiguity may have been deliberate, or alternatively it may indicate that the different meanings were inextricably intertwined. Indeed, given that the overwhelming majority of chapters in the *Devisement* (including this one) are rubricated 'Ci devise de',[15] and given that the text in BNF f.fr. 1116 is entitled 'Le divisiment dou monde',[16] which is usually taken to mean 'the description of the world' but which could equally well mean 'the division of the world', 'division' and 'description' are always already imbricated in the *Devisement*. In the case of Chapter XXXVI, on the one hand, the diversity (or division) that is marked is that between the foreign and the familiar, 'us' and 'them': 'they' have fruits that do not grow in 'our' cold climates. On the other, the text is equally attentive to Asia's *internal* difference: the francolins of Rudbar are different from the francolins of other countries. However, the phrase 'que l'en appelle francolin' indicates that the reader is not necessarily expected to know what a francolin is, and since the bird (a type of partridge) is indigenous to Asia and Africa but not Europe, the focus here is clearly as much on the diversity of the world *outside* Europe as it is on Asia's diversity *from* Europe. Perhaps most tellingly, remarking on diversity in both cases triggers description: in the case of the oxen, a detailed description (XXXVI, 6–9).

If the spelling does not necessarily have a bearing on the meaning of words in the semantic cluster *diversité / diviser / deviser*, in some instances labile spelling nonetheless leads to a more obvious but nonetheless implicit collapsing of the different senses the words may imply:[17]

---

[15] The rubric of fourteen of the twenty chapters that follow the prologue begins 'Ci devise'.

[16] As noted, this is corrected by both Benedetto and Ronchi to 'Le divisament'.

[17] Cf. also : CLXXIV, 64 ('ont toutes bestes et oisiaus deviséç des nostres'); CLXXX,

Quant l'en a alés les xx jornee des montagnes que je voç a dit desovre, e por ponent, adonc treuve une plaine et une provence que est encore de le confin dou Mangi, que est apellé Sindinfa; et la mestre cité a a non Sindinfu, que mout fu jadis grant et nobles e mout hi a ja eu grant et riches rois. E[l]le gire environ bien xx miles; mes orendroit est devisé en tel mainere com je voç deviserai. (CXIV, 1–2)

(When one has crossed the mountains for twenty days as I just told you, to the west one finds a plain and a province that is still on the edges of Manzi and which is called Chengdu, the main city of which is Chendufu, which once was great and noble and had a great and powerful king. It is 20 miles in circumference but now is divided up [or possibly 'described'] in such a way as I will now tell you [or possibly: 'divide for you'].)

Here, although one instance is a past participle and the other a future, *deviser* ('to divide') and *deviser* ('to describe') have an identical spelling within the same clause. Are we in fact simply dealing with the same verb? If so, we can see here how its various meanings become imbricated with and leak into each other.

The descriptive technique of the *Devisement* does not always run to the same level of detail given for the francolins or oxen of Rudbar. Descriptions of places, in particular, often seem to spill over into cataloguing. As we saw in Chapter 2 (pp. 107–8), extensive sequences of chapters may be devoted to a series of similar-sounding places that are situated spatially and temporally in relation to each other, with sometimes relatively sparse details given, according to a relatively formulaic pattern about language, religion, trade, goods produced, currency and language. I will be returning to currency and language in more detail in the next section. For now let me return to a point I made in Chapter 2, namely that the difference in some instances between different places seems to come down to just one letter in the name, since otherwise they sound so similar, both in terms of their names and in terms of how they are described. Thus we learn in very similar terms that the people of Singiu (Zenzhou, CXXXV), Pingiu (Pizhou, CXXXVII) and Cingiu (Tongzhou, CXXXVIII) all have fine hunting, are idolaters and use the Great Khan's paper money; in addition, the people of Pingiu and Cingiu burn their dead, and the *mercandie* and *granz arz* of both Singiu and Cingiu are remarked upon, as are the fine castles one encounters on the way to Singiu and Pingiu. A reader who knows none of these places and may never have heard of them before might be forgiven for confusing them, or even

---

9 ('maintes deverses bestes devisees a toutes les autres dou monde'); CLXXXI, 4–5 ('Il hi a bestes de diverses faisonz e propemant singes, car il hi n'i a si deversemant faites, que voç dirois que ce soit home. Il hi a gat paul si deviséç que ce estoit mervoille'); CXCII, 9 ('il ont toutes bestes devisez a toutes les autres dou monde'); and CXCIII, 49 ('et maintes autres bestes ont il encore moutitude, deviséç a celz de nostres contrés').

for being indifferent to their supposed singularity. While indifference to the singularity of others may on one level have ethical implications,[18] on another level the effect here is to stress how the singularity of different places and things is established in relation to other places and things.

This differential account of the world suggests a multitude of variety, with shades of finely tuned distinctions, which in some respects is infinitely extensible beyond the confines of the text. Jacopo d'Aqui's anecdote (c. 1334) of Marco Polo saying on his deathbed that he had only recounted a fraction of what he had seen picks up on this implication,[19] a scenario that is repeated in Mandeville's *Le Livre des Merveilles* in terms that undoubtedly echo the *Devisement*'s use of the notion of diversity quite precisely.[20]

> Il y a plusours autres diversez pays et mout d'autres mervailles par dela qe jeo n'ay mie tout veu, si n'en saveroie proprement parler. Et meismement en païs ouquel j'ay esté y a plusours diversetés dont jeo ne fais point mencioun, qar trop seroit longe chose a tout deviser. Et pur ceo qe jeo vous ay deviseez d'ascunes pays vous deit suffyr quant au present. Qar si jeo devisoie tant quantquez y est par dela, un autre qe se peneroit et travailleroit le corps pur aler en celles marches et pur cercher le pays seroit empeschez par mes ditz a recompter nulles choses estranges, qar il ne porroit rien dire de novel en quoy ly oyantz y puissent prendre solacz. Et l'em dit toutdis qe choses novelles pleisent. Sy m'en taceray atant sanz plus racompter nulles diversetez qe soient par dela, a la fin qe cis qe vourra aler en celles parties y troeve assez a dire. (pp. 478–9)

> (There are many other diverse countries and many other marvels besides, so I have not seen everything and would not even be able to speak about them. And even in the countries I have visited there are diversities I have not mentioned, for it would take too long to describe everything. And because I have described many countries to you, this will have to be enough for you for the time being. For if I were to describe the rest, someone else who took the trouble and suffered to go to those regions and to seek out those countries would be prevented by my words from telling of anything strange, for he would have nothing new to say to please his audience. And as one always says, new things are pleasing. So I will stop now without talking about the other diversities beyond, so that the one who wishes to travel there may have something to say.)

---

[18] See Emmanuel Levinas, *Totalité et infini: essai sur l'extériorité* (The Hague: Martinus Nijhoff, 1961).

[19] See John Larner, *Marco Polo and the Discovery of the World* (New Haven, CT, and London: Yale University Press, 1999), pp. 44–5.

[20] Cited from Jean de Mandeville, *Le Livre des merveilles du monde*, ed. Christiane Deluz (Paris: CNRS, 2000).

I shall return to the relation of Mandeville's text to the *Devisement* in my Conclusion. The key point to note here is that the *Devisement* draws on the encyclopaedic tradition to inaugurate a discourse of diversity in which neither terminology nor descriptive technique suggests a reductive, oppositional view of a world, a discourse in which the European subject is not situated and defined in sharp contrast to others who become regarded collectively as the Other. On the contrary, she or he is invited to situate her- or himself as part (a very small part) of a larger system of differences to which she or he is both geographically and ontologically really quite marginal, and not the conceptual centre against which others are defined.

Generating meaning, or situating a subject, through difference and differentiation is, of course, a key feature of modern thought after the so-called 'linguistic turn' instantiated by Saussurian linguistics and then developed into a philosophical system by Derridean deconstruction. Meaning is both generated and deferred (another aspect of Derrida's neologism *différance*) along two parallel planes: perceived relations between material things or abstract ideas on the one hand, and the relation of signifiers along the signifying chain on the other (and the incessant movement along the signifying chain is why there will always be some element of diversity for which any one text fails to account). Nothing has meaning in and of itself, but only in relation to other things, with the plural here being vital, both for the medieval notion of diversity on which the *Devisement* draws and for Derrida. Thus both Marco Polo and Mandeville speak of *diversities* and not just diversity. The next section will explore the significance of this mode of conceiving of diversity with particular reference to two central themes in the *Devisement* – language and money – themes that turn out to be related, I argue, precisely because the text separates them so categorically.

Language and money

As already noted, given its insistence on diversity, one of the striking things about the *Devisement* is its uncanny knack for making places sound extremely similar. Even though the *Devisement*'s information is usually accurate in terms of the relative positions of different places, their political affiliations and main religions, their surrounding terrain and economic base, its descriptions are often highly formulaic. Two formulae in particular are used repeatedly in almost identical form. On the one hand, towns or provinces are said to have a language of their own; on the other, different towns or provinces are said to use the paper money of the Great Khan. For example:[21]

---

[21] In the first three quotations, *lengajes* and *rois* might seem plural. However, as noted in Chapter 2, the text's noun (and verb) morphology is highly mobile. In this instance, all translations and adaptations thought to be made directly from the Franco-

> Bangala est une provence ver midi [...] ont rois e lengajes por elz; il sunt pesimes ydres, ce entendés ydules. (CXXVI, 1–2)
>
> (Bengal is a province to the south [...] they have a king and language of their own: they are dreadful idolaters, which means they have idols.)
>
> Cangigu est une provence ver levant, il ha rois. Les jens <sunt> ydules et ont langajes por elz; il se renderent au grant <kan> et li font chascunz anz treu. (CXXVII, 1)
>
> (Jiaozhi Guo is a province to the east, with a king. The people are idolaters and have their own language; they are subjects of the Great Khan and each year pay him tribute.)
>
> Aniu est une provence ver levant, que sunt au grant kaan. Ils sunt ydules; il vivent de bestiames et dou profit de la tere; il ont langajes por elz.
> (CXXVIII, 1–2)
>
> (Heni is a province to the east, which belongs to the Great Khan. They are idolaters; they live from livestock and the land; they have their own language.)
>
> [S]uigiu est une tranoble cité e grant. Il sunt ydules et <sunt> au grant can et ont monoie de carte. (CLI 1)
>
> (Suzhoi is a very noble, big city. The people are idolaters, subjects of the Great Khan and have paper money.)
>
> Et ceste Vughin est encore une mout grant cité et noble. Il sunt ydres et <sunt> au grant kaan et ont monoie de carte. (CLI 13–14)
>
> (And this Wuxing is again a very large, noble city. They are idolaters, subjects of the Great Khan and have paper money.)
>
> Ceste cité de Ciangan est mout grant et rique. Il sunt ydres et sunt au grant kaan et ont monoie de carte. (CLI 15–16)
>
> (The city of Changxing is very large and rich. There are idolaters, subjects of the Great Khan and have paper money.)

Significantly, the role of race in Marco Polo's taxonomy of diversity is negligible: he comments on the black skin of people living near the equator but seems more interested in their nakedness than in their colour, while he dwells hardly at all on what today would be considered the racial characteristics

---

Italian redaction (the Tuscan, Venetian and French redactions, and *Z*) render *lengajes* and *rois* with a singular noun. What follows draws on my 'Coming Communities in Medieval Francophone Writing about the Orient', in Noah Guynn and Zrinka Stahuljak (eds), *Violence and the Writing of History in the Medieval Francophone World* (Cambridge: D.S. Brewer, 2013), pp. 187–201.

of Mongols, the Chinese, the Indo-Chinese, Tibetans, Arabs, Indians and so on. As Thomas Hahn notes, race is not always a key marker of difference in medieval culture.[22] Thus the main categories of difference and diversity that are deemed of interest in the *Devisement* are marked rather by other factors: religion, language, government and money.

Kublai Khan governed a myriad of different peoples, both in reality and in the *Devisement*'s account, and to varying degrees he drew these peoples into the Mongol empire's cultural norms and shared economy. However, these peoples practised a variety of different religions and spoke, it may be presumed, a very wide variety of languages. I have already discussed the representation of religious difference and syncretism in the *Devisement* (Chapter 3) and remarked in passing (in Chapter 2) that, when it is noted that the people of a city or a province 'have their own language', details about what this language is or how it differed from others are not given. It is thus linguistic difference *per se* that the text wishes to highlight rather than the specifics of any given instance, and the formula 'lengajes por elz' occurs no fewer than twenty-eight times. However, it is interesting to observe that it is never combined with the only other formula that is used of cities and provinces with an equal level of frequency, which is that 'they have paper money' – a reference to the bank notes Kublai famously introduced in China and elsewhere, money that is also described variously as 'la charte dou grant kaan' ('the paper of the Great Khan') or 'la monnaie du seignor' ('the lord's money'). There is striking geographic and stylistic symmetry here in that variations on 'they have paper money' occur twenty-nine times. There is no suggestion that paper currency meant everyone spoke the same language, and, as we have seen, the *Devisement* tells us Marco Polo learned to speak, read and write four Oriental languages in order to function effectively in his work as a functionary of some kind for Kublai Khan (XVI, 1), which suggests a keen awareness of the multilingual nature of the Mongol empire.[23] But there does nonetheless seem to be an implication that the barriers that linguistic diversity helps to erect between different groups of people dissolve with a shared currency, in that it is never remarked that a city or province where paper money is accepted has its own language. Perhaps, therefore, we can better understand the implications of the role of paper money in the

---

[22] Thomas Hahn, 'The Difference the Middle Ages Makes: Color and Race before the Modern World', *Journal of Medieval and Early Modern Studies*, 31 (2001), 1–37 (8). See also Robert Bartlett, 'Medieval Concepts of Race and Ethnicity', *Journal of Medieval and Early Modern Studies*, 31 (2001), 39–56: Bartlett argues that, because it was believed that all people shared common descent from Noah's three sons, environment (particularly climate) and culture were thought to be the main determiners of racial differences.

[23] Apart from Mongol, it is believed that Persian was used widely as an administrative language and that it quickly became the *lingua franca* of the Mongol empire. See Pierre Racine, *Marco Polo et ses voyages* (Paris: Perrin, 2012), 'De Gengis Khan à Kubilay'. See also Stephen G. Haw, *Marco Polo's China*, Chapter 1.

Devisement by considering why many of the communities that do not accept it are represented as constituted and defined either primarily or in part by having their own language.

One important question posed by theorists of community concerns the role of essence and/or identity in community formation. Jean-Luc Nancy, for example, suggests that modern philosophy has implicitly posited an (imperfect) idea of community grounded in an essential identity: 'la communauté n'est pas seulement la communication intime de ses membres entre eux, mais aussi la communication organique d'elle-même avec sa propre essence' ('community is grounded not only in the intimate communication of its members among themselves, but also in its inner organic communication with its own essence').[24] But, as Giorgio Agamben argues, drawing on medieval philosophy, 'non vi è differenza di essenza fra la natura commune e l'ecceità' ('there is no difference in essence between common nature and ipseity').[25] For Nancy '[la communauté] est faite avant tout du partage et de la diffusion ou de l'imprégnation d'une identité dans une pluralité dont chaque membre, par là même, ne s'identifie que par la médiation supplémentaire de son identification au corps vivant de la communauté' ('community is formed above all by the sharing and diffusion, or from the saturation, of an identity in a plurality with which each member, through this very process, only identifies by the supplementary mediation of his or her identification with the living body of the community'), suggesting that what has defined community historically is a shared but singular essence.[26] Yet for Agamben singularity is in essence elusive: 'l'idea et la natura commune non costituiscono l'essenza della singolarità [...] la singolarità è, in questo senso, assolutamente inessenziale' ('a common idea and nature do not constitute the essence of singularity [...] singularity, in this sense, is absolutely inessential').[27] This leads him to conclude that 'Il rapporto fra commune e singolare non è più allora pensabile come il permanere di una identica essenza nei singoli individui e il problema stesso dell' individuazione rischia di presentarsi come uno pseudoproblema' ('the relation between the common and the singular is no longer then thinkable as the residue of an identical essence in singular individuals and the very problem of individuation risks becoming a pseudo-problem').[28]

Although the two approaches differ on the role and value of singularity, there is nonetheless common ground on the need to realize the full potential of ideas of community. For Nancy, common essence may be realized only as a future potential, or indeed in some respects as a future perfect, since 'community', he suggests, is often represented as always already lost. Yet 'commu-

---

[24] *La Communauté désœuvrée*, 2nd edn (Paris: Christian Bourgeois, 1999), p. 30.
[25] *La comunità che viene*, 2nd edn (Turin: Bollati Boringhieri, 2001), p. 20.
[26] *La Communauté désœuvrée*, p. 30.
[27] *La comunità*, p. 20.
[28] *La comunità*, p. 20.

nity' thus conceived nonetheless relies on a common essence that requires exclusion as much as inclusion: notions of 'community' can therefore lead to totalitarian, brutal regimes that institutionalize violence, oppositional politics and ideologies. Rather than assuming a common essence, perhaps, what we therefore need to experience (or to aspire to), according to Nancy, is a utopic *être-en-commun* (being-in-common), an alternative model of community, *la communauté désœuvrée*, or 'inoperative community', that allows for difference and heterogeneity. Similarly, for Agamben the aim should be 'l'idea di una comunità *inessenziale*, di un convenire che non concerne in alcun modo un' essenza' ('the idea of an inessential community, of an accord that does not concern essence in any way'),[29] which is to say a 'coming community' yet to be realized, grounded in solidarity with being itself, one that might be likewise inimical therefore to totalitarian regimes and hegemonic ideologies. Both the 'inoperative community' and the 'coming community' are thus utopian notions that posit community as a potential good grounded in relationality itself, a potential good that has yet to be fully attained.

With this in mind, it is striking that if, on the one hand, the *Devisement* represents the myriad of communities that do not use paper money as distinguished by each having a language of their own, as therefore deriving their singularity from their language, on the other hand having a language of their own is precisely something they share. Language is thus accorded a special status here, in that whereas multiple communities are represented as Muslim, or Christian, or idolaters, or a mixture of different religions, or as merchants, farmers, bandits, dishonest or honest etc., when a group is said to have *langajes por elz*, this apparently differentiates them absolutely from others despite any internal differences and even though the language in question is not identified. Language *per se* thus becomes a marker of difference, decisive in the formation of the communities Marco Polo, Rustichello da Pisa and their readers encounter, suggesting a world fragmented into atomized but similar units, with some individuals (such as Marco himself) circulating among them. Yet if all these communities have in common having a 'language of their own', perhaps they have, potentially at least, structural similarities that mean they are not as divided as might at first glance seem? Perhaps there is a 'coming community' here yet to be realized? If so, what might this look like, and what could be the agent of unity?

This Babel contrasts with the vast array of lands and provinces that use paper money. As already noted, the two formulae 'ont lengajes por elz' and 'ont monoie de carte' are never combined. The *Devisement* thereby implicitly marks the distinction between the lands directly controlled by Kublai Khan and the rest of the world by noting where paper money circulates,

---

[29] *La comunità*, p. 20.

even though other peoples may pay tribute to him.[30] The frequency of the two formulae and their contrasting usage are clearly deliberate, particularly when it is considered that in other texts that certainly used the *Devisement* as a source (Hayton and Mandeville, for example), paper money is mentioned only briefly and either language is rarely an issue (as for Mandeville), or different scripts are as remarkable as different languages *per se* (as for Hayton).[31] In some senses paper money is thus *the* distinguishing feature of Kublai Khan's government and of his sovereignty.

The production, function and circulation of paper money are unusually accorded a whole chapter of the *Devisement* (XCVI), yet this chapter has received surprisingly little attention from an interpretive point of view. Whereas some historians have questioned how profoundly Marco Polo understood the economics and mechanisms of paper money, the chapter's real significance lies not in its accuracy as an account of paper money but rather in how it postulates an alternative economic order, which effectively is an alternative symbolic order. And given the frequency with which the use of paper money is signalled and its place in the account that is offered of the Mongol empire's technological wizardry, there can be little doubt that paper money should be counted among the most significant of the *merveilles* associated with Kublai Khan.

If Kublai's prosperity surpasses that of all other lords in the world put together, this is directly attributable, according to Marco, to his paper money:

> Or voç ai contés la mainere et la raison por coi le grant sire doit avoir et ha plus tresor que nuls homes de ceste monde; et si vos dirai une greignor chouse: que tuit les seignor de<u> siecle ne ont si grant richese come le grant sire a solemant. (XCVI, 15)

> (Now I have told you how and the reasons why the great lord has to have and has more treasure than any other in the world; and I will tell you something even greater: that all the lords of the world put together are not as rich as the great lord by himself.)

On the one hand, this clearly contributes to the hyperbolic and utopian description the *Devisement* offers of Kublai's magnificence: his court is larger, more elaborate and more wondrous than that of any Occidental lord, his hunts more extensive, his learning and appetites (for food, sex, power) more prodigious. On the other, is it just opulence that is admired here? Clearly the

---

[30] The division of the Mongol empire after the death of Genghis Khan meant that much of the Middle East and Central Asia paid tribute to the Great Khan rather than being controlled directly by him. Kublai's main power base was, of course, China.

[31] For passing references to paper money see: Hayton, *Flor*, p. 121; and Mandeville, *Livre*, pp. 396–7. Hayton frequently remarks on different scripts, and Mandeville manuscripts often contain alphabets in different languages.

social order that paper money symbolizes is every bit as crucial to the sense of wonder.[32]

The *Devisement* articulates a clear awareness of the symbolic value of paper money as opposed to coins, precious stones, precious metals, silk or other commodities. First and foremost, the value of paper money is not grounded in the intrinsic or essential value of the material from which it is made: thus the equivalence of different notes to Occidental coins is carefully calibrated, and it is pointed out that value is not dependent on weight (XCVI, 3 and 6). Secondly, value depends on title and more specifically is guaranteed by the authority of Kublai himself, since his seal goes on each note, to show it is genuine (XCVI, 11).[33] Thirdly, value is explicitly defined as exchange value: it is not the notes themselves that are valuable, but what you can exchange them for (XCVI, 5–8). The whole system works through a network of substitutions and exchanges, such that paper money becomes symbolic of the symbolic order itself, a symbolic order that Kublai's subjects are said to embrace 'willingly': 'Et si voç di que toutes les jens et regionz d'omes que sunt sout sa seignorie prennent voluntier cestes chartre en paiemant' (XCVI, 5: 'And I tell you that all the people and all the regions of men who are under his sovereignty willingly accept this paper in payment'). Indeed, it is as if they would in fact rather have the paper money than the goods given up in exchange: 'et les mercaant le prennent moult voluntieres, por ce que il le metent puis en toutes les chouses qu'il achatent, por toutes les teres do grant sire' (XCVI, 9: 'and the merchants take it very willingly, because with it they are able to buy everything in all the lands of the great lord'). This utopian vision of the effects of paper money is tempered, however, by the threat of violence: 'nulz ne le ose refuser a poine de pardre sa vie' (XCVI, 4: 'no one dares refuse it on pain of death'). Paradoxically, Kublai's subjects are free to accept paper money but not free to refuse it. Although the better, more prosperous world instantiated by paper money thus apparently depends on a subliminal threat of violence, as Slavoj Žižek argues of precisely this kind of *choix forcé,* 'there is nothing totalitarian about it. The subject who thinks he can avoid this paradox and really have a free choice is a *psychotic* subject, one who retains a kind of distance from the symbolic order – who is

---

[32] See Racine, *Marco Polo*, 'Marco Polo au service du grand khan': 'la circulation du papier-monnaie dans la majeure partie de la Chine atteste que le souverain entendait unifier l'empire chinois' ('the circulation of paper money throughout most of China demonstrates that the sovereign aimed to unite the Chinese empire').

[33] The seal as signifier would therefore be the main distinction between paper money and the porcelain tokens or stones that the *Devisement* notes are used elsewhere: see, for example, CXXIX, 6.

not really caught in the signifying network.'³⁴ The refusal of paper money is tantamount to enacting self-banishment.³⁵

Paper money allows Kublai's subjects to buy things, but more importantly, as Suzanne Conklin Akbari suggests, it allows them to buy into a social network of exchange, a network that concerns the circulation of signs as much as commodities, binding individuals from different places and cultural outlooks together in a symbolic community.³⁶ For in Marco Polo's world it would seem that communities have *either* a language of their own *or* paper money. As Yunte Huang suggests in passing, 'money may be a universal language',³⁷ as if the circulation and acceptance of paper money in itself makes any linguistic differences unworthy of remark, or even as if paper money allows communities to transcend linguistic difference, to form a larger, more fluid and yet peaceful and connected community, performatively constituted by the acceptance of the paper currency. Is this perhaps a kind of 'comunità *inessenziale*' as envisaged by Agamben, one that 'non concerne in alcun modo un' essenza' ('does not concern in any way an essence')?³⁸ If so, it is interesting that Kublai's regime apparently avoids the fragmentation marked by every town and province having 'a language of its own' only through the threat that rejecting the symbolic order represented by paper money may lead to violence.

In his discussion of Baudelaire's *La fausse monnaie* Jacques Derrida argues that all money – whether counterfeit or genuine – depends on an *acte de foi* (act of faith),³⁹ requiring both credit and creditability, which is constitutive of authority as well as guaranteed by it. Money, in other words, instantiates and yet is a product of shared belief. It is thereby a prototype for, as well as a form of, fiction, profoundly analogous to both language and literature.⁴⁰ Michel Foucault also underlines these points: 'Dire que la monnaie est un gage, c'est dire qu'elle n'est rien de plus qu'un jeton reçu de consentement commun – pure fiction par conséquent' ('to say that a coin's value is guaranteed is to say that it is nothing more than a token with commonly recognized

---

[34] Slavoj Žižek, *The Sublime Object of Ideology* (London and New York: Verso, 1989), pp. 165–9 ('The Forced Choice of Freedom').

[35] See Giorgio Agamben's influential *Homo Sacer: il potere sovrano e la nuda vita* (Turin: Einaudi, 1995), pp. 116–23, on the ban and its relation to violence and power.

[36] 'Currents and Currency in in Marco Polo's *Devisement dou monde* and *The Book of John Mandeville*', in Suzanne Conklin Akbari and Amilcare A. Iannucci (eds), *Marco Polo and the Encounter of East and West* (Toronto: University of Toronto Press, 2008), pp. 110–30 (pp. 124–8).

[37] 'Marco Polo: Meditations on Intangible Economy and Vernacular Imagination', in Conklin Akbari and Iannucci (eds), *Marco Polo and the Encounter of East and West*, p. 276.

[38] *La comunità*, p. 20.

[39] *Donner le temps 1: La fausse monnaie* (Paris: Galilée, 1991), p. 124.

[40] *Donner*, p. 113.

value – and thus pure fiction').[41] Money, for Foucault as for Derrida, functions primarily as a sign, as a form of representation that grounds reciprocity and mutual belief.[42] As such, it also partakes of the economy of the gift as conceived anthropologically: it thus dissolves the distinction between giving and taking, as in the scene in which Kublai's subjects exchange their precious stones (offered to him as a 'present', XCVI, 7) for his paper money, which they take (XCVI, 9). Who is giving what to whom here? Who is giving, who taking? The wealth may in some senses flow in only one direction, but there is no doubt that paper money is empowering for those who use it, that it binds them together.

The *Devisement* thus implies both an analogy and a contrast between language and currency that invite reflection. Both allow for exchange; both engender (while also reflecting) community formation, but the latter on a larger and more inclusive scale. It might be tempting to see Marco Polo's preoccupation with money simply as a reflection of his outlook as a merchant. Indeed, as we have seen, one influential reading of the *Devisement* sees it as an elaborate 'merchants' manual' or primarily as a merchant's view of the world.[43] However, as I have suggested any strictly 'mercantile' interpretation fails to account for the complex problems of interpretation posed by its indeterminate narrative voice, by its alternation of description and narrative, by the way it draws on the conventions of a range of disparate genres (prose romance, chronicle, encyclopaedias, as well as merchants' manuals) and by its languages of transmission. The 'coming community' Marco portrays in the Far East is not simply a proto-capitalist paradise for merchants, but rather an alternative symbolic order interested in a new way of exchanging signs as much as in the traffic of objects.

Others who eat others

Travel and accounts of travel have always had ethical implications, even before the age of carbon footprints and eco-tourism. To travel is to encounter others, and how one treats and reacts to those others, not just in what is called the contact zone of the actual encounter but also in the virtual contact zone of the textual account of that encounter, is an ethical challenge.[44] In his thought-provoking *The Ethics of Travel from Marco Polo to Kafka*, Syed

---

[41] *Les Mots et les choses: une archéologie des sciences humaines* (Paris: Gallimard, 1966), p. 194.
[42] *Les Mots et les choses*, pp. 187 and 191–2.
[43] See F. Borlandini, 'Alle origini del libro di Marco Polo', in *Studi in onore di Amintore Fanfani*, 6 vols (Milan: Giuffrè, 1962), I, pp. 107–47.
[44] On the 'contact zone', see Mary Louise Pratt, *Imperial Eyes: Travel Writing and Transculturation* (London and New York: Routledge, 1992), pp. 6–7.

Islam attempts to think through the ethical implications of travel writing with particular reference to the *Devisement* by adopting a distinction between what he calls sedentary and nomadic travellers. Sedentary travellers, however far they may wander from home, gaze at others over an unbridgeable chasm always already put in place between themselves and the others, between their culture and the other; they thus cannot help 'othering' the others, underlining their strangeness, their lack of civilization, their barbarism. Others are thus *unheimlich* in a literal sense – unhomely – and no true home or refuge is ever to be found among them. Sedentary travel, then, is a narcissistic undertaking since it is about confirming one's own identity and since any engagement with others, despite the obsessive othering in which sedentary travellers engage, in fact fails to see their true alterity. For Islam, Marco Polo inaugurates a tradition of Western travel writing to which almost all subsequent texts in the tradition belong: thus, to quote Islam, 'all these intrepid travellers, despite moving so much and so far in space, did not seem to have travelled at all'.[45]

Nomadic travel, on the other hand:

> is to do with encounters with otherness that fracture both a boundary and an apparatus of representation: it is a performative enactment of becoming other. In the ethical sense, only nomadic travel deserves the name 'travel' [...] And on the cross-cultural plane, nomadic travel also impels one to come face to face with the other, without the paranoia of othering that represents the other in relation to oneself.[46]

Islam is indexing two main theoretical frameworks here: Levinas on the one hand, for whom the other is fundamentally unknowable, and whose alterity therefore should be acknowledged by the ethical subject through a 'face-to-face', rather than made into an object of knowledge;[47] then, on the other hand, Deleuze and Guattari, for whom the designation of others as an object of knowledge effectively deterritorializes them, only to reterritorialize them within a binary (and eurocentric) epistemological framework of self and other.[48] The ideal of nomadic travel that Islam expounds, largely though through the negative exemplum of the *Devisement* as an instance of sedentary travel, is paradoxically – by implication at least – best represented for Islam by Kafka, an author largely sedentary in life. Thus the *Devisement*, which is motivated by the movements of a globe-trotter by anyone's standards, is emblematic of a mode of travel that 'settles for a representational practice

---

[45] Islam, *Ethics of Travel*, p. vii.

[46] Islam, *Ethics of Travel*, p. vii.

[47] For example, see Islam, *Ethics of Travel*, pp. 87–94, drawing mainly on Levinas, *Totalité et infinie*.

[48] For example see Islam, *Ethics of Travel*, pp. 40–1 and 101–111, drawing mainly on Gilles Deleuze and Félix Guattari, *Kafka: pour une littérature mineure* (Paris: Editions de Minuit, 1975).

that scarcely registers an encounter with the other'; Kafka, on the other hand, 'shows us both the imprisoning spaces of power and how to escape them'.[49]

Others have taken issue with Syed Islam's reading. For example, John Larner is critical of his argument that Marco is 'holding up for inspection the "disorders" of the East'[50] and that he postulates 'a total "otherness" between Christianity and non-Christianity',[51] and, by implication at least, he is also highly dismissive of Islam's theoretical framework. For my part, while I agree with Larner that Islam's presentation of Marco Polo's text may be 'unjust' in the sense that I do not believe the *Devisement* is ideologically retrograde and offensive in the way Islam seems to think,[52] I do on the other hand think that Islam's theoretical framework and indeed many of the insights on individual passages that it enables are suggestive, even if I do not agree with his reading of *Devisement*.

For Islam, as for many others, cannibalism represents a limit case of 'othering':

> Marco Polo's text abounds in dietary transgressions [...], which reach their limit in anthropophagy. The nature of this taboo is so fundamental to a civil order that it cannot be named in a list of dietary prohibitions. Leviticus and Deuteronomy, therefore, despite being meticulous in drawing an exhaustive taxonomy of dietary prohibitions, passed over it in silence. But the othernesss of the other as the mark of exorbitant abomination can be named with it. It signals the extreme point of the relative difference between habitudes, where the degree zero of 'our' manners and customs rises up from its absolute silence to become the sonorous norm among 'them'.
>
> Just as dietary pollution is widespread among the uncivil races, so is the habit of man-eating. Moreover, the civil races, following their own dietary abominations, practice cannibalism too.[53]

Islam is not, of course, alone in according such importance to cannibalism in the analysis of pre-modern European culture from a post-colonial perspective. An impressive body of scholarship examines Europe's fascination with cannibalism during and since the age of discovery; similarly, it has been argued that the stress anthropology places upon the, in reality rather rare, phenomenon of cannibalism has played a key role in continuing to propagate the myth that outside civilized Europe cannibalism was rampant, and that in places where the veneer of civilization is thin cannibalism could resurface, so ubiquitous is our primitive urge to devour each other.

---

[49] Islam, *Ethics of Travel*, p. 42.
[50] Larner, *Marco Polo*, p. 98.
[51] Larner, *Marco Polo*, p. 102.
[52] Larner, *Marco Polo*, p. 103.
[53] Islam, *Ethics of Travel*, pp. 161–2.

As William Arens has argued, cannibalism is always located at the furthest and latest outposts of Western expansion (in the Caribbean and South America in the fifteenth and sixteenth centuries, in Africa in the nineteenth, in New Guinea and Polynesia in the twentieth).[54] Thus, as Peter Hulme puts it, cannibalism should be understood as existing primarily as a discourse, the main question being: 'Why were Europeans so desirous of finding confirmation of their suspicions of cannibalism?'[55] In other words cannibalism is, to cite Hulme again, 'a trope of exceptional power'.[56]

Early modernists have a tendency to claim cannibalism as a peculiarly early modern trope. Thus Frank Lestringant states: 'Columbus can be credited with the discovery not only of America, but also of the cannibal.'[57] He goes on to acknowledge forebears of the early modern cannibal among classical and medieval monstrous races, but for Lestringant 1492 is nonetheless a watershed, 'a curious metamorphosis' in the history of the trope of cannibalism, so that the coining of a new term for anthropophagy reflects the emergence of a new episteme, that of colonialism.[58] According to this account, cannibalism is a graphic corporeal metaphor that projects on to others the sublimated impulse of Western colonialism to consume, while articulating a primordial fear that the tables may at any point be turned. This, of course, situates literary representations of cannibalism firmly in what Islam calls sedentary travel.

Medievalists, however, are suspicious of the evocation of the 1492 watershed, which is often invoked, as María Rosa Menocal has argued so eloquently, precisely to occlude persistent aspects of medieval culture that early modernists find troublesome and would prefer to brush under the carpet of history.[59] To what extent, one might ask, is there an epistemological rupture in the history of representations of cannibalism? In fact, Columbus's and his contemporaries' authorities and sources are very familiar to medievalists when it comes to descriptions of cannibals and monstrous races: the influence of Pliny, Isidore and so on is palpable. Furthermore, Geraldine Heng, in her influential *Empire of Magic*, puts an argument concerning cannibalism that is similar in many ways to that made by early modernists, with the additional

---

[54] William Arens, 'Rethinking Anthopophagy', in Francis Barker, Peter Hulme and Margaret Iversen (eds), *Cannibalism and the Colonial World* (Cambridge: Cambridge University Press, 1998), pp. 39–62 (p. 40).

[55] Peter Hulme, 'The Cannibal Scene', in Barker, Hulme and Iversen (eds), *Cannibalism and the Colonial World*, pp. 1–38 (p. 4).

[56] Hulme, 'The Cannibal Scene', p. 4.

[57] Frank Lestringant, *Cannibals: The Discovery and Representation of the Cannibal from Columbus to Jules Verne* (Berkeley and Los Angeles: University of California Press, 1997), p. 15.

[58] Lestringant, *Cannibals*, p. 16.

[59] María Rosa Menocal, *Shards of Love: Exile and the Origins of the Lyric* (Durham, NC, and London: Duke University Press, 1994), pp. 1–54.

twist, she suggests, that romance – that privileged medieval textual space where history meets cultural fantasy – seeks (unsuccessfully) to repress the traumatic memory of a real-life episode of cannibalism in Syria in 1098, in which crusaders roasted and ate the flesh of enemy soldiers rather than face starvation. For Heng, romance is thus 'a genre of *the nation*' and specifically 'a genre of the English nation in the Middle Ages', fearful of a barbarous other but instantiating an 'English communal identity by presenting Englishmen as a unity of Christian military aggressors who gleefully gobble up the Islamic Levantine enemy'.[60]

Heng's account is suggestive, but also highly selective. Surprisingly, given her post-colonial perspective, her view of romance as genre has decidedly anglocentric horizons, and there are a number of points on which I would take issue with her.[61] But she does show how cannibalism is a primary mechanism of othering in medieval culture, how it is an unspeakable repressed that nonetheless always returns. And within Islam's framework it is also an index of the extent to which romance may be inscribed in a tradition of sedentary travel writing, in that any encounter with the other inevitably leads to a proto-Imperialist consume-or-be-consumed confrontation, not to a Levinasian 'face-to-face'.

Medieval mechanisms of othering, in both Heng and Islam's accounts,[62] share a tendency to lump all others together as representative of a 'malignant otherness' against which a dominant Christian identity is defined according to a logic that is rigidly binary: us and them. This in turn means that Islam's reading of the *Devisement* is troubled by one aspect of the text: its focus on the myriad of diversities (*diversités*, plural) that Marco Polo encounters on his travels. I have argued throughout this book – and this is my main point of disagreement with Islam – that the *Devisement* does *not* divide the world according to a binary logic (Christians vs. the rest) and that consequently the othering that is clearly enacted in this text has far more ethical potential than that of many comparable medieval texts. This is because, on the one hand, in the *Divisement* difference is never allowed to sit within a binary logic, and on the other, because the narrative impetus of the text (as opposed to its narrated content) moves as much towards an othering of the self as an othering of the others that are represented. In other words, the division of the world the *Devisement* proposes is one of deferral rather than opposition, a deferral that effectively decentres the centre from which Marco ostensibly departs, and one which, as I have suggested, is as much concerned with what Homi Bhabha calls a 'difference within' as with underlining the radical alterity of others.[63] Indeed, if Marco himself figures this 'difference within' both at the

---

[60] Heng, *Empire*, pp. 6, 7, 9.
[61] See further Gaunt, 'Can the Middle Ages Be Postcolonial?'
[62] See Heng, *Empire*, pp. 28–9, and Islam, *Ethics of Travel*, p. 140.
[63] Homi Bhabha, *The Location of Culture* (London and New York: Routledge, 1994),

Great Khan's court, where he claims to have resided for almost two decades as one of his foreign administrators, thus as one who both belonged and yet did not, and then upon his return home, where his time abroad makes him a perpetual outsider, whose tales of otherness are not to be believed by all, then his journey is genuinely nomadic, in that he moves inexorably towards the *Unheimlich* and can never truly return home.

The *Devisement*'s penchant for differential as opposed to binary logic is illustrated by its formal properties (narrative voice, language) as well as by its treatment of a range of themes (religion and money, for example). What then of cannibalism? Are cannibals represented as 'the basic index of cultural limit', and are they then the ultimate sign of 'the exorbitant difference' that is the object of what Islam calls Marco's 'singular pursuit', which in turn means that he 'never breaches this mask to risk an encounter with the other'?[64]

The first thing to say is that cannibalism is not represented in the *Devisement* as widespread in Asia (as Islam suggests). In fact, there are just six instances of it in the Franco-Italian redaction:[65]

1 LXXV, 19–23 Tibetan and Kasmiri *astroniques* and *enchanteor* who reside in the Great Khan's court at Ciandu (Shangdu) 'ont une tel uçance com je vos dira: car je voç di que quant un home est jugiés a mor, et soit mors par la seignorie, il le prenne\<n\>t et le font cuire et le menuient; mes [s]e il morust da sa mort il ne le mengient mie' (LXXV, 23: 'have a custom such as I will now relate for you: for I tell you that when a man is condemned to die and dies at the hands of the law, they take him and cook him and eat him; but if he dies a natural death, they do not eat him'). This first mention of cannibalism is introduced as 'une mervoille'.

2 CLV, 6–8 The inhabitants of Fugiu (Fuzhou), at the limits of Cathay, 'menuient de toutes brutes couses; e menuient ausi cars d'ome mout voluntieres, puis que il ne soit mors de sa mort; mes celes que sunt ocis de fer il le menuient tuit e le ont por mout bone carne [...] il vont tout jors occiant homes, et boivent le sang, puis le menuient tuit; et ce porcacent tout jor, d'aler occir homes por boier le sang et por

p. 13.
[64] Islam, *Ethics of Travel*, p. 162.
[65] Just five in the French and Z redactions. The equivalents to these passages in the French, Tuscan and Z redactions are as follows. French redaction: 1) 74, 84–7 (much abbreviated); 2) no equivalent; 3) 160, 21–9; 4) 165, 19–28; 5) 165, 104–34; 6) 167, 6–9. Tuscan redaction: 1) 74, 21 (much abbreviated); 2) 151, 6–8; 3) 157, 3–5; 4) 162, 9–10; 5) 164, 3–8; 6) 168, 5. Z redaction: 1) no equivalent; 2) 88, 10–16; 3) 94, 9–10; 4) 99, 12; 5) 101, 8–13; 6) 105, 4.

mangier le cars' (CLV, 6 and 8: 'they eat many vile things; and they also willingly eat human flesh, as long as the man has not died a natural death; but they will eat those who have died by the sword in their entirety and they consider it very good meat [...] they go about killing men all the time in order to drink their blood and eat their flesh'). They are 'les plus cruelz homes dou monde' (8: 'the cruellest men in the world').

3 CLXI, 6–8   With reference to the inhabitants of the Japanese islands, Marco notes that 'Les fais de cestes ydules sunt de tantes deversités et de tantes [e]vres de diables qu'il ne fait pas a mentovoir en nostre livre, por ce que trop seroit mauvés chouse a oir por les cristienz; et por ce en laieron de cestes ydres e voç conteron d'autres couses. / Mes tant vos en dirai seulamant que je vuoil que voç sachiés que cesti ydres de cestes ysles, quant il prennent aucun homes que ne soit lor amis, se il ne se puet rachater por monoie, il convoie tuit sez parens e seç amis; et dit «je vuoil que voç veignés mengier ho moi a mon astiaus». Et adonc fait occire le home qu'il a pris et le menuie con seç parenç, et entendés qu'il le fait cuire: et ceste chars d'ome ont il por la meilor viande qu'il peusent avoir.' ('The deeds of these idolaters are so diverse and so much the work of the devil that it is not suitable to relate them for Christians to hear; and for this reason we will leave these idolaters and tell you of other things. But I will say only that I want you to know that these idolaters from these islands, when they capture men who are not among their friends, if they cannot be bought by ransom, they summon all their relations and friends and say "I want you to come and eat at my house". And then they kill the man they have captured and eat him with their relations, and you should realize that they cook him: and they consider this human flesh among the best meat that one can have.')

4 CLXVI, 8   Those who live in the cities of Java are civilized because they have converted to Islam, 'mes celes des montagnes sunt tiel como bestes, car je voç di tout voiramant qu'il menuient cars d'onmes et toutes autres cars e bonne e mauvase' ('but those from the mountains are like beasts, for I tell you truly that they eat human flesh and any other flesh, whether it be good or bad').

5 CLXVIII, 3–9   The people of Sumatra will suffocate a terminally ill relative. 'Et quant il est mort, il le font cuire: et puis tuti les parens

dou mors vienent et le menuient tout. Et si voç di qu'il menuient encore toutes les meroles que sunt dedens les osse; et ce font il por ce que il ne velent que en remagne aucune sustance, car il dient, se il hi remansist aucune sostance, que cel sostance feroit vermes, les <quel> mor<r>oient por defaute de mangier; et de la mort de cesti vermes dient que l'arme dou mort en auroit grande donmajes e peicés; e por ce le menuient tout. Et aprés [qu]e le ont mangiés, il prenent les oses, et le metent en une belle archete, et puis le portent et l'apennent en grant cavernes des montagnes, en tel leu que nulle beste ne autre mauvese choise le peusse tochere. / Et encore voç di, se il puet prendre des autres homes que ne soient de lor contrée, il le prenent; e se celui ne se poit rachater, il les occient et le menuient tot maintenant; or ce est mult mavese mainiere et male uçanse' (6–9: 'And when he is dead they will have him cooked: and then all the relations of the dead man come and eat him all. And I tell you that they eat all the bone marrow: and they do this because they do not want any substance to remain, for they say that if any substance remains, this substance will make worms, which would die due to lack of food; and they say that from the death of these worms the soul of the dead man would come to great harm and agony; and for this reason they eat him entirely. And when they have eaten him, they take the bones and place them in a fine casket, and then they take it and place it in great caves in the mountains, in such a place where no beast or evil thing may touch it. And I tell you too that if they can capture men who are not from their country, they capture him and if he cannot be ransomed, they kill him and eat him all up at once, and this is a bad custom and habit.')

6 CLXXII, 3–4   The inhabitants of the Andaman islands 'ont chief come chienz et dens et iaux come chiens; car je voç di qu'il sunt tuit senblable a chief de grant chien mastin. Il ont especeries aseç; il sunt mout cruel jens; il menuient les omes, tuit cil que il puent prandre, puis qu'il ne soient de lor jens' ('have heads like dog and teeth and eyes like dogs; for I tell you that their faces look just like those of great mongrel dogs. They have plenty of spices; they are very cruel people; they eat men, any they can capture as long as they are not of their own race'.)

The spectre of cannibalism is evoked here in a number of traditional ways, which it is worth briefly reviewing in order to highlight how the *Devisement*'s use of cannibalism differs from that of near contemporary or subsequent medieval sources.

Examples 2 and 3 are relatively straightforward instances of othering: the people of Fugiu and the Japanese apparently break the most fundamental of taboos primarily because they like the taste of human flesh, and in the case of the Japanese they also break the rules of fair play that govern the taking and exchange of hostages among civilized peoples. Example 4 then plays on one strand of the medieval iconography of cannibals identified by Debra Strickland, which represents them as living in the wilderness, outside the civilizing influence of city walls,[66] while example 6 may play on a tradition of cannibalistic and monstrous cynocephali deriving from Pliny, although, as I have already suggested, it is not clear that cynocephali are necessarily evoked here, and this may even be an instance of the *Devisement* seeking to correct previous knowledge of Asia.[67] These, then, are conventional representations of man-eaters, examples perhaps of cannibalism as 'a trope of exceptional power'. Of course, the presence of the trope here has played a role in long-standing scholarly debates about the authenticity of the *Devisement*. Did Marco really go to all the places he claims to have visited, and did he really encounter cannibals? But such questions are to my mind beside the point (given that, as with Columbus, it is relatively unlikely that Marco did in fact encounter cannibals), a more pertinent question being: why did he feel the need to place cannibals in the East at all? And then: how does he do this? After all, no one doubts that Columbus went to the West Indies, yet there is general consensus that the cannibals he claims to have encountered are drawn from his imagination and from literary sources.

The simple answer to the first question is that his readers expected there to be cannibals in the East. All surviving thirteenth-century Latin sources about the Mongols (Peter of Russia, John of Plano Carpini, Simon of St-Quentin, Vincent of Beauvais, William of Rubruck and Matthew Paris) accuse them of cannibalism, but, as Gregory Guzman demonstrates, their descriptions are generally lifted almost verbatim from widely disseminated classical sources (particularly Pliny) and while some of these writers were sedentary in every sense of the term, several of those who did actually journey to the East and encounter Mongols did at least concede that they were relaying hearsay.[68] This also seems then like standard othering, and, as Guzman notes, Latin writers such as John of Plano Carpini and Simon of St-Quentin who report

---

[66] Debra Higgs Strickland, *Saracens, Demons and Jews: Making Monsters in Medieval Art* (Princeton and Oxford: Princeton University Press, 2003), p. 45.

[67] See Chapter 3, pp. 121–2, n. 14.

[68] Gregory G. Guzman, 'Reports of Mongol Cannibalism in the Thirteenth-Century Latin Sources: Oriental Fact or Western Fiction', in Scott D. Westrem (ed.), *Discovering New Worlds: Essays on Medieval Exploration and Imagination* (New York and London: Garland, 1991), pp. 31–68.

ritual funerary cannibalism, analogous to example 5 from the *Devisement*, clearly do not understand it, failing to see the filial piety and respect it might be read as enacting.[69] The *Devisement*, on the other hand, conspicuously does not overtly condemn the ritual funerary cannibalism of the Sumatrans, preferring instead to detail the beliefs of those it says perform the ritual concerning the protection of their relatives' *sustance*. On the hand, it is difficult not to wonder whether attentive readers would have seen a parallel between funerary cannibalism and the eucharist, which is also concerned with a *sustance*. On the other hand, it has just before this been explained that Marco Polo's party barricaded itself in at night 'por doutance de cel mauvais homes bestiaus que menuient les homes' (CLXVII, 4) and afterwards this leads into an additional accusation that the Sumatrans, like the Japanese, devour hostages who cannot pay their ransoms, describing this as a *male uçanse* (CLXVIII, 9). Are we to infer from this that there are degrees of cannibalism, that some forms of cannibalism are worse than others?

It is interesting, if this is the case, that before we learn about the cannibalism of the Japanese, we are informed that we will not in fact be told about the worst things they do (CLXI, 6). So there is something worse than cannibalism, it would seem, making cannibalism here precisely *not* the totally unspeakable taboo that Islam and Heng suggest it is. Example 1, which to my knowledge is unprecedented as well as exceptional, may also suggest that different types of cannibals may be scattered along a relative scale of iniquity, rather than simply defining its limit. As Jill Tattersall points out, 'there is some confusion here', in that this account comes in the middle of Marco's lengthy description of the Great Khan's court, but it is nonetheless clearly *not* the Mongols who are being accused of cannibalism, which already makes Marco exceptional among thirteenth-century writers about the Mongols, who are usually all too quick to level charges of cannibalism, drawing on literary sources.[70] Those who are being accused of cannibalism, rather, are Tibetan and Kasmiri 'astrologers' and 'magicians' employed at the Great Khan's court. They are therefore tolerated right at the centre of this utopian regime. Moreover – and most strikingly – their cannibalism follows strict rules in that they eat only executed criminals. Their practices are not condemned but rather described as 'une mervoille', therefore something to be wondered at, to be sure, but also perhaps something to be understood. Thus, whereas some of the *Devisement*'s cannibals are represented as breaking rules and others as not having any rules at all (they might eat anyone), these cannibals are clearly

---

[69] Guzman, 'Reports', p. 51. For example, see Christopher Dawson, *Mission to Asia* (Toronto: Toronto University Press, 1980), p. 23, for John of Plano Carpini's account, though he reports funerary cannibalism (possibly among Tibetans) as hearsay.

[70] Jill Tattersall, 'Anthropophagi and Eaters of Raw Flesh in French Literature of the Crusade Period: Myth, Tradition and Reality', *Medium Aevum*, 57 (1988), 240–53 (p. 245).

not to be feared (provided, of course, you are not a convicted criminal). There is clearly no need to erect a barricade against them.

These cannibals' position at the centre of civilization is also exceptional, because, as noted, cannibals are usually placed at the limits of the civilized world, as indeed they are elsewhere in the *Devisement*: Fugiu (at the limits of Cathay), Japan, Java, Sumatra, the Andaman islands. These geographical locations point to another telling innovation in the *Devisement*'s anthology of cannibalism. As we saw in the Introduction, the *Devisement* pushes the limits of the known world back considerably from those laid out by one of its main vernacular intertexts, the *Roman d'Alexandre*. When Marco Polo bowls past either the Alexandrian Gog and Magog, or his own relocated Gog and Magog, the *Devisement* fails to mention that among the peoples Alexander sought to confine were allegedly the hideously cannibalistic people of Gog and Magog. As we have seen, Marco pointedly and explicitly goes well beyond the traditional Gog and Magog relatively early in his narrative, but without making any mention of the alleged cannibalism of its inhabitants. What is more, the peoples beyond these limits turn out to be civilized. In other words, precisely because the *Devisement* seeks to push back the limits of the known world, he has also to relocate cannibals to its new frontiers, with the troublesome exception of the Tibetan and Kasmiri 'astrologers' and 'magicians'.

Does their position at the centre of civilization uniquely make these astrologers and magicians ethical cannibals? This seems unlikely. But along with the relocation of cannibals to new liminal territories (albeit literary ones), these cannibals at the heart of civilization, where one might least expect them, show that boundaries and limits are never absolute, that they may be moved and redrawn, that they may invoke internal as well as external divisions and differences, that they need not observe a binary logic. And this is not a bad basis for ethics.

Conclusion

In his recent *Marco Polo y la cruzada* Antonio García Espada reads the *Devisement du Monde* as an instance of crusade propaganda (which had something of a renaissance after the fall of Acre in 1292) and alongside fourteenth-century missionary writing about Asia.[71] In his conclusion he argues that the turn of the thirteenth century was a key moment in the solidification of ideas of 'us' and 'them' in Europe; the East is defined exclusively as a place populated by monsters and prodigies from which the Holy Land

---

[71] Antonio García Espada, *Marco Polo y la cruzada: historia de la literatura de viajes a las Indias en el siglo XIV* (Madrid: Marcial Pons Historía, 2009).

must at all costs have be rescued, and this inaugurates seven centuries of focusing on *alteridad* ('alterity'), grounded in reading texts such as Marco Polo's, which was to determine the course of Europe's interactions with the rest of the world.[72] His alignment with Anglo-American critics such as Islam and Heng is, in the final pages of his book, quite explicit,[73] but, as we have seen, a close reading of the *Devisement* does not bear out the proposition that the text inscribes 'exorbitant otherness'. Thus the interest of Espada's book lies, in my view, less in his reading of the *Devisement* than in the material alongside which he places Marco Polo, for there can be no doubt that during the fourteenth century xenophobic texts about the rest of the world, often drawing heavily on the kind of written source the *Devisement* sought to correct, continued to be produced in Europe, and also that there was a vogue for what Espada calls *tratados de recuperación* – which is to say, treatises on the recuperation of the Holy Land. Hayton's *Le Flor des histoires* is a case in point. The disparity in outlook between the *Devisement* and these texts is, however, striking. So, rather than suggesting that the *Devisement* prefigures, or indeed is one of them (as is the case with Espada), I would suggest that it becomes associated with this tradition in some branches of its transmission and often assimilated to its agenda: hence the modifications that the text undergoes in the French redaction, for example, but in particular in Pipino.

For *alteridad* or 'otherness' is not a category in which the *Devisement* seems interested. *Diversité* is the main category the *Devisement* uses to elaborate its view of the world, and this certainly cannot be mapped on to 'otherness' as construed by modern scholars such as Islam, Heng or Espada. The *Devisement* does not posit a binary view of the world but represents, rather, a world variegated by differences that may nonetheless be transcended given a more propitious symbolic order. And even cannibals, usually the 'other' *par excellence*, may be assimilated to the differential view of the world as opposed to the traditional oppositional one against which the *Devisement* reacts.

---

[72] Espada, *Marco Polo*, pp. 351–67, p. 353 for the comment on *alteridad* and Marco Polo.

[73] Espada, *Marco Polo*, pp. 366–7; he also references Campbell on medieval travel writing.

Conclusion: 'et ipse non notavit nisi pauca aliqua, que adhuc in mente retinebat'[1]

> Dans quelle langue écrire des mémoires dès lors qu'il n'y a pas de langue maternelle autorisée? Comment dire un «je me rappelle» qui vaille quand il faut inventer et sa langue et son *je*, les inventer *en même temps*, par-delà même ce déferlement d'amnésie qu'a déchaîné le *double interdit*? (Jacques Derrida)[2]
>
> Non è detto che Kublai Kan creda a tutto quel che dice Marco Polo quando gli descrive le città visitate. (Italo Calvino)[3]

My two epigraphs encapsulate the main cruces of reading *Le Devisement du Monde* that I have explored in this book. For some scholars Marco Polo and Rustichello da Pisa chose to write in French because for Italians of the time it was the only available legitimate vernacular alternative to Latin: this case has been made most recently and persuasively with particular eloquence and erudition by Alison Cornish:

> because there was a literature in French a good hundred and fifty years before there was one in Italian, for a long time, French literature *was* vernacular literature. To adopt it was not to steal it, nor to be dominated by it, but to use it as if it were one's own. French was a literary (and performative) instrument, not a birthright.[4]

Yet the force of Derrida's argument in *Le Monolinguisme de l'autre* is that

---

[1] 'And he did not note more than a few things that he was able to recall.'

[2] Jacques Derrida, *Le Monolinguisme de l'autre ou la prothèse d'origine* (Paris: Galilée, 1996), p. 57: 'In what language is one to write memoirs, given there is no authorized mother tongue? How is one to utter an "I remember" that means something when one has to invent both one's language and one's *I*, invent them *at the same time*, through and beyond that unfurling of amnesia that is unleashed by a double interdiction.'

[3] Italo Calvino, *Le città invisibili* (Turin: Einaudi, 1972), p. 13 (original emphasis): 'it is not certain that Kublai Khan believes everything Marco Polo says when he describes for him the cities he visited.'

[4] See her 'Translatio Galliae: Effects of Early Franco-Italian Exchange', *Romanic Review*, 97 (2006), 309–30 (p. 310). See also (more extensively) her *Vernacular Translation in Dante's Italy: Illiterate Literature* (Cambridge: Cambridge University Press, 2011).

the adoption of any language for the narration of one's experiences (whether this be one's mother tongue or not) entails displacement and deferral, since one never *possesses* language. The language one speaks is nonetheless not exactly a foreign language:[5] it is simply all one has to work with, it inhabits one, but *belongs* to others. The subject not only struggles to speak this 'langue de l'autre' in a first layer of interdiction (a term that in and of itself evokes language as prohibition); in a second layer of interdiction she or he also has to struggle to produce an '*I*' that belongs uniquely to her or his own experiences, largely because '*I*' represents a position that can never belong uniquely to one person, a position that always slips away from the speaker in any act of narration, particularly when the narration is written down and the text goes into circulation. The ambiguous narrative voices of the *Devisement* that I explored in Chapter 1 dramatize this predicament particularly starkly. Their first-person pronouns range from the specifically identified to the spectacularly labile; as we saw in Chapter 2, the 'nostre langaje' to which they refer denotes an idiom that is uniquely theirs in the specifics of its syntax, morphology, lexis and so on, yet palpably not their own in that one identifies himself as Venetian, the other as Pisan, and they are using a form of *fransois*, a language that in the thirteenth century, rather like English today in much of the world, was up for grabs by a wide range of diverse peoples outside its indigenous territories. And as if to confirm the extent to which French was by definition up for grabs, the process of eliminating the singularity of the *Devisement*'s use of French seems to have begun as soon as people started to transcribe and translate it.

The effect of the double displacement produced by Marco Polo and Rustichello da Pisa speaking in the first person and in French then also needs to be considered in relation to the position from which they speak and their subject-matter, as we saw in Chapters 3 and 4. Italo Calvino's celebrated *Le città invisibili* (1972) is inspired by his reading of the Tuscan redaction of the *Devisement*, *Il Milione*, and particularly by the account in the prologue of Marco finding favour by narrating his missions to the Great Khan (see Chapter 1). The novel portrays Marco Polo locked in dialogue with Kublai Khan, narrating and cataloguing the many wondrous and sometimes fantastic cities of Kublai's empire that Marco has visited on Kublai's behalf – visited precisely in order to describe them to his new lord and master. The second epigraph to this conclusion is the opening sentence of the book, raising from the outset the question of authenticity and belief: because Marco tells of distant lands, lands Kublai has never seen – invisible therefore – but descriptions of which he avidly desires, how is Kublai to know Marco tells the truth? It is customary in post-colonial scholarship to evoke the *other* and *alterity* in relation to a scenario such as this, but *Le città invisibili* foregrounds at an

---

[5] Derrida, *Le Monolinguisme*, p. 18.

early stage a related, but nonetheless distinct, term, *elsewhere*: 'L'altrove è uno specchio in negativo' ('elsewhere is a mirror in negative').[6] This highly ambiguous sentence (is the mirror seen in negative, or does it work as a negative?) seems to invite the reader to think about what s/he seeks when, like Kublai, s/he is avid for tales of elsewhere. For Calvino, Marco Polo's tales offer a path both to the past and to the future, to the recognition of 'il poco che è suo' ('the little that is one's own') as well as to the revelation of 'il molto che non ha avuto e non avrà' ('the much one has not had and will never have'),[7] but this is less to do with concrete other places than with what they are made to signify: 'l'occhio non vede cose, ma figure di cose che significano altre cose' ('the eye does not see things, but rather figures of things that signify other things').[8] Cities in *Le città invisibili* are tellingly categorized according to a range of key terms, most notably: memory, desire, signs, exchanges, name ('il nome'). The point seems to be that, whether or not these elsewhere places really exist, when they are encountered in textual form it is not the places themselves that are encountered, but a signifying system ('figure di cose che significano altre cose').

Kublai Khan certainly questions the authenticity and truthfulness of Marco's descriptions and stories in *Le città invisibili* (and, unlike the places described in the *Devisement*, Calvino's cities are often quite fantastic), but Marco explains repeatedly that authenticity and truthfulness are really not the point. When Kublai protests that '*Le tue città non esistono*' (original emphasis, 'your cities do not exist'), Marco retorts that 'se vuoi sapere quanto buio hai intorno, devi aguzzare lo sguardo sulle fioche luci lontane' ('if you want to know how much darkness surrounds you, you must fix your gaze on dim lights in the distance'),[9] adding 'Nessuno sa meglio di te, saggio Kublai, che non si deve mai confondere la città col discorso che la descrive' ('No one knows better than you, oh wise Kublai, that one should never confuse the city with the discourse that describes it').[10] You look into the distance to understand the here and now (Calvino seems to be saying), but at the same time you must realize that your account of what you see is an artifice, a discourse, that may not correspond to what is there.

Calvino was, as others have noted, an extremely intelligent reader of the *Devisement*.[11] He highlighted the risks of incomprehension and the oppor-

---

[6] *Le città invisibili*, p. 35.
[7] *Le città invisibili*, p. 35.
[8] *Le città invisibili*, p. 21.
[9] *Le città invisibili*, p. 65.
[10] *Le città invisibili*, p. 67.
[11] Calvino scholars do not often give the question of his reading of Marco much detailed attention, being more preoccupied with the postmodern agenda of the novel, but I have found the following extremely illuminating: Valeria Bertolucci Pizzorusso, 'Le meraviglie inquietanti: Marco Polo, Sklovskij, Calvino', *Studi Mediolatini e Volgari*, 51 (2005), 7–26; and Steven Shankman, *Other Others: Levinas, Literature, Transcultural*

tunities for creativity when listening to, and recounting, stories in foreign languages (see Chapter 2);[12] he pinpointed the tendency of many readers to read only for the familiar and expected, to reject the unexpected (see Chapters 2 and 3).[13] But above all, his novel responds with eloquent poise to the discursive nature of the encounter with elsewhere that the *Devisement* – and any text like it that describes unknown foreign lands – offers its readers (see Chapter 1). The scholarly and popular preoccupation with the historical authenticity (or inauthenticity) and veracity of the *Devisement* is perfectly legitimate in some respects and eloquent testimony to the success of the text's rhetoric of authenticity and veracity, but it nonetheless may prevent a thorough-going consideration and understanding of how the *Devisement* works as a text, and why it has been so successful down the ages, since this probably has little to do with veracity. After all, boring and uninteresting texts may tell the truth, and literary masterpieces may be utterly mendacious, but in neither case is there a direct relation between the two qualities. While it may be true that it is more interesting to be interesting than it is to be right, it is also true that it is possible to be interesting *and* right!

It may be objected to the stress I have placed on the discursive nature of the world the *Devisement* describes that this is a way of side-stepping the ethical and historical questions of how the *Devisement* mediates the actual encounter between medieval Europe and Asia that it records, and how this may offer a prehistory to the violent and exploitative early modern and modern encounters between Europeans and others. I would contend, however, that in order to understand fully the nature of these later encounters, one needs first to understand how Europeans imagined the rest of the world. To evoke imagination in relation to the *Devisement* is not to beg the question of whether or not 'tutto quel che dice Marco' ('everything Marco Polo says') is true or not. My own view, as I have intimated and for what it is worth, is that the *Devisement* does tell the truth, that Marco Polo did go to China and also that the *Devisement* does describe, as accurately as memory and possibly incomplete notes allowed, what Marco Polo and his travelling companions saw in Asia. I do thus believe that the *Devisement* is an incomparable source

---

Studies (Albany: SUNY Press, 2010), pp. 37–56 ('The Difference between Difference and Otherness: *Il Milione* of Marco Polo and Calvino's *Le città invisibili*').

[12] Of Marco's predecessors as storytellers to Kublai, Calvino writes: 'In lingue incomprensibili al Kan i messi riferivano notizie intese in lingue a loro incomprensibili' (*Le città invisibili*, p. 29: 'the messengers relayed to the Khan in incomprehensible languages news that they had heard in languages that were incomprehensible to them'); Marco, on the other hand, learns the Tartar language, and so his stories become 'i più precisi e minuziosi che il Gran Kan potesse desiderare' (p. 30: 'the most precious and meticulous that the Great Khan could desire').

[13] 'Io parlo parlo, – dice Marco, – ma chi m'ascolta ritiene solo le parole che aspetta' (*Le città invisibili*, p. 143: 'I talk and talk, says Marco, but whoever listens to me only retains the words he is expecting').

for information about many parts of Asia in the thirteenth century. But in some respects this is beside the point, in that I think the parameters of the critical and scholarly debate on Marco Polo need changing somewhat, for the *Devisement* is a text in which the distinction between truth and fiction is deliberately blurred, a text that challenges us to ask (along with Calvino's Kublai) whether or not we should believe what we read, and if so, what we should do with this belief and the knowledge it imparts. The *Devisement* is, in other words, a text that challenges its readers to question what they know as well as the status of what they read, a challenge that is, as we have seen, sometimes articulated quite explicitly, but is in fact ubiquitously embedded in its very form and style.

Scholarship on accounts of medieval encounters with, and understanding of, the world outside Europe tends to make a distinction between, on the one hand, those texts that are grounded in experience or first-hand knowledge and, on the other, those that derive their knowledge of the rest of the world from other texts. On one side of this divide we might range most famously the texts by John of Plano Carpini, William of Rubruck (whose account of his trip to the Mongol court in 1253–5 is justly celebrated for its factual basis and keen eye for detail), Hayton and (contentiously for some) Marco Polo; on the other, again just to stick with the most famous examples, Mandeville, a large number of encyclopaedic texts and also the many texts in the Alexander tradition that literary historians classify as fictional and/or romance. However, this distinction perhaps occludes the fact that all of these texts draw on other texts in some way and signify through their relation to a textual tradition (even if they correct rather than follow it); moreover, precisely because of the dynamic nature of this intertextuality, which spans the fact/fiction divide that modern scholarship has in my view inappropriately imposed, even the most 'factual' of accounts may evoke the spectre of fiction, while all the 'fictional' accounts nonetheless claim historical veracity. All these texts also aspire to affect the view of the world of those they address: this is perhaps most obviously the case with a text such as Hayton's *La Flor des estoires*, with its overt crusading agenda, but it is equally true of both Marco Polo and Mandeville – the former 'factual', the latter 'fictional'. I have alluded on a number of occasions during this book to the historical and cultural circumstances that might explain why the *Devisement* came to be viewed by some as fictional, while Mandeville's *Le Livre des Merveilles*, again for some, became a trusted source of facts about the world: Marco Polo's travels in Asia were undertaken at an exceptionally timely moment, but the account of them in the *Devisement* was destined quickly to evoke a world beyond the experience of European travellers, owing to the disintegration of the Mongol empire, the rise of hostile Islamic empires in the Middle East and the Black Death; Mandeville's account, on the other hand, went into circulation at a moment in time when Europe was facing an exceptional crisis (again the Black Death), and so, perhaps not coincidentally, readers seem to have been willing to embrace a more familiar (if far more fantastic) account of other places, their exotic monstrous races and the threat or possibilities these places and their legendary wealth might represent.[14] What this goes to show, I think, is not that medieval readers were necessarily more credulous than modern readers, but rather that, if these texts have quite a lot in common in terms of their rhetoric, style and what they represent for their readers, the *Devisement* is nonetheless unusual, particularly in the vernacular, in its tenacious drive to challenge received wisdom. Yet for a reader who had no prospect of ever going to China, Marco Polo and Mandeville's rival accounts of Asia are just that: rival accounts. And whereas Mandeville offers the reader a familiar sacred geography of the world centred on Jerusalem and a time-honoured account of its peoples deriving ultimately from Pliny,[15] the *Devisement* systematically challenged premises about the world and about different religions that medieval Christendom held dear. The *Devisement* also does not, as I have argued, give a particularly privileged position to a European perspective; indeed, it continually troubles any conventional notion of a centre, whether this be Jerusalem (the centre of the world in medieval visual and textual *mappae mundi*), which is barely mentioned in the *Devisement*, or the more Eurocentric cultural outlook familiar from post-medieval writing and cartography. The *Devisement*, as I hope I have demonstrated throughout this book, offers a uniquely and radically different view of the world from other texts, one to which readers with many different outlooks and desires have responded over the centuries.

The radical nature of the *Devisement* can be briefly illustrated through a comparison with Mandeville's *Le Livre des Merveilles*, but with recourse once again to Calvino's insights on Marco Polo as a teller of tales of 'elsewhere': 'L'altrove è uno specchio in negativo.' I have already commented on the ambiguity of this formulation, and Calvino is no doubt also playing on the ambivalence of the mirror in medieval culture as a surface that enables the beholder to see not only himself, but also a vision of perfection or truth. If, in a mirror, the beholder sees himself in reverse (if one raises one's left hand when looking in a mirror, one's mirror image's right hand is raised), one might then wonder if a 'mirror in negative' allows the beholder to see himself uncannily as he really is, to see, in other words a truth about himself, or a true perspective of himself, that is otherwise unavailable. How do the *Devisement* and the *Livre des Merveilles* compare as 'mirrors'?

One of the most dramatic and intriguing passages in Mandeville is his

---

[14] See above, pp. 115–17 and 121–2.

[15] For stimulating accounts of Mandeville's world view, see the remarks interspersed throughout Suzanne Conklin Akbari, *Idols in the East: European Representations of Islam and the Orient (1100–1450)* (Ithaca, NY, and London: Cornell University Press, 2009), and Iain Macleod Higgins, *Writing East: The 'Travels' of Sir John Mandeville* (Philadelphia: University of Pennsylvania Press, 1997).

excursus on circumnavigation. Mandeville is not alone among medieval writers in raising the possibility of circumnavigation.[16] Thus, although no direct source for everything he says about circumnavigation has been identified, given his plagiaristic practices elsewhere in his book, it seems unlikely that the Mandeville-author came up with what he says about this topic all by himself. In addition to bemused comments on gravity and calculations about the size of the earth, which he probably took from Brunetto Latini (but which have their origin in Ptolemy and which are more or less right in their scale but wrong in their actual dimensions because they take no account of America),[17] the Mandeville-author tells the story of a man who *almost* circumnavigated the world:[18]

> Et quant homme vait outre celles jorneies vers Ynde et vers les isles foraches, tout est environnant la rondesse de la terre et de la mer par dessouz noz pays de cea. Et pur ceo m'ad il souvenuz mointefoiz d'une chose qe jeo oÿ compter quant jeo fuy jeovenes, comment un vaillant homme s'em party jadis de noz parties pur aler cercher le mounde. Si passa Ynde et les isles outre Ynde ou il y plus de V^m isles, et tant ala par mer et par terre et tant environa le mounde par mointes saisouns q'il troeva un isle ou il oÿ parler soun langage et toucher les boefs en disant tieles paroles come l'em fait en son pays dont il s'enmerveilla moult. Qar il ne savoit coment ceo poait estre. Mes jeo dy q'il avoit tant irré par terre et par mer q'il avoit environé toute la terre, q'il estoit revenuz envyronant jusqes a ses marches, et s'il vousist avoir passé avant q'il eust troevé et son pays et sa conissaunce. Mes il retorna ariere par illecques ou il estoit venu, si perdy assez de ses peines si come il mesmes le disoit un gran piece après q'il fust revenuz. Qar il avient après qu'il aloit en Norveye, si ly prist tempeste en mer et arriva en une isle, et quant il fust en celle isle il reconust qe ceo estoit l'isle ou il avoit oÿ parler son langage a mener les boefs a la charue. (pp. 337–8)

> (And when a man travels for many days towards India, then towards the distant islands, he is girding the earth's and the sea's roundness, underneath our own country. And for this reason I have often remembered a story I heard when I was young, about how a worthy man once left our parts to explore the world. He went past India and the islands beyond, where there are more than 5,000 islands, and he so travelled, over sea and over land, and so went round the world for many seasons that he came to an island,

---

[16] See Jean de Mandeville, *Le Livre des Merveilles du monde*, ed. Christiane Deluz (Paris: CNRS, 2000), p. 342, n. 16.

[17] See Mandeville, *Le Livre des Merveilles*, ed. Deluz, p. 342, n. 18.

[18] Cited from ed. Deluz. For particularly stimulating readings of this episode, see: Frank Grady, *Representing Righteous Heathens in Late Medieval England* (Basingstoke: Palgrave, 2006), pp. 69–70; Stephen Greenblatt, *Marvelous Possessions: The Wonder of the New World* (Oxford: Clarendon Press, 1991), pp. 47–8; and Geraldine Heng, *Empire of Magic: Medieval Romance and the Politics of Cultural Fantasy* (New York: Columbia University Press, 2003), p. 305.

where he heard his own language spoken by a ploughman who addressed and drove his oxen as they do in his own land, and this amazed him greatly. Yet he could not understand how this could be so. But I say to you that he had travelled so far over land and sea that he had been right round the world and returned to a place very close to where he came from so that if he had wanted to go further he would have come to his own land and his own knowledge. But instead he turned back the way he came, and so wasted his efforts, as he himself would say long after he had returned home. For at a later stage he happened to go to Norway, but there was a storm and he was landed on an island, which he recognized as the island where he had heard his own language used by the ploughman to his oxen.)

This story particularly interests me because it seems to figure a deliberate turning away from the uncanny, whereas, as I argued in Chapter 3, Marco Polo embraces the uncanny with alacrity. For what could be more uncanny than travelling as far as it possible to go away from home only to realize that you are back where you started? The marvel here ('il s'enmerveilla moult') is so incredible that the man turns back, apparently without speaking to the ploughman he hears speaking his own language, which is at one and the same time familiar and alarmingly foreign. This turning back is described as a return to his *conissaunce*, 'knowledge'. Yet retrospectively (when he realizes his mistake years later) he understands that a return to what he knows was also unwittingly a return to ignorance (a Freudian perception if ever there was one), and a failure to recognize the truth of what he saw: *conissaunce*, 'recognition' as well as 'knowledge', turns out spectacularly to be also Lacanian *méconnaissance*, 'misrecognition', here. What the man who almost circumnavigated the world fails to recognize is in fact himself, or rather an image of himself, or perhaps even himself as other. His travels have defamiliarized him (and his starting point), making him a stranger to himself (to use Kristeva's formulation), unrecognizable and yet tantalizingly familiar, or alternatively, recognizable yet worryingly foreign.[19]

The story is an account of what might have been, but I think it is interesting, given the Mandeville-author's persistent desire to show how he surpasses previous travellers and travel writers, that Mandeville does not claim to have circumnavigated the world himself, even though he insists it is possible. As we see elsewhere in the *Livre des Merveilles*, he is clearly attracted by the uncanny, yet ultimately his avatar here (described as 'un vaillant homme') turns away from it. But maybe what the Mandeville-author is acknowledging subliminally, through his story of the man who turned back, is that the knowledge that his *Livre des Merveilles* purveys about the world – the mirror that he holds up for his readers' contemplation – is illusory precisely because

---

[19] Julia Kristeva, *Etrangers à nous-mêmes*, 2nd edn (Paris: Gallimard, 1991).

he declines to go all the way and embrace the unfamiliar, which includes a failure to embrace the displacement of his own self through travel.

Marco Polo also does not claim to have circumnavigated the world, but, although he returned to Venice, he arguably never turned back towards the familiar, or away from the strangeness either of what he saw or what he became. On the contrary, the *Devisement* portrays a Marco who is irrevocably altered by his encounter with difference, becoming a marvel as well as a purveyor of marvels, a stranger if you will. He took a hard look at what he encountered, at least by his own account,[20] and when called upon to narrate what he saw (perhaps, indeed, while held captive in Genoa), he did so, embracing the difficulties of describing the unfamiliar in a language that was necessarily inadequate to the task and which, perhaps fittingly therefore, he mastered only imperfectly. And rather than looking at the other always through the lens of a European Christian observer, polarizing the world into 'us' and 'them', he created a framework that allows a myriad of different cultures and peoples, with a myriad of different languages, to consider each other differentially (see Chapter 4). Marco himself, as traveller and storyteller, thus never fully returns to his starting point.

When Kublai asks Marco in Calvino's *Le città invisibili*, '*Viaggi per rivivere il tuo passato?*' ('Do you travel to relive your past?), the narrator remarks that this question could be reformulated as '*Viaggi per ritrovare il tuo futuro*' ('Do you travel to retrieve your future?').[21] The prefix of the Italian verb *ritrovare* suggests one's future is something one has once owned but lost. If one finds it again or retrieves it by travelling, this suggests that the future is *altrove,* elsewhere, yet the equivalence of the two questions suggests the future is also ineluctably bound up with the past. How fitting, then, that Christopher Columbus should have gone looking for the future, inspired by a *past* journey he found in the *Devisement* (supplemented, of course, by Mandeville) and sailing west to get east. His inspiration was, in other words, profoundly medieval, backward-looking, then, in some respects rather than forward-looking, and grounded, as many have observed, in his covetousness of the riches of the East as described by both Marco Polo and Mandeville rather than in his curiosity. My sense, then, is that Marco Polo might well *not* have approved. Though not immune to the attractions of wealth, Marco was far more interested, as we saw in Chapters 3 and 4, in cultural diversity and in the sophisticated technological and social organization of the peoples he encountered. Though he never says so explicitly, the wonder he expresses at some cultural phenomena and artefacts (paper money, the Mongol transport infrastructure and so on) suggests strongly that he describes parts of Asia precisely as a vision for Europe's future.

---

[20] See CLII, 6: 'fu verité selonc ce que je Marc Poul vit puis apertemant a mes iaux' ('it was true, according to what I, Marco Polo, saw most clearly with my own eyes').

[21] *Le città invisibili*, p. 35.

'The past is a foreign country: they do things differently there.'[22] Thus begins a well-known English novel. In the *Devisement* it is perhaps implicitly the future that is the foreign country and where 'they do things differently'. The early modern *conquistadores* who followed Columbus to America and their colonial/imperial modern successors throughout the world wantonly exploited and destroyed other cultures they encountered as they travelled, squandering the alternative futures they might have represented from Calvino's perspective. But how interesting, then, from an early twenty-first-century perspective, that the foreign country that one remarkable thirteenth-century European traveller and writer identified as representing the future should be China.

[22] L.P. Hartley, *The Go-Between* (London: Penguin Classics, 2004), p. 5.

BIBLIOGRAPHY

Editions of Marco Polo

El Libro de Marco Polo anotado por Cristóbal Colon. El libro de Marco Polo, versión de Rodrigo de Santaella, ed. Juan Gil (Madrid: Alianza, 1987)

I viaggi di Marco Polo, gentiluomo veneziano, in Giovanni Battista Ramusio, *Navigazioni e viaggi*, ed. Marica Milanesi, 6 vols (Turin: Einaudi, 1978–88), III (1980), pp. 7–297

Marco Polo, *La Description du monde*, ed. Pierre-Yves Badel (Paris: Livre de Poche, 1998)

Marco Polo, *Le Devisement du monde*, ed. Philippe Ménard et al., 6 vols (Geneva: Droz, 2001–9): I, ed. Philippe Ménard (2001); II, ed. Jeanne-Marie Boivin, Laurence Harf-Lancner and Laurence Mathey-Maille (2003); III, ed. Jean-Claude Faucon, Danielle Quéruel and Monique Santucci (2004); IV, ed. Joël Blanchard and Michel Quereuil (2005); V, ed. Jean-Claude Delclos and Claude Roussel, (2006); VI, ed. Dominique Boutet, Thierry Delcourt and Danièle James-Raoul (2009)

Marco Polo, *Il milione*, ed. Luigi Foscolo Benedetto (Florence: Olschki, 1928)

Marco Polo, *Il «Milione» veneto: ms. CM 211 della Biblioteca Civica di Padova*, ed. Alvaro Barbieri and Alvise Andreose (Venice: Marsilio, 1999)

Marco Polo, *Milione. Le Divisament dou monde. Il milione nelle redazioni toscana e franco-italiana*, ed. Gabriella Ronchi, intro. by Cesare Segre (Milan: Mondadori, 1982)

Marco Polo, *Milione. Redazione Latina del manoscritto Z*, ed. Alvaro Barbieri (Parma: Fondazione Pietro Bembio, 1998)

Marco Polo, *Milione: versione toscana del trecento*, ed. Valeria Bertolucci Pizzorusso, with an 'indice ragionato' by Giorgio R. Cardona (Milan: Adelphi, 1975)

Marco Polo, *The Description of the World*, ed. A.C. Moule and Paul Pelliot, 2 vols (London: Routledge, 1938)

Milion: Dle jediného rukopisu spoly s příslušným základem latinským. Vydal, ed. Justin V. Prášek (Prague: Česká, Akademie Císaře Františka Josefa, 1902)

The Travels of Marco Polo, trans. with an introduction by Ronald Latham (Harmondsworth: Penguin, 1958)

The Travels of Marco Polo, with an introduction by Paul Smethurst (New York: Barnes and Noble, 2005)

Editions of other texts

Brunetto Latini, *Tresor*, ed. Pietro Beltrami, Paolo Squillacioti, Plinio Torri and Sergio Vatteroni (Turin: Einaudi, 2007)
Calvino, Italo, *Le città invisibili* (Turin: Einaudi, 1972)
La Chanson de Roland, ed. Ian Short (Paris: Le Livre de Poche, 1990)
Hartley, L.P., *The Go-Between* (London: Penguin Classics, 2004)
Hayton, *La Flor des estoires*, in *Recueil des historiens des croisades: documents latins et français relatifs à l'Arménie*, II (Paris: L'Académie des Inscriptions et des Belles Lettres, 1906)
L'Image du Monde de Maître Gossouin: rédaction en prose, ed. O.H. Prior (Lausanne and Paris: Payot, 1913)
Jean de Mandeville, *Le Livre des Merveilles du monde*, ed. Christiane Deluz (Paris: CNRS, 2000)
Joinville, Jean de, *Histoire de Saint Louis*, in *Historiens et chroniqueurs du moyen âge: Robert de Clari, Villehardouin, Joinville, Froissart, Commynes*, ed. Albert Pauphilet (Paris: Gallimard, 1952), pp. 195–366
Martin da Canale, *Les Estoires de Venise*, ed. Alberto Limentani (Florence: Olschki, 1972)
Prester John, *La Lettre du Prêtre Jean: les versions en ancien français et en ancien occitan, textes et commentaires*, ed. Martin Gosman (Groningen: Bouma Boekhuis, 1982)
Robert de Clari, *La Conquête de Constantinople*, in *Historiens et chroniqueurs du moyen âge: Robert de Clari, Villehardouin, Joinville, Froissart, Commynes*, ed. Albert Pauphilet (Paris: Gallimard, 1952), pp. 1–81
Rustichello da Pisa: *Il romanzo arturiano di Rustichello da Pisa*, ed. Fabrizio Cigni (Ospedaletto: Pacini, 1994)
Thomas de Kent, *Le Roman d'Alexandre ou Le Roman de toute chevalerie*, ed. Brian Foster and Ian Short, trans. Catherine Gaullier-Bougassas and Laurence Harf-Lancner (Paris: Champion, 2003)
Villehardouin, Geoffroi de, *La Conquête de Constantinople*, in *Historiens et chroniqueurs du moyen âge: Robert de Clari, Villehardouin, Joinville, Froissart, Commynes*, ed. Albert Pauphilet (Paris: Gallimard, 1952), pp. 83–194

Secondary sources

Abeydeera, Ananda, 'Le voyage de Marco Polo dans le pays du bouddhisme', *Corps Ecrit*, 34 (1990), 19–28
Abu-Lughod, Janet L., *Before European Hegemony: The World System AD 1250–1350* (New York and Oxford: Oxford University Press, 1989)
Agamben, Giorgio, *Homo Sacer: il potere sovrano e la nuda vita* (Turin: Einaudi, 1995)
Agamben, Giorgio, *La comunità che viene*, 2nd edn (Turin: Bollati Boringhieri, 2001)
Akbari, Suzanne Conklin, and Iannucci, Amilcare A. (eds), *Marco Polo and the Encounter of East and West* (Toronto: University of Toronto Press, 2008)
Akbari, Suzanne Conklin, 'Currents and Currency in Marco Polo's *Devisement*

dou monde and *The Book of John Mandeville*', in Akbari and Iannucci (eds), *Marco Polo*, pp. 110–30
Akbari, Suzanne Conklin, *Idols in the East: European Representations of Islam and the Orient (1100–1450)* (Ithaca, NY, and London: Cornell University Press, 2009)
Allsen, Thomas T., 'The Cultural Worlds of Marco Polo', *Journal of Interdisciplinary History*, 31 (2001), 375–83
Apter, Emily, *The Translation Zone: A New Comparative Literature* (Princeton and Oxford: Princeton University Press, 2006)
Arens, William, 'Rethinking Anthopophagy', in Barker, Hulme and Iversen (ed.), *Cannibalism*, pp. 39–62
Ashcroft, Bill, Griffiths, Gareth, and Tiffin, Helen, *Post-Colonial Studies: The Key Concepts* (London and New York: Routledge, 2000)
Aslanov, Cyril, *Le Français au Levant, jadis et naguère: à la recherche d'une langue perdue* (Paris: Honoré Champion, 2006)
Auerbach, Erich, *Mimesis: The Representation of Reality in Western Literature*, trans. Willard Trask (Princeton: Princeton University Press, 1953)
Avril, François, Gousset, Marie-Thérèse, Monfrin, Jacques, Richard, Jean, and Tesnière, Marie-Hélène, *Marco Polo Das Buch der Wunder. Handschrift Français 2810 der Bibliothèque Nationale de Paris/Le Livre des merveilles. MS fr. 2810 de la Bibliothèque Nationale de France* (Lucerne: Faksimile Verlag, 1996)
Badel, Pierre-Yves, 'Lire la merveille selon Marco Polo', *Revue des Sciences Humaines*, 183 (1981), 7–16
Barbieri, Alvaro, *Dal viaggio al libro. Studi sul 'Milione'* (Verona: Fiorini, 2004)
Barbieri, Alvaro, 'Il "narrativo" nel *Devisement dou Monde*: tipologia, fonti, funzioni', in Conte (ed.), *I viaggi del 'Milione'*, pp. 49–75
Barker, Francis, Hulme, Peter, and Iversen, Margaret (eds), *Cannibalism and the Colonial World* (Cambridge: Cambridge University Press, 1998)
Barthes, Roland, 'L'effet de réel', *Communications*, 11 (1968), 84–9
Bartlett, Robert, 'Medieval Concepts of Race and Ethnicity', *Journal of Medieval and Early Modern Studies*, 31 (2001), 39–56
Beltrami, Pietro G., Capusso, Maria Grazia, Cigni, Fabrizio, and Vatteroni, Sergio (eds), *Studi di filologia romanza offerti a Valeria Bertolucci Pizzorusso*, 2 vols (Pisa: Pacini, 2006)
Benjamin, Walter, 'The Task of the Translator: An Introduction to the Translations of Baudelaire's *Tableaux Parisiens*', in Venuti (ed.), *The Translation Studies Reader*, pp. 15–25
Bergreen, Laurence, *Marco Polo: From Venice to Xanadu* (London: Quercus, 2008)
Berman, Antoine, 'Translation and the Trials of the Foreign', in Venuti (ed.), *The Translation Studies Reader*, pp. 284–97
Bertolucci Pizzorusso, Valeria, 'Enunciazione e produzione del testo nel *Milione*', *Studi Mediolatini e Volgari*, 25 (1977), 5–43
Bertolucci Pizzorusso, Valeria, 'Lingue e stili nel *Milione*', in Renzo Zorzi (ed.), *L'epopea delle scoperte* (Venice: Leo S. Olschki, 1994), pp. 61–73
Bertolucci Pizzorusso, Valeria, 'Pour commencer à raconter le voyage: le prologue de la relation de Marco Polo', in Baumgartner, Emmanuèle, and

Harf-Lancner, Laurence (eds), *Seuils de l'œuvre dans le texte médiéval* (Paris: Presses de la Sorbonne Nouvelle, 2002), pp. 115–30

Bertolucci Pizzorusso, Valeria, 'La réception de la littérature courtoise du XIIème et XIIIème siècle en Italie: nouvelles propositions', in Altmann, Barbara K., and Carroll, Carleton W. (eds), *The Court Reconvenes: Courtly Literature across the Disciplines* (Cambridge: D.S. Brewer, 2003), pp. 3–13

Bertolucci Pizzorusso, Valeria, 'Le meraviglie inquietanti: Marco Polo, Sklovskij, Calvino', *Studi Mediolatini e Volgari*, 51 (2005), 7–26

Bertolucci Pizzorusso, Valeria, 'Le versioni storiche del *Milione* in Italia. La versione toscana', in Masini, Salvatori and Schipani (eds), *Marco Polo 750 anni*, pp.199–208

Bertoni, Giulio, 'L'istituto di filologia di Roma', *Cultura Neolatina*, 1 (1941), 5–12

Bhabha, Homi K., *The Location of Culture* (London and New York: Routledge, 1994)

Bianchi, Vito, *Marco Polo: storia del mercante che capì la Cina* (Bari: Laterza, 2007)

Borlandini, F., 'Alle origini del libro di Marco Polo', in *Studi in onore di Amintore Fanfani*, 6 vols (Milan: Giuffrè, 1962), I, pp. 107–47

Burgio, Eugenio, 'Marco Polo e gli idolatri', *L'immagine riflessa*, 8 (2005), 31–62

Burgio, Eugenio, and Mascherpa, Giuseppe, '«Milione» latino. Note linguistiche e appunti di storia della tradizione sulle redazioni Z e L', in Oniga and Vatteroni (eds), *Plurilinguismo letterario*, pp. 119–58

Burgio, Eugenio, and Eusebi, Mario, 'Per una nuova edizione del *Milione*', in Conte (ed.), *I viaggi del 'Milione'*, pp. 17–48

Butler, Judith, *Gender Trouble: Feminism and the Subversion of Identity* (London and New York: Routledge, 1990)

Bynum, Caroline Walker, 'Wonder', *American Historical Review*, 103 (1997), 1–26

Calabrese, Michael, 'Between Despair and Ecstasy: Marco Polo's Life of the Bhudda', *Exemplaria*, 9 (1997), 189–229

Campbell, Mary B., *The Witness and the Other World: Exotic European Travel Writing, 400–1600* (Ithaca, NY, and London: Cornell University Press, 1988)

Capusso, Maria Grazia, *La lingua del "Devisament dou Monde" di Marco Polo: 1 morfologia verbale* (Pisa: Pacini, 1980)

Capusso, Maria Grazia, 'La mescidanza linguistica del *Milione* franco-italiano', in Conte (ed.), *I viaggi del 'Milione'*, pp. 263–83

Chow, Rey, 'Reading Derrida on Being Monolingual', *New Literary History*, 39 (2008), 217–31

Cigni, Fabrizio, 'La ricezione della letteratura francese nella Toscana nord-occidentale', in Werner, Edeltraud, and Schwarze, Sabine (eds), *Fra toscanità e italianità* (Tübingen and Basel: Francke, 2000), pp. 71–108

Cigni, Fabrizio, 'Copisti prigionieri (Genova, fine sec. XIII)', in Beltrami, Capusso, Cigni and Vatteroni (eds), *Studi di filologia*, I, pp. 425–39

Cigni, Fabrizio, '"Prima" del *Devisement dou Monde*. Osservazioni (e alcune ipotesi) sulla lingua della *Compilazione arturiana* di Rustichello da Pisa', in Conte (ed.), *I viaggi del 'Milione'*, pp. 219–31

Conte, Silvia (ed.), *I viaggi del 'Milione': itinerari testuali, vettori di trasmissione e metamorfosi del Devisement du monde di Marco Polo e Rustichello da Pisa nella pluralità delle attestazioni. Convegno internazionale Venezia, 6–8 ottobre 2005* (Rome: Tiellemedia, 2008)

Cornish, Alison, 'Translatio Galliae: Effects of Early Franco-Italian Exchange', *Romanic Review*, 97 (2006), 309–30

Cornish, Alison, *Vernacular Translation in Dante's Italy: Illiterate Literature* (Cambridge: Cambridge University Press, 2011)

Critchley, John, *Marco Polo's Book* (Aldershot: Variorum, 1992)

Cruse, Mark, *Illuminating the* Roman d'Alexandre*: Oxford, Bodleian Library, MS Bodley 264: The Manuscript as Monument* (Cambridge: D.S. Brewer, 2011)

Curtius, Ernst Robert, *European Literature and the Latin Middle Ages*, trans. Willard R. Trask (London: Routledge and Kegan Paul, 1953)

Daston, Lorraine, and Park, Katherine, *Wonders and the Order of Nature, 1150–1700* (New York: Zone Books, 1998)

Dawson, Christopher, *Mission to Asia* (Toronto: Toronto University Press, 1980)

Delcorno Branca, Daniela, *Tristano e Lancillotto in Italia: studi di letteratura arturiana* (Ravenna: Longo, 1998)

Deleuze, Gilles, and Guattari, Félix, *Kafka: pour une littérature mineure* (Paris: Les Editions de Minuit, 1975)

Derrida Jacques, *De la Grammatologie* (Paris: Les Editions de Minuit, 1967)

Derrida, Jacques, *L'Ecriture et la différence* (Paris: Les Editions de Minuit, 1967)

Derrida, Jacques, *Donner le temps 1: La fausse monnaie* (Paris: Galilée, 1991)

Derrida, Jacques, *Le Monolinguisme de l'autre ou la prothèse d'origine* (Paris: Galilée, 1996)

Derrida, Jacques, 'Des Tours de Babel', in *Psyché: Inventions de l'autre* (Paris: Galilée, 1998), pp. 203–35

Dictionnaire du Moyen Français, consulted on-line at http://www.atilf.fr/dmf/

Dutschke, Consuelo W., 'Francesco Pipino and the Manuscripts of Marco Polo's *Travels*', unpublished Ph.D. dissertation, University of California at Los Angeles, 1993

Dutschke, Consuelo W., 'The Truth in the Book: The Marco Polo Texts in Royal 19 D 1 and Bodley 264', *Scriptorium*, 52 (1998), 278–300

Duval, Frédéric, 'Les néologismes', in Galderisi (ed.), *Translations médiévales*, I, pp. 499–534

Espada, Antonio García, *Marco Polo y la cruzada: historia de la literatura de viajes a las Indias en el siglo XIV* (Madrid: Marcial Pons Historia, 2009)

Fleischman, Suzanne, 'Philology, Linguistics and the Discourse of the Medieval Text', *Speculum*, 65 (1990), 19–37

Fleischman, Suzanne, *Tense and Narrativity: From Medieval Performance to Modern Fiction* (London: Routledge, 1990)

Folena, Gianfranco, *Culture e lingue nel Veneto medievale* (Padua: Editoriale Programma, 1990)

Foucault, Michel, *Les Mots et les choses: une archéologie des sciences humaines* (Paris: Gallimard, 1966)

Foucault, Michel, 'Qu'est-ce qu'un auteur?', *Bulletin de la Société Française de Philosophie*, 63 (1969), 73–104

France, Peter (ed.), *The New Oxford Companion to Literature in French* (Oxford: Clarendon Press, 1995)
Freud, Sigmund *The Uncanny*, trans. David McClintock, with an introduction by Hugh Haughton (London: Penguin, 2003)
Friedman, John Block, *The Monstrous Races in Medieval Art and Thought* (Cambridge, MA, and London: Harvard University Press, 1981)
Frisch, Andrea, *The Invention of the Eyewitness: Witnessing and Testimony in Early Modern France* (Chapel Hill: University of North Carolina Press, 2004)
Galderisi, Claudio (ed.), *Translations médiévales: cinq siècles de traduction en français au Moyen Âge (XIe–XVe siècles). Etude et répertoire*, 3 vols (Turnhout: Brepols, 2011)
Gaunt, Simon, and Weiss, Julian, 'Cultural Traffic in the Medieval Romance World', *Journal of Romance Studies*, 4 (2004), 1–12
Gaunt, Simon, '*La greigneur merveille du monde*: Marco Polo and French as a Marker of Cultural Relativity', *French Studies Bulletin*, 100 (2006), 63–6
Gaunt, Simon, 'Can the Middle Ages be Postcolonial?', *Comparative Literature*, 61 (2009), 160–76
Gaunt, Simon, 'Translating the Diversity of the Middle Ages: Marco Polo and John Mandeville as "French" Writers', *Australian Journal of French Studies*, 46 (2009), 235–48
Gaunt, Simon, 'L'inquiétante étrangeté de la littérature de voyage en français au moyen âge', *Medioevo Romanzo*, 36 (2010), 57–81
Gaunt, Simon, 'Untranslatable', in Campbell, Emma, and Mills, Robert (eds), *Rethinking Medieval Translation: Ethics, Politics, Theory* (Cambridge: D.S. Brewer, 2012), pp. 243–55
Gaunt, Simon, 'Coming Communities in Medieval Francophone Writing about the Orient', in Guynn, Noah and Stahuljak, Zrinka (eds), *Violence and the Writing of History in the Medieval Francophone World* (Cambridge: D.S. Brewer, 2013), pp. 187–201
Godefroy, Frédéric, *Dictionnaire de l'ancienne langue française et de tous ses dialectes*, 10 vols (Paris: F. Vieweg, 1880–1902)
Gosman, Martin, 'Marco Polo's Voyages: The Conflict between Confirmation and Observation', in von Martels, Zweder (ed.), *Travel Fact and Travel Fiction: Studies in Fiction, Literary Tradition, Scholarly Discovery and Observation in Travel Writing* (Leiden: Brill, 1994), pp. 72–84
Gosman, Martin, *La Légende d'Alexandre le Grand dans la littérature française du 12e siècle* (Amsterdam: Rodopi, 1997)
Grady, Frank, *Representing Righteous Heathens in Late Medieval England* (Basingstoke: Palgrave, 2006)
Greenblatt, Stephen, *Marvelous Possessions: The Wonder of the New World* (Oxford: Clarendon Press, 1991)
Guéret-Laferté, Michèle, 'Le vocabulaire exotique du *Devisement du Monde*', in Conte (ed.), *I viaggi del 'Milione'*, pp. 287–305
Guzman, Gregory G., 'Reports of Mongol Cannibalism in the Thirteenth-Century Latin Sources: Oriental Fact or Western Fiction', in Westrem, Scott D. (ed.), *Discovering New Worlds: Essays on Medieval Exploration and Imagination* (New York and London: Garland, 1991), pp. 31–68
Hahn, Thomas, 'The Difference the Middle Ages Makes: Color and Race before

the Modern World', *Journal of Medieval and Early Modern Studies*, 31 (2001), 1–37

Harf-Lancner, Laurence, 'From Alexander to Marco Polo, from Text to Image: The Marvels of India', in Maddox, Donald, and Sturm-Maddox, Sara (eds), *The Medieval French Alexander* (Albany: State University of New York Press, 2002), pp. 235–57

Harf-Lancner, Laurence, 'Divergences du texte et de l'image: l'illustration du *Divisement du monde* de Marco Polo', *Ateliers*, 30 (2003), 39–52

Haw, Stephen G., *Marco Polo's China: A Venetian in the Realm of Khubilai Khan* (London and New York: Routledge, 2006). Consulted as an e-book (Kindle); references are to chapters.

Heers, Jacques, *Marco Polo* (Paris: Fayard, 1983)

Heng, Geraldine, *Empire of Magic: Medieval Romance and the Politics of Cultural Fantasy* (New York: Columbia University Press, 2003)

Higgins, Iain Macleod, *Writing East: The 'Travels' of Sir John Mandeville* (Philadelphia: University of Pennsylvania Press, 1997)

Hobson, John M., *The Eastern Origins of Western Civilisation* (Cambridge: Cambridge University Press, 2004)

Holtus Günter, and Wunderli, Peter, *Franco-Italien et épopée franco-italienne* (Heidelberg: Universitätsverlag Winter, 2005) (= *Grundriss der Romanischen Litteraturen des Mittelalters*, vol. I.2, fasc. 10)

Huang, Yinte, 'Marco Polo: Meditations on Intangible Economy and Vernacular Imagination', in Akbari and Iannucci (eds), *Marco Polo*, pp. 262–79

Hulme, Peter, 'The Cannibal Scene', in Barker, Hulme and Iversen (eds), *Cannibalism*, pp. 1–38

Ineichen, Gustav, 'La mescolanza delle forme linguistiche nel "Milione" di Marco Polo', in Holtus, Günter, Krauss, Henning, and Wunderli, Peter (eds), *Testi, cotesti e contesti del franco-italiano: in memoriam Alberto Limentani* (Tübingen: Niemeyer, 1989), pp. 65–74

Islam, Syed Manzarul, *The Ethics of Travel from Marco Polo to Kafka* (Manchester and New York: Manchester University Press, 1996)

Jackson, Peter, *The Mongols and the West, 1221–1410* (Harlow: Longman, 2005)

Jacoby, David, 'Marco Polo, His Close Relatives, and His Travel Account: Some New Insights', *Mediterranean Historical Review*, 21 (2006), 193–218

Kappler, Claire, and Thiolier-Méjean, Suzanne (eds), *Le Plurilinguisme au moyen âge: Orient-Occident: de Babel à la langue une* (Paris: L'Harmattan, 2009)

Kay, Sarah, 'La seconde main et les secondes langues dans la France médiévale', in Galderisi (ed.), *Translations médiévales*, I, pp. 461–85

Kinoshita, Sharon, *Medieval Boundaries: Rethinking Difference in Old French Literature* (Philadelphia: University of Pennsylvania Press, 2006)

Kinoshita, Sharon, 'Marco Polo's *Le Devisement dou Monde* and the Tributary East', in Akbari and Iannucci (eds), *Marco Polo*, pp. 60–86

Kosta-Théfaine, Jean-François, 'Du récit de voyage et de sa mise en image: l'exemple du manuscrit de New York (Pierpont Morgan Library M 723) du *Devisement du Monde* de Marco Polo', in Korzilius, Jean-Loup (ed.), *Art et Littérature: le voyage entre texte et image* (Amsterdam: Rodopi, 2006), pp. 31–60

Kristeva, Julia, *Etrangers à nous-mêmes*, 2nd edn (Paris: Gallimard, 1991)

Lacan, Jacques, 'L'instance de la lettre dans l'inconscient ou la raison depuis Freud', in *Ecrits* (Paris: Seuil, 1966), pp. 493–528

Lacan, Jacques, 'The Insistence of the Letter in the Unconscious', *Yale French Studies*, 36/7 (1966), 112–47

Lacan, Jacques, *Le Séminaire livre X: l'angoisse* (Paris: Seuil, 2004)

Larner, John, *Marco Polo and the Discovery of the World* (New Haven, CT, and London: Yale University Press, 1999)

Léglu, Catherine E., *Multilingualism and Mother Tongue in Medieval French, Occitan and Catalan Narratives* (University Park: Penn State University Press, 2010)

Le Goff, Jacques, *L'Imaginaire médiéval* (Paris: Gallimard, 1985)

Leonardi, Lino, 'Il testo come ipotesi (critica del manoscritto-base)', *Medioevo Romanzo*, 35 (2011), 5–34

Lestringant, Frank, *Cannibals: The Discovery and Representation of the Cannibal from Columbus to Jules Verne* (Berkeley and Los Angeles: University of California Press, 1997)

Levinas, Emmanuel, *Totalité et infini: essai sur l'extériorité* (The Hague: Martinus Nijhoff, 1961)

Lodge, R. Anthony, *French: From Dialect to Standard* (London and New York: Routledge, 1993)

Lusignan, Serge, *La Langue des rois au Moyen Age: le français en France et en Angleterre* (Paris: PUF, 2004)

Marnette, Sophie, *Narrateurs et points de vue dans la littérature française médiévale: une approche linguistique* (Bern: Peter Lang, 1998)

Marroni, Sergio, 'La meravilgia di Marco Polo. L'espressione della meraviglia nel lessico e nella sintassi del *Milione*', in Conte (ed.), *I viaggi del 'Milione'*, pp. 233–62

Masini, Federico, Salvatori, Franco, and Schipani, Sandro (eds), *Marco Polo 750 anni. Il viaggo. Il libro. Il diritto. Congresso internazionale (*Rome: Tiellemedia, 2006)

Ménard, Philippe, 'L'illustration du *Devisement du Monde* de Marco Polo: étude d'iconographie comparée', in Moureau, François (ed.), *Métamorphose du récit de voyage* (Paris: Champion/Slatkine, 1986), pp. 17–31

Ménard, Philippe, 'Réflexions sur l'illustration du texte de Marco Polo dans le manuscrit fr. 2810 de la bibliothèque nationale de Paris', in *Mélanges in memoriam Takeshi Shimmura* (Tokyo: France Tosho, 1998), pp. 81–92

Ménard, Philippe, 'Le prétendu remaniement du *Devisement du Monde* de Marco Polo', *Medioevo Romanzo*, 11 (1998), 332–51

Ménard, Philippe, 'Marco Polo en Angleterre', *Medioevo Romanzo*, 24 (2000), 189–208

Ménard, Philippe, 'Le problème de la version originale du "Devisement du Monde" de Marco Polo', in Livi, François (ed.), *De Marco Polo à Savinio : écrivains italiens en langue française* (Paris: Presses de l'Université de Paris-Sorbonne, 2003), pp. 7–19

Ménard, Philippe, 'Marco Polo en images: les représentations du voyageur au moyen âge', in Beltrami, Capusso, Cigni and Vatteroni (eds), *Studi di filologia*, II, pp. 993–1021

Ménard, Philippe, 'Intérêt et importance de la version française du *Devisement du Monde* de Marco Polo', in Masini, Salvatori and Schipani (eds), *Marco Polo 750 anni*, pp. 183–97

Ménard, Philippe, *Marco Polo: à la découverte du monde* (Paris: Glénat, 2007)

Ménard, Philippe, 'Le mélange des langues dans les diverses versions du *Devisement du Monde* de Marco Polo', in Kappler and Thiolier-Méjean (ed.), *Le Plurilinguisme au moyen âge*, pp. 233–49

Meneghetti, Maria Luisa, 'Scrivere in carcere nel medioevo', in Francia, P. (ed.), *Studi di filologia e letteratura in onore di Maria Picchio Simonelli* (Alessandria: Edizioni dell' Orso,1992), pp. 185–99

Meneghetti, Maria Luisa, 'Quando l'immagine dice di più: riflessioni sull'apparato decororativo del *Livre des Merveilles du monde*', in Beltrami, Capusso, Cigni and Vatteroni (eds), *Studi di filologia*, II, pp. 1023–49

Menocal, María Rosa, *Shards of Love: Exile and the Origins of the Lyric* (Durham, NC, and London: Duke University Press, 1994)

Meyer, Paul, 'De l'expansion de la langue française en Italie pendant le moyen âge', in *Atti del Congresso Internazionale di Scienze Storiche IV: sezione storia delle letterature* (Rome: Accademia dei Lincei, 1904), pp. 61–104

Minervini, Laura, 'La lingua franca mediterranea: plurilinguismo, multilinguismo, pidginizzazione sulle coste del Mediterraneo tra tardo medioevo e prima età moderna', *Medioevo Romanzo*, 20 (1996), 231–301

Monfrin, Jacques, *Etudes de philologie romane* (Droz: Geneva, 2001)

Münkler, Marina, *Marco Polo: vita e leggende*, trans. Giuliana Cavallo-Guzzo (Milan: Vita e Pensiero, 2001)

Niemeyer, Jan Frederik, *Mediae Latinitatis Lexicon Minus* (Leiden: Brill, 1954–77)

Nancy, Jean-Luc, *La Communauté désœuvrée*, 2nd edn (Paris: Christian Bourgeois, 1999)

O'Doherty, Marianne, '"They Are Like Beasts, For They Have No Law": Ethnography and the Construction of Human Difference in Late Medieval Translations of Marco Polo's *Book*', in Kosta-Théfaine, Jean-François (ed.), *Travels and Travelogues in the Middle Ages* (Brooklyn: AMS Press, 2009), pp. 59–93

Olschki, Leonardo, *L'Asia di Marco Polo: introduzione alla lettura e allo studio del 'Milione'* (Venice: Fondazione Cini, 1957)

Oniga, Renato and Vatteroni, Sergio (ed.), *Plurilinguismo letterario* (Soveria Mannelli: Rubbettino, 2007)

Orlandini, Giovanni, 'Marco Polo e la sua famiglia', *Archivio Veneto-Tridentino*, 9 (1926), 1–68

Paris, Gaston, 'Romani, Romania, lingua romana, romancium', *Romania*, 1 (1872), 1–22

Park, Katherine, 'The Meaning of Natural Diversity: Marco Polo on the "Division" of the World', in Sylla, Edith, and McVaugh, Michael (eds), *Texts and Contexts in Ancient and Medieval Science: Studies on the Occasion of John E. Murdoch's Seventieth Birthday* (Leiden and New York: Brill, 1997), pp. 134–47

Pelliot, Paul, *Notes on Marco Polo*, 3 vols (Paris: Imprimerie Nationale, 1959–73)

Pfister, Max, 'Le bilinguisme de Brunetto Latini: *Le Livre du Trésor*', in Kappler and Thiolier-Méjean (ed.), *Le Plurilinguisme au Moyen Âge*, pp. 203–216.

Phillips, J.R.S., *The Medieval Expansion of Europe*, 2nd edn (Oxford: Clarendon Press, 1998)
Posner, Rebecca, *Linguistic Change in French* (Oxford: Clarendon Press, 1997)
Pratt, Mary Louise, *Imperial Eyes: Travel Writing and Transculturation* (London and New York: Routledge, 1992)
Rachewiltz, Igor de, 'Marco Polo Went to China', *Zentralasiatische Studien*, 27 (1997), 34–92
Racine, Pierre, *Marco Polo et ses voyages* (Paris: Perrin, 2012). Consulted as e-book (I-books); references are to chapters.
Renzi, Lorenzo, 'Il francese come lingua letteraria e il franco-lombardo: l'epica carolingia nel Veneto', in Araldi, Girolamo, and Folena, Gianfranco (eds), *Storia della cultura Veneta I: delle origini al trecento* (Vicenza: Neri Pozza Editore, 1976), pp. 563–89
Rieger, Dietmar, 'Marco Polo und Rustichello da Pisa: der Reisende und sein Erzähler', in von Ertzdorff, Xenia (ed.), *Reisen und Reiseliteratur im Mittelalter und in der Frühen Neuzeit* (Amsterdam: Rodopi, 1992), pp. 289–312
Roques, Mario, 'Les manuscrits de Marco Polo', *Romania*, 76 (1955), 399–408
Ross, David J.A., 'Methods of Book Production in a XIVth-Century French Miscellany (London, B.M. Royal 19.D.1)', *Scriptorium*, 6 (1952), 63–75
Rossabi, Morris, *Khubilai Khan: His Life and Times* (Berkeley and Los Angeles: University of California Press, 1988)
Rouse, Richard H. and Mary A., *Manuscripts and their Makers: Commercial Book Producers in Medieval Paris, 1200–1500*, 2 vols (London: Harvey Miller, 2000)
Ruggieri, Ruggero, *Marco Polo e l'oriente francescano* (Rome: Edizioni Porziuncola, 1984)
Segre, Cesare, 'Marco Polo: filologia e industria culturale', in Ronchi, Gabriella, Milanesi, Marica, and Segre, Cesare (eds), *Avventure del 'Milione'* (Parma: Zara, 1983), pp. 9–20
Segre, Cesare, 'Chi ha scritto il *Milione* di Marco Polo?', in Conte (ed.), *I viaggi del 'Milione'*, pp. 5–16
Shankman, Steven, *Other Others: Levinas, Literature, Transcultural Studies* (Albany: SUNY Press, 2010)
Smethurst, Paul 'The Journey from Modern to Postmodern in the *Travels of Sir John Mandeville* and Marco Polo's *Divisament dou Monde*', in Utz, Richard, and Swan, Jesse G. (eds), *Studies in Medievalism XIII: Postmodern Medievalisms* (Cambridge: D.S. Brewer, 2005), pp. 159–79
Spiegel, Gabrielle M., *Romancing the Past: The Rise of Prose Historiography in Thirteenth-Century France* (Berkeley and Oxford: University of California Press, 1993)
Steinicke, Marion, 'Marco Polo's *Devisement dou monde* as a Narcissistic Trauma', in Akbari and Iannucci (eds), *Marco Polo*, pp. 87–109
Strickland, Debra Higgs, *Saracens, Demons and Jews: Making Monsters in Medieval Art* (Princeton and Oxford: Princeton University Press, 2003)
Strickland, Debra Higgs, 'Artists, Audience, and Ambivalence in Marco Polo's *Divisament dou Monde*', *Viator*, 36 (2005), 493–529
Strickland, Debra Higgs, 'Text, Image, and Contradiction in the *Devisement dou monde*', in Akbari and Iannucci (ed.), *Marco Polo*, pp. 23–59

Tattersall, Jill, 'Anthropophagi and Eaters of Raw Flesh in French Literature of the Crusade Period: Myth, Tradition and Reality', *Medium Aevum*, 57 (1988), 240–53

Terracini, B., 'Richerche e appunti sulla più antica redazione del *Milione*', *Rendiconti della Reale Accademia Nazionale dei Lincei*, ser. VI, 9 (1933), 369–428

Tobler, Alfred, and Lommatzsch, Erhard, *Altfranzösisches Wörterbuch*, 11 vols (Berlin: Weidmannsche, 1925–2002)

Tucci, Ugo, 'I primi viaggiatori e l'opera di Marco Polo', in Araldi, Girolamo, and Folena, Gianfranco (eds), *Storia della cultura veneta: dalle origini al Trecento*, 8 vols (Vicenza: Neri Pozza, 1976), I, pp. 633–70

Uebel, Michael, *Ecstatic Transformation: On the Uses of Alterity in the Middle Ages* (New York: Palgrave, 2005)

Varvaro, Alberto, 'Language and Culture', in Abulafia, David (ed.), *Short Oxford History of the Middle Ages: Italy in the Central Middle Ages* (Oxford: Oxford University Press, 2004), pp. 195–211

Venuti, Lawrence, *The Scandals of Translation: Towards an Ethics of Difference* (London and New York: Routledge, 1998)

Venuti, Lawrence (ed.), *The Translation Studies Reader* (London and New York: Routledge, 2000)

Vitullo, Juliann, *The Chivalric Epic in Medieval Italy* (Gainsville, FL: University of Florida Press, 2000)

Wartburg, Walther von, *Franzözisches Etymologishes Wörterbuch*, 25 vols (Tübingen: Niemeyer, 1922–2005)

Wehr, Barbara, 'A propos de la genèse du "Devisement dou monde" de Marco Polo', in Selig, Maria, Frank, Barbara, and Hartmann, Jörg (eds), *Le Passage à l'écrit des langues romanes* (Tübingen: Gunter Narr Verlag, 1993), pp. 299–326

Wehr, Barbara, 'Venetismi e toscanismi nel MS. B.N. FR. 1116 del testo di Marco Polo', in Oniga and Vatteroni (eds), *Plurilinguismo letterario*, pp. 205–23

Wittkower, Rudolf, *Allegory and the Migration of Symbols* (London: Thames and Hudson, 1977)

Wood, Frances, *Did Marco Polo Go to China?* (London: Martin Secker and Warburg, 1995)

Wunderli, Peter, 'Un luogo di "interferenze": il franco-italiano', in Morini, Luigina (ed.), *La cultura dell'Italia padana e la presenza francese nei secoli XII–XV* (Alessandria: Edizioni dell'Orso, 2001), pp. 55–66

Young, Robert J.C., *Colonial Desire: Hybridity in Theory, Culture, and Race* (London and New York: Routledge, 1995)

Yule, Henry, *The Book of Ser Marco Polo the Venetian concerning the Kingdoms and Marvels of the East*, revised by Henri Cordier, 2 vols (London: John Murray, 1903)

Zhou, Gang, 'Small Talk: A New Reading of Marco Polo's *Il Milione*', *Modern Language Notes*, 124 (2009), 1–22

Žižek, Slavoj, *The Sublime Object of Ideology* (London and New York: Verso, 1989)

Zorzi, Alvise, *Vita di Marco Polo veneziano*, 2nd edn (Milan: Bompiano, 2000)

Zumthor, Paul, 'The Medieval Travel Narrative', *New Literary History*, 25 (1994), 809–824

INDEX

Note: whereas the names of countries and some cities that most readers will find easily recognizable (e.g. Japan, Baghdad) are indexed under their modern English forms, the majority of place names are indexed using the orthography of the Franco-Italian redaction. A modern form is then given in brackets. The modern form of Chinese and Indochinese place names are taken from Stephen Haw's useful catalogue in *Marco Polo's China: A Venetian in the Realm of Khubilai Khan* (London and New York: Routledge, 2006). Modern forms of other place names are taken from Wikipedia. Modern theorists are indexed selectively, with only those whose work is referenced substantially appearing.

Abyssinia 140
Acre 4, 5, 145, 171
Adam's Peak 97–8, 101–2
Aden 140
Africa 69, 114, 150, 164
Agamben, Giorgio 156–7, 160
Alau (Hülegü) 72, 122–3
Alexander the Great 31–2, 68–71, 114, 117, 171
Alexander tradition 29, 33–4, 107, 114, 121–2, 148 n. 8, 171, 177
Andaman Islands 121–2 n. 14, 168, 171
Aniu (Heni, in Vietnam) 154
Arghun (Persian Ilkhan) 5
Aristotle 148
Armenia 18, 32, 42, 73, 82–4, 114
Asia 1–3, 6–7, 32, 34, 67, 69–70, 70–1, 74, 113, 115, 122–3, 135, 148, 150, 158 n. 30, 166, 169, 176–8
Ayas 4

Babel 105–6, 157
Bactria 69–70
Baghdad 140
Baldasciam (Badakhshan) 63
Bangala (Bengal) 52, 59, 154
Berca 72
Bethlehem 70
Bhabha, Homi 39, 76 n. 79, 86, 103–4, 165
Black Death 6 n. 24, 115 n. 7, 177
Black Sea 3–4

Blemmyae 121
Brahmins 69, 95, 100 n. 55, 137–8
Brunetto Latini 14, 16, 26–7, 30, 68, 70–2, 81, 110, 179
 Le Tresor 14, 26, 27, 30, 68–72, 81, 110, 148 n. 8
Buddha 95–101, 138–9
Buddhism 95, 100
Bukhara 3, 122

Cacianfu (Hezhongfu, now Puzhou) 107
Caingiu (Changzhou) 107
Calvino, Italo 38, 173–8, 181
Candinfu (Dongpingfu, now Dongping) 107
Cangigu (Jiaozhi Guo, Northern Vietnam) 154
Cannibalism 147, 163–72
Caspian Sea 32
Cathay *see* China
Ceylon (Sri Lanka) 95–6, 100
Chanson de Roland 27, 96 n. 47, 100 n. 54, 131, 135
Charles de Valois 19
China 49, 74, 103, 115–6, 123–4, 134, 155, 158 n. 30, 159 n. 32, 166, 171, 176, 178, 182
Christianity 17, 19, 32–3, 37, 70, 88, 95 n. 43, 96, 100–1, 116–17, 126–35, 137–44, 145–6, 157, 163, 181
Chronicles 33, 46–8, 54, 55 n. 33, 56 n. 38, 57, 61

Ciandu (Shangdu) 166
Ciangan (Changxing) 154
Ciangli (Jiengling, now Dezhou) 107
Cianglu (Changlu, now Cangzhou) 107
Cingiu (Tongzhou, now Nantong) 107, 108, 151
Clari, Robert de 47–8, 57, 61
Clement IV 4
Coigangiu (Huai'anzhou, now Huai'an) 66
Columbus, Christopher 1, 38, 74–5, 164, 169, 181–2
Comanians 31, 117
Creman (Kerman) 63–4
Crusading 29, 33–4, 46, 57, 133–4, 139, 145, 165, 171, 177
Curzola, Battle of 5
Cynocephalus 121–2 n. 14, 169
Cyprus 135

Dante 26–7, 81, 111
David Melic (King David) 78
Derrida, Jacques 38, 89–91, 104–7, 109, 111, 147, 153, 160–1, 173–4
Devisement du Monde
 Franco-Italian redaction 3, 11, 14–22, 25, 30–1, 42–6, 49–62, 63–73, 81–9, 91, 94–102, 108, 111, 113, 118–19, 124–5, 139–40, 143, 149, 152–4 n. 21, 166–8
 French redaction 2, 12, 14–15, 18–9, 21–2, 24–6, 33–5, 45, 59–61, 64 n. 57, 66 n. 62, 67 n. 63, 78, 83, 86–9, 91–2, 94–6, 97–102, 111, 121–2, 124, 131–3, 139–40, 144, 154 n. 21, 166 n. 65, 172
 L redaction 12, 20–1
 Language of 12–19
 Pipino version 1 n. 3, 6 n. 23, 6 n. 24, 12–13, 19–21, 96, 114 n. 3, 124 n. 21, 135, 139, 144
 Prologue 16–17, 54 n. 32, 75–7, 174
 Ramusio version 5 n. 18, 6 n. 22, 6 n. 24, 10 n. 36, 12, 20, 22, 74–7
 Reception of 2, 6–10, 12 n. 46, 15–6, 18, 20–1, 33–5, 45, 61–2, 66 n. 62, 67 n. 63, 74, 78, 81–9, 95–102, 114–15, 123–5, 131–3, 135–7, 139, 141–3, 144, 166 n. 65, 172
 Transmission of 11–28, 144, 172
 Tuscan redaction 2, 12, 16 n. 54, 18, 45, 58, 66 n. 62, 67–8 n. 63, 78, 83–5, 92, 94, 95 n. 45, 98, 118–19, 124–5, 136 n. 40, 154 n. 21, 166 n. 65, 174
 Venetian redaction 2, 12, 13, 15, 18–19, 21, 58, 67–8 n. 63, 78 n. 1, 79, 96, 124–5, 136 n. 40, 154 n. 21
 Z redaction 12, 13, 20–22, 23, 45 n. 7, 61–2, 66 n. 62, 67 n. 63, 78, 95, 111, 124–5, 137, 141–3, 154 n. 21, 166 n. 65
 See also Marco Polo, Narrative voice and Rustichello da Pisa
Diversity 30, 37, 111, 113, 145, 147–53, 172
Dominicans 4, 20

Egypt 69–70
Eli (Ely) 57
Encyclopaedias 29–31, 33, 68, 109, 113, 148, 153
Ethnography 29, 71, 86
Euphrates 114

Faits des Romains 16 n. 54
Foucault, Michel 46, 160–1
Franco-Italian 13–16, 27, 93 n. 40
 See also *Devisement du Monde*, Franco-Italian redaction
French 14, 16, 24–8, 36, 79, 84, 87–9, 92–3, 110–11, 173–4
 See also *Devisement du Monde*, Franco-Italian redaction and French redaction
Freud, Sigmund 39, 127–8, 180
Fugiu (Fuzhou) 49, 141, 166, 171

Geography 29, 71
Georgia 18, 78
Genoa 5, 10 n. 36, 16, 18, 26, 36, 43, 51, 58 n. 45, 84, 181
Genghis Khan 3–4, 17, 20, 71–2, 127 n. 23, 134, 158 n. 30
Gervase of Tilbury 71, 120
Gog and Magog 32, 69, 171
Golden Horde 3, 131
Gossouin
 L'Image du Monde 68–71, 148 n. 8
Gregory X 4

Hayton 34, 133–4, 139, 145–6, 158, 172, 177
Hercules 69–70

Hinduism   100, 137
Histoire ancienne jusqu'à César   16 n. 54
Hülegü (Persian Ilkhan)   3, 122–3
Hungary   145
Hybridity   16, 24, 28, 35–6, 39, 85–6, 92–4, 146

Idolatry   95, 97–101, 135–43, 146, 154, 157, 167
Ilkhan *see* Arghun *and* Hülegü
India   4–5, 17, 19, 32,42, 49–51, 56, 58, 62 n. 53, 63, 66–70, 73, 83–4, 95, 114, 118, 121–2, 137, 141, 148, 155, 179
Indochina   4, 19, 155
Iran   131
Iraq   131
Isidore of Seville   71, 164
Islam   19, 100 n. 54, 131, 133, 134–5, 138–40, 145–6, 165, 167, 177
Italian   2, 14–16, 18, 19, 26–8, 80–1, 84–8, 93, 98, 104, 118 n. 10, 137, 173, 181
   See also Devisement du Monde, Tuscan redaction and Venetian redaction, Tuscan and Venetian

Jacopi d'Aqui   6 n. 23, 152
Jacques d'Armagnac   34
Jains   137
Japan   4, 66, 167, 169–71
Java   65, 118, 167, 171
Jean, Duc de Berry   34
Jean sans Peur   34
Jerusalem   70, 135, 178
Jews   130–1, 139–41
Joinville, Jean de   51–2, 57, 135
John of Plano Carpini   2 n. 6, 34, 135, 169, 177
Josaphat   100 n. 53
Judaism   135
Judea   70

Keshigten (imperial body guard)   4 n. 15
Kristeva, Julia   127–8, 180
Korea   4
Kublai Khan   3–4, 6, 17, 32, 52, 59, 72, 75–77, 95 n. 43, 101, 103, 113, 116, 119, 122–3, 125–33, 135, 141–2, 147, 155, 157–61, 173–7, 181

Lacan, Jacques   108, 128, 180

Lancelot en prose   15 n. 52
Latin   2, 5, 14–16, 19–21, 45 n. 7, 71, 78, 81, 103, 110, 133, 148
   See also Devisement du Monde, *L* redaction, Pipino version and *Z* redaction
Liber   69–70
Ligin (Liucheng)   107
Linguistic difference   82, 104–5, 153–5, 160
Louis IX   2 n. 6, 135

Maffeo Polo   2, 3, 6 n. 23, 122–3, 141, 142
Mandeville, Jean de   146 n. 3
   Le Livre des Merveilles du Monde   34, 38, 74, 115, 146 n. 3, 152–3, 158, 177–81
Mangi (Manzi)   49, 66, 124, 151
Manuscripts
   Berlin, Staatsbibliothek, Hamilton 424   22
   Florence, Biblioteca Nazionale, II.IV.88   13 n. 47
   London, British Library, Cotton Othon D V   11 n. 39
   London, British Library, Royal 19 D 1   34, 87, 114, 131–3
   New York, Pierpont Morgan M 723   133 n. 35
   Oxford, Bodley 264   33–4, 120–2
   Paris, Arsenal 5219   35
   Paris, BNF f.fr. 1116   11–16, 19–23, 25, 36, 58 n. 43, 79, 85, 93 n. 38, 98, 102, 124, 136 n. 40, 150
   Paris BNF f.fr. 2810   29 n. 97, 34, 114, 121–2, 133 n. 35
   Paris BNF f.fr. 5649   33
Mappae mundi   30, 178
Marco Polo
   Authenticity and truthfulness   6, 7, 74–5, 116, 119, 141–3, 169, 177
   Biography   1–2, 3–4, 38
   Linguistic ability   78, 102–3, 143, 155
   Nickname   75, 119
   Oriental sources   29 n. 91
   Protagonist   52–3, 54, 56–58, 60, 91, 115, 141–2, 147, 157, 166, 181
   Reputation   1, 27
   Scholarship on   6–9, 24, 26–7, 28, 29–30, 162–3, 171–2, 177

Storyteller   35, 37, 41–4, 49–61,
    73–6, 84–5, 113, 116, 123, 142–3
  Travels   32, 63, 66, 67, 70, 141, 180
  Venetian origins   1, 3, 174
  See also Calvino, Italo, *Devisement du
    Monde*, Kublai Khan, Rustichello
    da Pisa, Yangiu
Martin da Canale   16 n. 55, 110
Marvels   29, 37, 113–26, 179–81
Matthew Paris   169
Mercantile culture   18, 26, 72 n. 69, 93,
    149, 161
Merchants' manuals   29, 30–1, 149, 161
Missionaries   2, 20, 29, 95 n. 43, 171
Mongolia   19, 32
Mongol Empire   3–4, 6 n. 24, 17, 19,
    103, 115 n. 7, 119, 123, 131, 133, 135,
    145, 155, 158, 177
Mongol court   131, 177
Mongol (language)   103, 155
Mongols   3–5, 6, 46, 100, 116, 119,
    122–4, 131, 133–5, 145, 155, 169–70

Nancy, Jean-Luc   156–7
Narrative voice   42–62, 65, 174
Nayan   32–3, 72 n. 71, 127, 128–33
Nestorian Christians   124, 131, 139
Niccolò Polo   2, 3, 4, 122–3
Nile   69, 114

Odoric of Pordenone   34
Old Man of the Mountain   52

Pandia   69–70
Paper money   147, 151, 153–5, 157–61,
    181
Persia   6, 32, 42, 73, 82–4, 114, 124
  Persian ruler *see* Arghun
Peter of Russia   169
Philology   28, 79–81, 93, 128
Picard   87–8
Pingiu (Pizhou, now Gupi)   107, 108,
    151
Pipino, see *Devisement du Monde*, Pipino
    version
Pliny   113, 115, 148–9, 164, 169, 178
Poland   145
Prester John   17, 32, 71, 72, 134
Ptolemy   179

Quisai (Xingzai)   49
Quis (Kais)   64

Ramusio, Giovanni Battista   5 n. 18, 12,
    74–6, 77 n. 80
  See also Devisement du Monde,
    Ramusio version
Reobar (Rudbar)   149, 151
Roman d'Alexandre
  See Alexander tradition
Roman de Troie   16 n. 54
Rustichello da Pisa
  Collaboration with Marco Polo   5, 10,
    16, 18, 42–62
  Compilazione arturiana   5, 72–3,102
  Linguistic abilities   78, 84–5, 87, 89,
    103, 110, 173
  See also Devisement du Monde, Marco
    Polo, narrative voice
Russia   4, 145

Salamander   53, 60, 117
Sanyanfu (Xiangyangfu)   46, 48, 123–5,
    142
Sciapod   121
Scotra (Socotra)   141
Semiramis   69, 70
Simon of St-Quentin   169
Sindinfa   151
Sindinfu (Chengdufu, now Chengdu)
    151
Singiu (Zhenzhou, now Yizheng)   107,
    108, 151
Soldaia (Sudak)   3
Solinus   71, 113
Sri Lanka *see* Ceylon
Suigiu (Suzhoi)   154
Sumatra   167, 170–1
Syria   131, 165

Tangut (Tangout)   139
Taoism   100, 137
Tartars   31, 42, 43, 72 n. 71, 73, 82, 84,
    88, 102, 114, 117, 122, 123, 124, 125,
    134, 176 n. 12
Tedaldo Visconti *see* Gregory X
Thibaut de Chepoy   19, 133 n. 35
Thomas de Kent
  Roman de toute chevalerie   114, 148
    n. 8
  See also Alexander tradition
Tibet/ Tibetans   155, 166, 170–1
Tigris   69
Translation   15, 38, 78–9, 82, 86 n. 18,
    89–94, 102–111

Travel writing   2, 29, 35, 38, 108, 115 n. 5, 161–2, 165, 172 n. 73, 180
Tristan en prose   15 n. 52, 16 n. 54, 45 n. 6, 103
Turkey   4, 17, 64
Turkish   53, 60, 103 n. 60, 109, 135 n. 30
Tuscan   2, 26–7, 58, 83, 88, 93, 154 n. 21
  See also Devisement du Monde, Tuscan redaction and Italian

Uzbekistan   3

Venice   1, 4–6, 10 n. 36, 18, 19, 42, 47, 56, 60, 73, 76, 77, 83, 84, 114, 181

Venetian   2, 10, 20, 21–2, 27, 59, 77, 78, 93
  See also Devisement du Monde Venetian redaction and Italian
Villehardouin, Geoffroi de   47–8, 57, 61
Vincent of Beauvais   34, 169
Vughin (Wuxing or Huzhou)   154

William of Boldensale   34
William of Rubruck   2 n. 6, 135, 169, 177

Yangiu (Yangzhou)   49, 53 n. 28
Yogis   137, 138

Gallica
Already Published

1. *Postcolonial Fictions in the* Roman de Perceforest*: Cultural Identities and Hybridities*, Sylvia Huot
2. *A Discourse for the Holy Grail in Old French Romance*, Ben Ramm
3. *Fashion in Medieval France*, Sarah-Grace Heller
4. *Christine de Pizan's Changing Opinion: A Quest for Certainty in the Midst of Chaos*, Douglas Kelly
5. *Cultural Performances in Medieval France: Essays in Honor of Nancy Freeman Regalado*, eds Eglal Doss-Quinby, Roberta L. Krueger, E. Jane Burns
6. *The Medieval Warrior Aristocracy: Gifts, Violence, Performance, and the Sacred*, Andrew Cowell
7. *Logic and Humour in the Fabliaux: An Essay in Applied Narratology*, Roy J. Pearcy
8. *Miraculous Rhymes: The Writing of Gautier de Coinci*, Tony Hunt
9. *Philippe de Vigneulles and the Art of Prose Translation*, Catherine M. Jones
10. *Desire by Gender and Genre in Trouvère Song*, Helen Dell
11. *Chartier in Europe*, eds Emma Cayley, Ashby Kinch
12. *Medieval Saints' Lives: The Gift, Kinship and Community in Old French Hagiography*, Emma Campbell
13. *Poetry, Knowledge and Community in Late Medieval France*, eds Rebecca Dixon, Finn E. Sinclair with Adrian Armstrong, Sylvia Huot, Sarah Kay
14. *The Troubadour* Tensos *and* Partimens*: A Critical Edition*, Ruth Harvey, Linda Paterson
15. *Old French Narrative Cycles: Heroism between Ethics and Morality*, Luke Sunderland
16. *The Cultural and Political Legacy of Anne de Bretagne: Negotiating Convention in Books and Documents*, ed. Cynthia J. Brown
17. *Lettering the Self in Medieval and Early Modern France*, Katherine Kong
18. *The Old French Lays of* Ignaure, Oiselet *and* Amours, eds Glyn S. Burgess, Leslie C. Brook
19. *Thinking Through Chrétien de Troyes*, Zrinka Stahuljak, Virginie Greene, Sarah Kay, Sharon Kinoshita, Peggy McCracken
20. *Blindness and Therapy in Late Medieval French and Italian Poetry*, Julie Singer
21. Partonopeus de Blois*: Romance in the Making*, Penny Eley
22. *Illuminating the* Roman d'Alexandre*: Oxford, Bodleian Library, MS Bodley 264: The Manuscript as Monument*, Mark Cruse
23. *The* Conte du Graal *Cycle: Chrétien de Troyes'* Perceval, *the Continuations, and French Arthurian Romance*, Thomas Hinton
24. *Marie de France: A Critical Companion*, Sharon Kinoshita, Peggy McCracken

25. *Constantinople and the West in Medieval French Literature: Renewal and Utopia*, Rima Devereaux
26. *Authorship and First-Person Allegory in Late Medieval France and England*, Stephanie A. Viereck Gibbs Kamath
27. *Virgilian Identities in the French Renaissance*, eds Philip John Usher, Isabelle Fernbach
28. *Shaping Courtliness in Medieval France: Essays in Honor of Matilda Tomaryn Bruckner*, eds Daniel E. O'Sullivan, Laurie Shepard
29. *Violence and the Writing of History in the Medieval Francophone World*, eds Noah D. Guynn, Zrinka Stahuljak
30. *The Refrain and the Rise of the Vernacular in Medieval French Music and Poetry*, Jennifer Saltzstein
31. *Marco Polo's* Le Devisement du Monde: *Narrative Voice, Language and Diversity*, Simon Gaunt
32. *The* Pèlerinage *Allegories of Guillaume de Deguileville: Tradition, Authority and Influence*, eds Marco Nievergelt, Stephanie A. Viereck Gibbs Kamath
33. *Rewriting Arthurian Romance in Renaissance France: From Manuscript to Printed Book*, Jane H. M. Taylor
34. *Unsettling Montaigne: Poetics, Ethics and Affect in the* Essais *and Other Writings*, Elizabeth Guild
35. *Machaut and the Medieval Apprenticeship Tradition: Truth, Fiction and Poetic Craft*, Douglas Kelly
36. *Telling the Story in the Middle Ages: Essays in Honor of Evelyn Birge Vitz*, eds Kathryn A. Duys, Elizabeth Emery, Laurie Postlewate
37. *The Anglo-Norman Lay of* Haveloc: *Text and Translation*, eds Glyn S. Burgess, Leslie C. Brook
38. *Sacred Fictions of Medieval France: Narrative Theology in the Lives of Christ and the Virgin, 1150–1500*, Maureen Barry McCann Boulton
39. *Founding Feminisms in Medieval Studies: Essays in Honor of E. Jane Burns*, eds Laine E. Doggett and Daniel E. O'Sullivan
40. *Representing the Dead: Epitaph Fictions in Late-Medieval France*, Helen J. Swift
41. *The* Roman de Troie *by Benoît de Sainte-Maure: A Translation*, translated by Glyn S. Burgess and Douglas Kelly
42. *The Medieval Merlin Tradition in France and Italy: Prophecy, Paradox, and Translatio*, Laura Chuhan Campbell

HENRI VIII,

DRAME HISTORIQUE EN CINQ ACTES.

PERSONNAGES.

HENRI VIII, roi d'Angleterre.
LE CARDINAL WOLSEY.
LE CARDINAL CAMPEIUS.
CAPUCIUS, ambassadeur de l'empereur Charles-Quint.
CRANMER, archevêque de Canterbury.
LE DUC DE NORFOLK.
LE DUC DE BUCKINGHAM.
LE DUC DE SUFFOLK.
LE COMTE DE SURREY.
LE LORD CHAMBELLAN.
LE LORD CHANCELIER.
GARDINER, évêque de Winchester.
L'ÉVÊQUE DE LINCOLN.
LORD ABERGAVENNY.
LORD SANDS.
SIR HENRI GUILDFORD.
SIR THOMAS LOVELL.
SIR ANTONY DENNY.
SIR NICOLAS DE VAUX.
DEUX SECRÉTAIRES DE WOLSEY.
CROMWELL, au service de Wolsey.
GRIFFITH, gentilhomme, écuyer de la reine Catherine.

TROIS AUTRES GENTILSHOMMES de sa maison.
LE DOCTEUR BUTTS, médecin du roi.
LA JARRETIÈRE, roi d'armes.
L'INTENDANT DU DUC DE BUCKINGHAM.
BRANDON.
UN SERGENT D'ARMES.
L'HUISSIER DE LA CHAMBRE DU CONSEIL.
UN CONCIERGE ET SON VALET.
UN PAGE, au service de Gardiner.
UN AUDIENCIER.
LA REINE CATHERINE, d'abord femme d'Henri VIII, puis répudiée.
ANNE BULLEN, d'abord dame d'honneur de la reine, puis reine.
UNE VIEILLE DAME, amie d'Anne Bullen.
PATIENCE, suivante de la reine Catherine.
Plusieurs Lords et Ladies, personnages muets.
Femmes de la suite de la reine Catherine.
Esprits qui lui apparaissent.
Bourgeois, Huissiers, Greffiers, Officiers, Gardes, etc.

La scène se passe en Angleterre.

PROLOGUE.

Je ne viens plus vous faire rire [1] ; nous vous présentons aujourd'hui des objets sérieux et graves, des événements importants et tragiques, de ces scènes nobles et touchantes qui font couler les larmes. Ceux dont le cœur est ouvert à la pitié pourront ici verser des pleurs ; le sujet en est digne : ceux qui donnent leur argent dans l'espoir qu'on leur offrira des faits réels et dignes de foi, pourront ici trouver la vérité ; ceux qui ne demandent qu'une ou deux scènes faisant tableau, et, moyennant cela, trouvent la pièce passable, s'ils veulent rester tranquilles,

[1] Ceci faisait sans doute allusion à quelque comédie en vogue, récemment représentée.

et avoir un peu de bonne volonté, je leur promets que dans l'espace de deux petites heures, ils en auront amplement pour leurs schellings[1]. Quant à ceux qui viennent pour assister à une pièce gaillarde et ordurière, pour entendre le cliquetis des boucliers, ou pour voir un drôle en longue robe bigarrée, bordée de jaune[2], ceux-là seront trompés dans leur attente; car, sachez, auditeurs bénévoles, que si nous mêlions la vérité historique avec des scènes aussi insignifiantes que celles d'un bouffon ou d'un combat, outre que ce serait ravaler notre intelligence, et démentir notre réputation, que nous avons, au contraire, à cœur de justifier, nous nous exposerions à ce qu'il ne nous restât plus le suffrage d'un seul ami éclairé. Vous donc, auditoire d'élite, et le premier de la ville, soyez assez bon pour être aussi tristes que nous vous désirons : imaginez que vous voyez les personnages de notre imposante histoire tels qu'ils étaient de leur vivant ; imaginez que vous les voyez puissants, suivis de la foule et entourés de milliers d'amis empressés à leur plaire ; puis voyez comme en un instant le malheur s'attaque à toute cette grandeur ; et alors, si vous conservez encore votre gaieté, je dirai qu'un homme peut pleurer le jour de ses noces.

ACTE PREMIER.

SCÈNE I.

Londres. — Une antichambre du palais.

Entrent par une porte LE DUC DE NORFOLK ; par l'autre, LE DUC DE BUCKINGHAM et LORD ABERGAVENNY.

BUCKINGHAM. Salut, mylord ; je suis enchanté de vous voir. Comment vous êtes-vous porté depuis que nous nous sommes vus en France ?

NORFOLK. Je remercie votre seigneurie ; j'ai toujours été

---

[1] Les places se payaient un schelling, ou vingt-quatre sous de France. Il y en avait sans doute à meilleur marché ; on sait que du temps de Boileau les places du parterre étaient à quinze sous.

Un clerc pour quinze sous, sans craindre le holà,
Peut aller au parterre insulter Attila.

[2] C'était le costume des bouffons.

www.ingramcontent.com/pod-product-compliance
Lightning Source LLC
Chambersburg PA
CBHW070805230426
43665CB00017B/2494